W9-ABF-785

Chicano Discourse:
Socio-historic Perspectives

Rosaura Sánchez
Department of Literature
University of California, San Diego

Salem Academy and College
Gramley Library
Winston-Salem, N.C. 27108

NEWBURY HOUSE PUBLISHERS, INC.
ROWLEY, MASSACHUSETTS 01969
ROWLEY • LONDON • TOKYO

1 9 8 3

Library of Congress Cataloging in Publication Data

Sánchez, Rosaura.
    Chicano discourse.

    Summary: Examines factors which contribute to
the bilingualism found in the Mexican American
community of the Southwest.
    1. Bilingualism--Southwestern States.
2. Mexican Americans—Language.   3. Spanish language—Dialects--Southwestern States.   4. Discourse
analysis. [1. Bilingualism--Southwestern States.
2. Mexican Americans--Language.   3. Spanish
language--Dialects--Southwestern States] I. Title.
P115.5.S65S2   420'.4261   82-2238
ISBN 0-88377-215-9   AACR2

Cover design by Leslie Bartlett

Salem Academy and College
Gramley Library
Winston-Salem, N.C. 27108

NEWBURY HOUSE PUBLISHERS, INC.

Language Science
Language Teaching
Language Learning

ROWLEY, MASSACHUSETTS 01969
ROWLEY • LONDON • TOKYO

Copyright © 1983 by Newbury House Publishers, Inc. All rights reserved. No part of this book may
be reproduced or transmitted in any form or by any means, electronic or mechanical, including
photocopying, recording, or by any information storage and retrieval system, without permission
in writing from the Publisher.

First printing: March 1983
Printed in the U.S.A.   5   4   3   2   1

PREFACE

This work is a study of Chicano bilingualism from a historical, social, ideological and semiotic perspective. It comes several years after completion of a dissertation on Spanish varieties in the Southwest from a generative grammar perspective. Since then my work has taken a different direction, following the work of sociolinguists and semioticians, particularly that of William Labov, M. A. K. Halliday, Joshua Fishman, Glyn Lewis and Umberto Eco.

I would like to acknowledge my indebtedness to Rosa Kestelman, to whom this work is dedicated, as her work in bilingual education and second language instruction and her ideas on linguistic and cognitive development have influenced and stimulated my thinking for over sixteen years. It was at her suggestion that I first turned to a linguistic analysis of the Spanish varieties of my own community.

Another important influence on my thinking has been the work and teaching of Carlos Blanco, whose Marxist criticism has provided insights into the study of language and society. I wish to thank him for all his helpful comments.

The review of a previous version of this manuscript by Gary Keller also provided invaluable information in rewriting and reorganizing this material.

I would also like to note the specific contribution of the many Chicano students here at the University of California at San Diego and at the University of Texas at Austin, whose exchanges with me, in and outside of class, increased my understanding of the Chicano language situation. For their help in collecting recorded data used in this work I am particularly indebted to Yolanda Guerrero, Mariana Marín, Jaime Salazar, Robyn Richter, María Ibarra, Yolanda Padilla, Alfredo Mancha, Pas Peña, Yolanda Róblez, María Rojas, Norma Corvera, Lynne Sullivan, Olga Villanueva, Reymundo Gomeztagle, Connie Campos, Martha Martínez, Sigrid Overstreet, Wendy Borst and Miguel Salas. I also wish to thank Barbie Reyes for her help in the transcription of four dialogues partly incorporated in the text of this manuscript.

Since this manuscript has undergone several revisions, I have several typists to thank. I therefore wish to thank Sandra Salcido from Chicano Studies, UCSD, who typed one complete version, and Marge Pacheco from Third World Studies, who typed several sections and several drafts. A special note of thanks goes to Teri Lamothe, who patiently waited to type the final version of this manuscript.

Rosaura Sánchez

La Jolla
1980

For Rosa Kestelman

INTRODUCTION

A study of Chicano bilingualism is a study of the Chicano community and its patterns of communication in two languages. It is therefore as much a study of the relation between social organization and verbal interaction as it is an analysis of the discourse of Chicanos, since verbal communication is both a social and a linguistic process. To examine this relation we have incorporated the methods used in various disciplines in order to consider the numerous interdependent factors and contradictions within society which affect the Chicano community and provide the specific context within which verbal and social interaction occurs.

Previous sociolinguistic work on Chicano bilingualism has consisted primarily of descriptive studies of language variation and language shift. What has not yet been formulated is a theoretical framework for these studies which goes beyond quantitative analyses of particular variables and explains the relation between verbal interaction and macrosocietal factors. Such a formulation would allow us to study language choice and language shift not merely in terms of language competence but in terms of those social factors which promote and limit competence. Thus shifts between two languages can also assume a semiotic function. What follows then is the presentation of a social, linguistic and ideological framework for the analysis of Chicano bilingualism.

Our analysis of taped dialogues, surveys and personal observations is based on certain theoretical assumptions about language as a linguistic, social and ideological sign system. We recognize that the bilingualism phenomenon could be analyzed from various perspectives. Our analysis will follow sociolinguistic, semantic, historical and Marxist perspectives, as all of these provide important tools for a comprehensive analysis of the people of Mexican origin (hereafter called Chicanos).

The present study begins with a historical review of the social and economic reality of the Chicano population. Chapter one, then, is a study of the Chicano population as a lingual and national minority residing primarily in the Southwest under stratified social and economic conditions. This historical perspective will allow us to consider the effect of a changing Southwest economy on Mexican immigration, labor segmentation, and social mobility, all factors which determine various types of social relations, intensive or limited language contact, and the functions of language. In their interconnection, these social and economic factors make up the material culture of the population of Mexican origin and consequently determine the cultural meaning attached to use of one or the other language. In discussing the relation between language and culture, we also examine the various cultural positions which the Chicano population has expressed throughout this century.

In chapter two we focus specifically on language use and language domains by looking at available statistical information on the background of speakers continuing to use Spanish as their informal language. This general overview provides us with contextual information necessary for analyzing language shifts. In this chapter we also postulate four types of bilingualism currently prevalent in the Southwest and examine language use within particular domains, including that of education. The relation between cultural and ideological perspectives and language choice becomes evident as we explore the particular functions of Spanish in the Southwest.

The third chapter makes the interconnection between social variables and discourse analysis. We begin by looking rapidly at various theories on the functions of discourse which allow us to focus on the underlying sets of social relations which relate *what is said* to *what is done* in Chicano discourse. This chapter, highly influenced by the work of Labov, Halliday and Vološinov, determines the direction of this entire study as it establishes the need to study communication as a social act connected to other social phenomena which constantly affect it and determine its levels of meaning.

In chapter four we examine the Spanish of Chicanos in terms of varieties, fields of discourse and participants. This study reviews some of the salient characteristics of popular urban and rural Spanish varieties in the Southwest and postulates that Spanish shifts within the community occur primarily at the stylistic level, that is, at the phonetic and lexical levels, rather than at the morphosyntactic level. The chapter also includes a semiotic analysis of loans and the familiar *caló* style.

Chapter five discusses the overlapping of functions in intimate and informal situations during intra-group verbal interaction which have led to code-switching among bilingual Chicanos. Shifts in codes are analyzed in terms of language functions, speech acts, cohesion and coherence, and type of proposition as well as in terms of speaker characteristics and ideological positions. Since code-switching is the most common mode of interaction among bilingual Chicanos in the Southwest, we have analyzed this phenomenon extensively in several transcribed episodes of Chicano discourse. The various approaches used in examining the dynamic bilingualism of Chicanos are summarized in our Conclusion; this section includes a look at the attitudes of Chicanos towards use of the Spanish languge and summarizes the various social factors which affect language choice.

These various essays have one common focus: a study of Chicano bilingualism within particular historical conditions in the Southwest. This examination of language in terms of content and social constraints allows us to go beyond form and grammar in examining the social and ideological message implicit and explicit in the bilingual verbal interaction of Chicanos.

CONTENTS

CHAPTER 1

The Mexican-Origin Population:
A National and Lingual Minority

The continued presence of the Spanish language in the Southwest is not the result of a conscious American language policy which strives for the maintenance of minority languages. The course of Spanish language development is rather the result of a historical process initiated in the early part of the nineteenth century with the westward movement of the United States (U.S.) population into Mexican territory. American penetration into the Southwest was not only political and economic but territorial and military so that by 1848 the Southwest was part of the United States. In the process the small dominant Mexican population residing in the Southwest was engulfed and relegated to a subordinate status. Our study is concerned with what occurred thereafter, for the particular development of the Southwest within a growing capitalist economy led to social stratification, social and geographical mobility, and low socioeconomic positions for particular national and racial minorities. Since language is a social product, it will be important to focus first on the effects of this social development on the population of Mexican origin in order to show how particular conditions and social relations led to the present course of Spanish language development in the Southwest.

To begin with, we will define the Mexican-origin population as a national and lingual minority. Next we will examine specific historical and economic factors which have determined the status of this population as well as the continued presence of the Spanish language in the Southwest. Finally we will look at the relation between language and culture. Realizing that it would be deterministic and mechanistic to attribute primary importance to one single factor, we will examine from a historical perspective both demographic and economic conditions as well as cultural, ideological and functional factors. Together all of these considerations will be seen to affect and determine social and language contact and separation, type of bilingualism, degree of cultural and linguistic absorption, language use and language rights.

1

THE CHICANO POPULATION:
A NATIONAL AND LINGUAL MINORITY

Lingual minorities have been variously defined but one European linguist has proposed defining a lingual minority as "a group of people whose everyday speech is definitely another language than the language or languages spoken by the majority of the population of the country in which these people live."[1] This definition implies that the minority language is not on an equal footing with the majority language, that it has no official status, that the minority population continues to have oral proficiency in the language, and that the minority population has not been culturally or linguistically absorbed by the dominant population. "Minority" status for the population is not however necessarily determined quantitatively but rather in terms of the group's social, economic and political status.

Today there are numerous lingual minorities throughout Asia, Europe, Africa and the Americas. Sociolinguists studying this phenomenon have concentrated on two primary questions: 1) language planning for newly emerging or developing nations where modernization requires the selection of a language of wider communication or the standardization of a national language, or 2) policies of multilingual countries towards the various language groups within their borders. Policies can range from those protecting the cultural and linguistic rights of nations (as in several socialist countries) to those favoring and facilitating the linguistic and cultural absorption of lingual minorities by the majority population of the region or country (as in some European states and in the United States). In some cases, however, the minority population can be marginalized, isolated, or suppressed culturally and linguistically to such a degree that it is neither protected nor assimilated, as is the case with some indigenous tribes in the Americas or with Lapps in Scandinavia.[2] Policies towards lingual minorities are also subject to change as in the case of Catalonia where language rights suppressed by the fascist Franco regime were restored by the new constitutional monarchy. Lingual minorities also continue to be formed. The presence of lingual minority groups in the Western world, for example, has increased with world capitalism's need for and attraction of thousands upon thousands of foreign workers to highly industrialized centers. Current estimates indicate the presence of several million people from Southern Europe and the Mediterranean area in the industrialized nations of Northwestern Europe.[3] A similar situation exists in the United States, as we shall see later. The development of minority enclaves for this international reserve army of labor has generally meant the presence of millions of immigrant laborers in the slums of industrialized centers with considerable barriers of language and culture to face.

Awareness of these worldwide social, economic and lingual situations, particularly those affecting peoples of the Third World, led to our examination of the Mexican-origin population from the perspective of its status within the larger society and of other Spanish-speaking groups whose historical context is basically different.

Defining the situation of Chicanos in the Southwest has generated a great deal of controversy given the varying perspectives from which analyses can be made. Some political scientists have studied the Chicano population as an internal colony as evident in the work of Blauner, Barrera and Almaguer. The present context of Chicanos, however, unlike that of Puerto Ricans in Puerto Rico, is not colonial.[4] Nor for that matter can we say that Chicanos constitute a nation, for they are scattered throughout the Southwest and even in the Midwest and Northwest as a national minority population in the midst of an English-speaking white majority. Although Mexicans in the Southwest were once a conquered population, subsequent economic development and increased immigration from Mexico have changed the original social and political relations between the populations of Mexican origin and the white population. The Mexican population was thus reduced in status from that of small and dominant to subordinate minority.

In traditional colonies, the actual foreign presence may be limited although the economic, social and political dependence of the colony on the colonial power is total. Thus the colonial administrators, foreign capitalists and foreign population generally constitute a small fraction of the total population in a colony. The Southwest, on the other hand, was only sparsely populated by Mexicans in 1848 when it was wrested from Mexico. As the Anglo population increased through westward expansion, Mexican immigration continued to be limited for a period of about fifty years (1850–1900). It is at the turn of the century that Mexican immigration begins to increase and to develop particular patterns that continue to the present day. Thus the Southwest territory, originally conquered, and colonized by Spaniards and Mexicans, underwent several transformations, political, economic, social, ethnic and to a large extent, linguistic in nature.

Yet, although their condition is not colonial like that of Puerto Ricans, Chicanos face similar oppressive conditions. Chicanos, Blacks, Puerto Ricans and Filipinos in the United States are descendants of immigrants from colonized or neo-colonized (economically dependent) nations, immigrants who, given their particular economic and political realities are *forced* to migrate from the dependent nation to the metropolis. Today, with the penetration of capitalist economic interests in the economies of Third World nations, we can no longer speak of national economic systems since these dependent nations provide the highly developed ones with raw materials, cheap labor and markets. With an internationalization of the production process, workers in the peripheral dependent nations are forced to migrate *internally*, from their mini-farms which no longer provide subsistence to the industrialized centers established by transnational corporations or to the highly mechanized farms controlled by United States agribusiness. But these workers also migrate *externally* to the highly developed nations as guest-workers and undocumented workers.[5] In effect this migrant labor force constitutes a reserve labor pool from which the capitalist nations, be it the United States, Northern Europe, or South Africa, draw a labor force to meet temporary needs. Previous periods of migration to the United States were characterized by incorporation of migrants into the regular labor market. During the nineteenth century, for example, expanding employment and urbanization, as industrialization developed rapidly in the United States, allowed for the absorption and eventual cultural and linguistic assimilation of a Southern European immigrant labor force, although initially it too faced discrimination and social rejection. Today, the capitalist economy in the United States meets its labor needs with temporary workers migrating from the less developed nations; when no longer needed these workers are immediately deported. As we shall see later, the United States also needs laborers in the secondary labor market sector, composed not only of these temporary workers but also of minority groups who are permanent residents and who constitute the cheap labor sector. These minorities are never completely assimilated. They are the descendants of Black slaves and Third World immigrants.

This analysis does not deny that acculturation has taken place among Third World immigrants, merely that assimilation has not been complete. In fact the degree of acculturation correlates with the extent of social mobility. Evidently, improvement of economic standing allows a Chicano the means to move out of the barrio and socialize in places where few or no minority individuals are to be seen. The capitalist system definitely allows for a small segment of these Third World immigrant groups to filter through into the middle class in order to support its contentions of opportunity and social mobility. Immigrant groups thus need to be studied in terms of the social and historical conditions under which each group immigrated and in terms of the degree of its subsequent absorption into the middle-income stratum.

The language choice of a particular immigrant group or nation can be accompanied by conscious language planning if the mechanism for the formulation of a formal language policy exists. In most countries language policy is formulated by the dominant class or group controlling the super-structure. If we look at the official languages of most of the African nations, we find that for the most part they have retained the colonial language as the official language after independence. To call these colonial languages—English or French or Portuguese—the language of wider communication is to deal in euphemisms from an international and Western perspective. These languages are generally retained not because they facilitate communication within the country but simply because under a neocolonial situation, the native elite or middle class, those intermediaries who facilitate the exploitation of the nation's natural resources and labor by foreign corporations and who under colonialism were acculturated to the colonial culture, are still in command. In formulating language policy these ruling classes reflect the cultural configurations of the whole nation or state. Since these Third World nations are primarily rural, consisting of huge masses of peasants with no direct access to the land, a small elite, whose interests are clearly aligned to those of the foreign bourgeoisie, determines language policy. The presence then of one or several great traditions[6] is at best only a secondary consideration in the formulation of language policy. It is the economic and political interests of the ruling classes which prevail in language policy. English, for example, is the official language of Zimbabwe although only 4% of the population is white.[7] The "great tradition" here is obviously Bantu, since 96% of the population speak Shona, a Bantu language. In South Africa, the white population constitutes 19.8% of the population with the Bantu forming 66.2%, Coloured 10.72% and Asian 3.3%[8]. Yet, although the Bantu languages predominate, Afrikaans and English are the official languages. Here again "great tradition" is equivalent to political and economic power. Language planning is, of course, also tied to modernization and therefore to mass education, developed to train the labor force for industry. Thus the training of a literate and skilled labor force for a technological society may involve acknowledging the importance of the indigenous languages and lead eventually to policy calling for bilingual education, as is occurring today in Peru.[9]

Political interests thus appear to be important considerations in language planning and to be interconnected with the economic. In this respect, there is another important example that we should consider, for it offers interesting insights relevant to this question and to the situation of Chicanos in the United States. That case is Ireland. As James Blaut has pointed out, the Irish people, emigrating to industrial areas in England in the nineteenth century constituted a colonial minority.[10] Their situation was very much like that of Puerto Ricans in the United States. Blaut points out that Ireland, like Puerto Rico today, suffered a population loss through destruction of its rural economy and endured forced emigration to the industrial sectors of the metropolis, where ghettos were established. In the case of Ireland, like that of Puerto Rico, there was a continual back-and-forth movement of the population between colony and oppressor nation.[11] In both of these cases, the political objective is decolonization and independence. What is interesting to note is that although language maintenance was an important issue in the Irish independence movement and, once independence was achieved, the Irish language was made the official language of the Republic of Ireland and a compulsory language of instruction, the restoration of Irish has not succeeded. John Macnamara indicates that Irish has not become the principal language of the country.[12] In fact, he states that less than 3% of the school-age population speak Irish as a home language and that many of these are bilingual. The reason for the triumph of English is clear. Ireland is completely dependent on the English economy and has been substantially assimilated by British culture through the media and through consumerism. Language loyalty was thus unable to compete with economic reality, for economic dependence created conditions which led to loss of the Irish language.

These worldwide examples point to the importance of considering economic and political factors in examining language policy and the actual language choice process. Language policy in itself clearly does not determine the course of development of a particular language. As we have seen, formal and political support of a particular national language does not automatically lead to the acquisition of that language by segregated and often illiterate masses. Generally, language policies reflect the dominant ideology and clearly indicate that social and economic upward mobility is limited to a select few. In other cases, language policy, although a symbol of aspirations for independence, is negated and doomed to failure by concrete material factors, like economic dependence and cultural saturation.

The language situation among Chicanos must be examined in light of these findings and in relation to the specific historical conditions present in the Southwest and in the United States. The Chicano population is a heterogeneous minority characterized by significant differences in generation, nativity, residency, occupation, income, education and language choice. To understand maintenance of the Spanish language in their communities despite overwhelming saturation by the dominant language, culture and ideology, we must consider their specific demographic and economic context. As we shall see, language choice is a question that can only be analyzed in terms of the contradictory forces operating within the Chicano community and in the larger American society. These will become clear as we analyze the social and economic factors which correlate with language use in the Chicano communities.

HISTORICAL AND SOCIAL FACTORS

The question of language choice, language maintenance and language shift is often discussed from a synchronic perspective which treats a given population at a particular moment in time. This approach, which would allow us to formulate the language question in terms of existing conditions, is insufficient and may in fact distort our conception of the total situation, giving a static picture of what is a complex, changing linguistic situation. The effects of particular social and historical factors on the Mexican-origin population, its culture and language, can be appreciated and crystallized through a historical approach which traces the population's initial and subsequent movements of migration from Mexico to the United States.

Bilingualism in the Southwest can be studied in terms of two general sets of factors which determine the conditions under which the two languages operate and the social pressures which promote particular language choices. The two include *demographic* factors which relate to the size, distribution and migration of the Mexican-origin population and *class* factors which determine the socio-economic standing of Chicanos in relation to the rest of the United States (U.S.) population. For an analysis of class factors we will be considering the status of Chicanos within the Southwest economy, their employment classification and income statistics. Demographic and class factors are necessarily interconnected and have to be analyzed in their interdependence.

Both determine the types of contact between the two language groups and the form of bilingualism. Those factors which promote social contact between the two language groups, even when the contact places Chicanos in a subordinate position, will be shown to promote language shift in the Chicano community. The effects of contact and distance among members of the Mexican-origin community itself will be studied as well, for the language of a first generation Chicano is not always that of a fourth generation Chicano. To establish the socio-economic and historical context within which the bilingualism of Chicanos has developed, it will be necessary to begin first with an analysis of the economic development of the Southwest.

ECONOMIC DEVELOPMENT OF THE SOUTHWEST SINCE 1848

The second half of the nineteenth century in the United States led to an expansion of the economy from a competitive, local-market-oriented capitalism to a twentieth century national and international market-oriented capitalism dominated by great corporate enterprises.[13] During this period the Southwest, however, continued to be dominated by agricultural, ranching, railroading and mining interests, labor-intensive enterprises which called for the hiring of unskilled, low-wage workers for seasonal or indeterminate periods of time. From 1900 to 1940 manufacturing developed in both California and Texas, but the rest of the Southwestern States continued to concentrate on the exploitation of natural resources.[14] Demand caused by the two World Wars created a labor shortage both in the manufacturing industry of the North (which led to the migration of Blacks from the South) and in the Southwest agricultural sector, which again looked to cheap immigrant labor. As modern capitalism developed, it sharply segmented its labor force into a dual labor market with primary and secondary markets. The primary labor market is characterized by stable employment and higher wages in areas governed by monopoly corporations. Those workers employed by peripheral firms with lower wages and little job security are said to be in the secondary labor market. Within the primary sector there are also two divisions which separate management and professional or technical jobs from semi-skilled blue-collar and white-collar jobs that involve repetitive tasks and specific supervision.[15] Immigrant labor has generally fed straight into the secondary labor market.

An increase in urbanization and industrialization in the Southwest after 1940 was paralleled by a drastic decline in agricultural jobs as a result of mechanization. Since then, employment increases have come in distribution, government, business, consumer and professional services. The Southwest, however, has not developed uniformly, for it is characterized by economic variations between and within the states themselves. California, for example, has the highest proportion of manufacturing jobs, whereas New Mexico has the lowest and continues to depend on its mining interests as well as on an increase in government employment.[16] The high employment situation in Houston,

Texas, on the other hand, does not compare with that of depressed South Texas, where the concentration of Chicanos is high. Basically, then, the last hundred years in the Southwest can be divided roughly into three phases of economic development: Phase I is characterized largely by agricultural, railroading, mining and ranching interests. Phase II is the transitional stage with manufacturing lagging behind that of the rest of the nation but with a shift towards urbanization and increased mechanization of agriculture. During Phase II, there was diversification in the economy although agriculture, railroads and mining continued to be of significant importance. The last period, Phase III, has seen the growth of urban-industrial complexes. Railroads have lost dominance and a number of manufacturing interests have replaced mining.[17] Today agri-business and monopoly corporate interests control the economy of the Southwest.

IMMIGRATION AND EMPLOYMENT

This brief summary of economic development in the Southwest leads to an examination of the patterns of Mexican immigration over the last century. An analysis of flow, the rhythms of both induced migration and forced deportation, the social status and place of origin of immigrants, their entry into the labor market and their rural or urban settlement will be seen to correlate with basic patterns of labor segmentation, or urbanization and of residential segregation. From this correlation we can arrive at hypotheses concerning the contradictions and the dominant trends which characterize bilingualism in the Chicano community at the present historical moment.

According to McWilliams, there were approximately 75,000 Mexicans in the Southwest in 1848.[18] Between 1848 and 1900 there was little immigration from Mexico; this was a period marked by the westward movement of thousands of Anglo settlers who inevitably came into conflict with the already-established Mexican population. During this period of labor-intensive work, Chicanos were hired as manual laborers in the fields, mines and railroads. After the Chinese Exclusion Act of 1882 and the Gentlemen's Agreement with Japan of 1907 ended the importation of cheap labor, it became necessary for the expanding economy to procure other sources of cheap labor for agriculture and the secondary labor sector. It was then and particularly after 1910 that growers and industrialists in the United States began a concerted effort to import cheap Mexican labor.[19]

Thereafter Mexican immigration to the United States increased steadily, ensuring the continued and growing presence of a Spanish-speaking population. Between 1900 and 1910 approximately 48,900 Mexican immigrants were admitted, but in the following decade, about 163,000 were allowed into the country. By 1920 Mexican immigrants constituted the principal source of labor for railroad maintenance crews and for agriculture in the Southwest.[20]

During the 1920s, as demand for cheap labor increased, approximately 487,700 Mexican immigrants were admitted. Policy towards the continued immigration of the Mexican laborers was continuously challenged by organized labor, which feared the displacement of white labor by Mexicans willing to work for lower wages. Racists who considered the Mexican an inferior, undesirable resident also opposed immigration. In 1901 the Industrial Commission on Immigration reporting on Mexican labor declared that "the Mexican peon laborer was little better than the Japanese coolie" and that "the competition of the Mexican was quite as disastrous to white labor as was that of the Chinese and Japanese."[21] Actually, as a result of labor segmentation the Anglo worker was not adversely affected, for he fell principally in the primary sector of the labor market where employment was more stable and wages higher. The segmentation of working conditions and of labor markets is possibly the single most important factor that has maintained a distance between English and Spanish speakers and thus reinforced the retention of the Spanish language. By 1908 the U.S. Department of Labor had concluded that the Mexicans were not really comparable to the Blacks in the South because "Mexicans were not permanent, did not acquire land and did not establish themselves in little cabin homesteads, but remained nomadic and outside of American Civilization."[22] Thus the Mexican worker was tolerated as a temporary source of cheap migrant labor.

The continued immigration of Mexicans to fill jobs in agriculture, industry, transportation and services did not modify their temporary status. During the Depression Mexicans faced massive deportations, with the "repatriation" of over 89,000. Later, as the United States prepared for war, it again sought out the Mexican laborer on a temporary restricted basis to fill its labor shortages in agriculture and agriculture-related industry. Documented and undocumented Mexican immigration continued nonetheless throughout the entire Bracero Program which extended from 1942 to 1964.[23] Today, thousands of Mexicans continue to cross the border throughout the year to work in the United States. These figures include commuters who cross the border on a daily or weekly basis but live permanently or seasonally in Mexico.

Estimates on the number of undocumented workers of Mexican origin in the United States vary anywhere from 2 to 7.4 million persons. Elaborate proposed plans for the deportation of these undocumented workers and for stricter border enforcement continue to reflect anti-Mexican sentiments generally disguised as interest in the "country's national security," in reducing unemployment or in reducing welfare and police costs. Evidence indicates, however, that these charges cannot be substantiated.[24] What is evident however is the willingness of U.S. business to exploit Mexican labor on both sides of the border. A special California task force investigating the exploitation of immigrant workers in Southern California found widespread violations of minimum-wage laws and other labor codes in the garment industries and local restaurants. Fortunately undocumented workers are beginning to organize and join labor unions throughout the Southwest, not only in the garment industries and in agriculture but in services, electronics and construction as well.[25]

Since undocumented immigration to the United States is a significant factor to consider in making prognoses for language maintenance in the Southwest, it is important to analyze present conditions contributing to its continuity. As in the case of Southern European and Mediterranean immigration to the capitalist industrial centers of Northwestern Europe, it is the availability of jobs in the secondary and tertiary (services) sectors of the labor market in the United States which has led to an international migrant labor force. Another important factor is the unemployment of nearly half of Mexico's work force, given its development of capital-intensive industrial projects rather than the development of labor-intensive industries.[26] Half of the shares of Mexico's 290 largest corporations, however, are controlled by transnational corporations.[27] The United States has also exported its technology, its labor-saving machinery to Mexican agriculture, developing agribusiness companies, especially in the Northwestern Mexican States. Modern agriculture enterprises have meant a reduction of the number of necessary farmworkers and increased the number of landless and unemployed farmworkers.[28] Another important consideration is the emergence of export-oriented industries along the Mexican border through the establishment of U.S. runaway shops *(las maquiladoras)*. Profits in these garment, electronics and other assembling industries are based on the exploitation of a cheap labor force and the low cost of transportation.[29] Initially only 12 shops were set up but by the mid-seventies there were over 400 shops in the urban centers along the Texas to California border.[30] Since these runaway shops are involved in only one aspect of production and can use an unskilled labor force, neither skills nor profits are left behind in Mexico. Unemployment does not diminish either, since 75% of the labor force in *maquiladoras* are young women. Unemployment rates are generally based on male employment.[31] Recently the number of these United States runaway shops has decreased, with a marked reduction in the number of workers as well.[32]

The presence of these shops together with large-scale unemployment in Mexico and the prospect of crossing the border into the United States have attracted massive migration to the border area. Although migrants to these areas were traditionally men, today entire families migrate, swelling the numbers of women in these border urban centers. Mario Margulis indicates that between 1940 and 1960 migrants in Reynosa, across the border from McAllen, Texas, were primarily men but by 1970, the number of women was slightly higher.[33] The border population is also younger. In cities across from the Texas border, migrants appear to come primarily from North and North Central Mexico, although a few come all the way from Guanajuato, Veracruz and Yucatán. A study of *maquiladoras* in Tijuana by Mónica Claire Gambrill, on the other hand, indicated that 67% of the interviewed employees came from the Pacific zone (Baja California, Sonora, Sinaloa, Nayarit, Jalisco, Colima, Michoacán, Guerrero and Oaxaca). From Central and Northern Mexico 30% came (Mexico D.F., Puebla, Guanajuato, Morelos, Durango, Zacatecas, Chihuahua and Coahuila).[34] The majority (55.49%) migrated directly to Tijuana from their place of origin; 58.48% came from urban areas rather than rural areas. In fact Gambrill found that those coming from rural areas had often had previous urban experience before coming to Tijuana so that a high 71.4% had migrated from an urban area or had previously resided in an urban area.[35] Additional information indicated that 65.8% of the men interviewed in Tijuana had finished primary school as compared to 67.3% of the women. Only 18.4% of the men had attended secondary school while 25.2% of the women had.[36] These statistics are not as low as those of Urquidi and Méndez which indicate that 20% of persons over 15 years of age residing in border Mexican municipalities have had no education at all and that 39% have had limited instruction.[37]

Information on these border residents is vitally important since these are both past and future potential immigrants to the United States. The growth of these border cities also reflects the urbanization of the entire Mexican population, which is about 58% urban today. In Table 1.1 taken from Bustamante's demographic tables, we can see that the border centers have grown quite rapidly in the last 50 years, at higher rates than the rest of the Mexican nation:[38]

Table 1.1   Population Growth in Mexican Border Centers

	Population		Rate of growth	
	1950	1970	1959–69	1960–70
Republic of Mexico	25,791,017	48,313,438	3.1%	3.3%
Border states	3,762,963	7,912,930	4.0	3.6
Some border municipalities				
Tijuana	65,364	340,583	9.8	7.4
Mexicali	124,362	396,314	8.4	3.4
Nuevo Laredo	59,496	151,253	4.9	4.6
Ciudad Juarez	131,308	424,135	11.1	4.4
Nogales	26,016	53,494	4.4	3.0

We find this demographic data quite useful as it allows us to assume continued immigration, both documented and undocumented, both male and female, from North, Central, Southern and Northwestern Mexico, but unlike earlier migration, primarily of urban origin and younger. These factors will not only affect language maintenance but Spanish varieties in the Southwest as well.

Thus throughout the twentieth century, Mexican immigration has been characterized by several features which have determined the type of contact between the two language groups in the Southwest: 1) Mexican immigration has been continuous; 2) Mexican immigration has been a source of cheap labor; and 3) Mexican immigration has been sought on a temporary basis. These factors have inevitably reinforced the maintenance of the Spanish language by creating propitious social conditions. The steady stream of incoming Mexicans as well as a continual mobility between the land of origin and this country has allowed Chicanos continued contact with a Spanish-speaking population. The low-wage status of these immigrants has led to the concentration of the Spanish-speaking

Salem Academy and College

Gramley Library

Winston-Salem, N.C. 27108

workers in low-income areas and in particular occupations. And finally, U.S. immigration policy, which clearly has not welcomed Mexicans as permanent residents, has served to augment societal discrimination of the Mexican-origin population in education, housing and employment. These conditions have only increased social distance between the two language groups.

Immigration from Mexico, however, is not the only type of migration relevant to a study of bilingualism. As indicated before, the Mexican-origin population has also been marked by geographic mobility within the country. Earlier seasonal migration from urban to agricultural centers led eventually to permanent settlement in urban areas for the vast majority of the Chicano population. By 1977, according to a Census Bureau report, about 79.5% of Mexican-origin families were concentrated in metropolitan areas.[39] The majority (about 85%) of the Mexican-origin population, estimated to number anywhere between seven and eleven million persons, still reside in the five southwestern states although there are at least a million Chicanos scattered throughout the industrial and agricultural centers of the Midwest, the Northwest and the migrant camps of Florida. In fact about 55.2% of the Chicano population in the Southwest reside within a radius of 250 kilometers (about 155 miles) from the Mexican border.[40] In Texas the concentration of Chicanos is especially strong along the border where 75.5% of persons of Mexican origin reside.[41] Yet although proximity to the border is an important consideration, so is urbanization of the Mexican-origin population. The latter diminishes in some instances the degree of social isolation characteristic of rural residence, although residence in the central cities of metropolitan areas has often meant residence in segregated barrios and ghettos, as in East Los Angeles, for the Spanish origin population. The continuation of separate Latin quarters is based on economics.

This urbanization, even in the face of labor segmentation, has accompanied an occupational shift and a penetration into employment categories where English speakers comprise a majority of the work force. Although the majority of the Mexican-origin population fell earlier into the farm worker category, today only 7.1% of Chicano males are involved in farm work. March 1977 statistics indicate that 63.3% of males of Mexican origin were employed as blue-collar, 12.9% as service and 16.8% as white-collar workers.[42] Although occupational mobility is evident from these statistics, there has been little economic mobility. Mexican-origin families continue to lag behind other groups in income. Families of Mexican origin had a median income of $11,700 as compared with $16,300 for U.S. families not of Spanish origin in 1977.[43] About one fourth of all Mexican-origin families fall below the low-income level. These statistics indicate that given existing labor segmentation, the Mexican-origin population has gone from the category of cheap-labor immigrants to that of low-wage residents. Thus in spite of urbanization, the promoting of contact between the two language groups has been constrained by economic factors which have

Salem Academy and College

Gramley Library

Winston-Salem, N.C. 27108

continued to segregate the Chicano labor force and relegated it to low-wage levels within broader employment categories.

This brief survey of the history of the Mexican-origin population in the United States shows a population characterized by various types of migration: migration from Mexico to the United States for permanent residence, recurring migration from Mexico on a temporary basis, regional migration from one state to another, seasonal migration to agricultural fields in the Northwest and Midwest, and massive urbanization with accompanying employment shifts which took the Chicano population from a primarily farm worker category to the blue-collar and service sectors. Most importantly, despite all these movements of migration, Chicanos have remained primarily concentrated in the Southwest.

The immigration patterns and occupational categories for the Mexican-origin population can be summarized as shown in Table 1.2. These various

Table 1.2   Immigration Patterns and Employment for the Mexican-origin Population

	Employment	Population
1848–1900	Agriculture Ranching Railroads Mining	Small Native Mexican Population Little Mexican Immigration Massive Anglo Westward Expansion
1900–1940	Agriculture Ranching Railroads Mining Services Blue Collar	Massive Mexican Immigration—Temporary and Permanent Extensive Deportations
1940–Present	Blue Collar Services White Collar Agriculture	Temporary Labor Immigration—Bracero Program Regular Mexican Immigration Undocumented Worker Immigration Commuters Continual Deportations

forms of mass migration provide the context for language maintenance and language shift, as do urbanization movements within the United States. It is important to understand that we are not discussing a minority population which coexists on equal terms with the dominant population. Instead we have a subordinate Spanish-speaking population struggling for economic, cultural and linguistic survival amidst an English-speaking superordinate population. If we bear in mind that attitudes towards a language reflect attitudes towards the speakers of that language, then to understand the low status of the Spanish language in the United States we only need to look at the status of the Mexican-origin population in American society, at Congressional policies towards Mexican immigration, and at the brutal treatment by the U.S. Immigration and Naturalization Service of both the documented and undocumented Mexican immigrant. As second-class citizens of this country, the Mexican-origin population has had a history of social isolation. It was not too long ago—as late as 15 years ago—that "No Mexicans Allowed" signs were still visible in Texas swimming pools and restaurants. This lack of social contact with the dominant English-speaking society, except in subordinate positions, has played an important role in the preservation of the Spanish language among several generations of the Mexican-origin population. Yet this century has brought occupational and residential shifts which have affected and changed the language, culture and education of all present generations in the Chicano community.

SOCIO-ECONOMIC-DEMOGRAPHIC FACTORS AND LANGUAGE

Spanish language use in the United States is significantly correlated with income status and nativity. Income status is a reflection of employment, educational attainment and wages, all of which are determined by the economic reality of this country. Nativity, in turn, must be analyzed in relation to given immigration patterns and trends. Although this study is concerned primarily with the Mexican-origin population, it will often be useful to compare statistics available for this population with those of other Spanish-origin persons.

As we will see later, not all Spanish-origin persons are Spanish-speaking; yet to project language trends it is important to note that official statistics estimate a Spanish-origin population in the United States of over 12 million.[44] Since this statistic does not include numerous undocumented workers from Mexico and Latin America, the total Spanish-origin population could amount to around 19 million. Statistics published in December, 1977, reflected the following distribution according to origin (Table 1.3). These vary in terms of millions from one quarterly report to the next but the breakdown is useful nonetheless.

Table 1.3   Spanish-origin Population in the United States: March 1977.[45]

Total Spanish-origin population	11.3 million
Mexican-origin	6.5 million
Puerto Rican	1.7 million
Cuban	0.7 million
Central or South American	0.9 million
Other Spanish	1.4 million

As is evident the Mexican-origin population is the largest group, concentrated primarily in the Southwestern states (California, Texas, Arizona, New Mexico and Colorado). Eighty-five percent of the Mexican-origin population resides in the Southwest.[46]

The statistics in Table 1.4 indicate the distribution of all Spanish-origin persons in the United States.

Table 1.4   Percent Distribution of Persons of
Spanish Origin by Residence in Selected
States: March: 1978.[47]

Texas	22
California	30
Arizona, Colorado and New Mexico	8
New York	13
Remainder of U.S.	27

Table 1.5   Median Age of all Persons and Persons
of Spanish Origin by Type of Spanish Origin:
March: 1976.[48]

	Median age
All persons	28.9
Total Spanish	20.9
Mexican origin	20.3
Puerto Rican	19.6
Cuban	36.8
Central and South American	25.5
Other Spanish	19.1
Not of Spanish origin	29.3

Table 1.6   Percent of Persons of Spanish Origin 25 Years Old and Over by Years of School
Completed and Type of Spanish Origin: March 1976.[49]

	Persons who completed less than 5 years of school %	Persons who completed 4 years of high school or more %
Total persons	3.8	64.1
Total Spanish origin	18.7	39.2
Mexican origin	24.2	32.5
Puerto Rican	18.7	29.8
Cuban	9.5	51.5
Other Spanish	7.0	60.3

The Mexican-origin population is fairly young in comparison to the general population (Table 1.5). This information becomes especially important when we observe that language maintenance is stronger among the older generations, as we shall discuss later. The educational attainment of these groups also varies (Table 1.6). Among younger Mexican-origin persons the level of education is increasing but as a whole the population continues to have the highest proportion with less than five years of school completed: in contrast, a greater proportion of Cuban, Central and South American and other Spanish-origin persons have completed four years of high school or more. As we shall see later, education and language maintenance also correlate.

The Mexican-origin population also has a low income level, although not as low as that of the Puerto Ricans, but lower than that of the other Spanish-origin

Table 1.7   Income in 1976 of Persons and Families of Spanish Origin: March 1977.[50]

	Total Spanish	Mexican	Puerto Rican	Cuban	Other Spanish
Median income of all families	$10,259	$10,322	$7,669	$11,773	$12,203
Median income of male persons	7,050	6,891	7,124	7,515	7,342
Median income of female persons	3,359	2,925	3,930	3,224	4,153

groups. Consider the 1977 Census Bureau statistics for families of Spanish-origin (Table 1.7).

The largest Spanish-origin group—the Mexican-origin population—is thus educationally and economically in the lower echelons.

CULTURAL AND IDEOLOGICAL CONSTRAINTS

The material conditions which surround the population of Mexican origin have determined not only their economic standing but the range of verbal contacts between English and Spanish speakers, between Mexicans and Chicanos, between rural and urban barrio residents, and between various generations of Mexican-origin persons in this country. These conditions in turn are reflected not only in the form and means of verbal communication, but in the cultural and ideological content of the verbal performance as well. Vološinov has stressed that language is an ideological sign system:

> Countless ideological threads running through all areas of social intercourse register effect in the word. It stands to reason, then, that the word is the most sensitive *index of social changes,* and what is more, of changes still in the process of growth, still without definite shape and not as yet accommodated into already regularized and fully defined ideological systems.[51] (Italics in original text)

Bilingualism thus registers the transitory phases of social changes for the Mexican-origin population, changes reflected not merely in geographical and occupational mobility but at the ideological and cultural levels as well. In this next section we will look at the historical relation between language and culture in the Chicano community.

LANGUAGE AND CULTURE

The relation between language and culture has been very much in the news in light of separatist action proposed by the majority French population in Quebec and as a result of opposition to federally funded programs allegedly established to preserve minority languages and cultures in this country. Language, culture and political solidarity are seen as interdependent ingredients fomenting nationalism and separatism.

The relation between language and culture is a complex question. Often the function of language vis-à-vis culture is simply symbolic; that is, language may serve as a symbol of the cultural, national or economic aspirations of a particular group. In the case of Ireland, for example, Gaelic symbolized the quest for political independence of the nation. Afterwards its symbolic status led to its being established as the national language. Its maintenance however was purely symbolic for hardly anyone speaks the language today. In the case of the Basques, the desire for autonomy and self-determination is being coupled with renewed interest in preserving and standardizing their language. Thus national-ists not speaking Basque consider it a duty to learn the language or teach it to their children. In an area with a large non-Basque population as a result of migration, only independence could lead to a conscious and full functional development of the Basque language, as in the case of Hebrew in Israel, where maintenance of the language would clearly be tied to interests of national unity and uniqueness. As a symbol, language can serve both to call attention to larger issues and to rally a group together to join in a common cause, or confuse the issue and lead to a false consciousness.

Language has never been a rallying symbol in the various labor and student protests in the Southwest throughout this century, although it has always served as a vehicle for expressing community concerns, as is clear from Spanish language newspapers published throughout this period. On the other hand, it has always served to identify the community, much like skin color, and to distinguish it from the Anglo community. The suppression of Spanish in the public schools of the Southwest prior to 1969 and the punishment of school children who insisted on speaking their native Spanish further polarized the Anglo and Mexican-origin communities, already divided along economic lines. Spanish was in fact a sign of being Mexican. Official school policies and attitudes towards Spanish were of course only a reflection of the dominant society's prejudicial attitudes toward the entire population of Mexican origin. Organized efforts during the Chicano Movement of the sixties, however, did not focus specifically on language but rather on the need for Chicano teachers and Chicano studies in the public schools and universities, on "equal opportunity" in employment and education, and on the myth of Aztlan.

Current interest in bilingual education however has given Spanish a symbolic status. It is now the banner of proponents of bilingual education, although not always that of the recipients of bilingual education who see English as the vehicle for upward mobility. As in the case of any system-oriented proposal, cultural pluralism is advocated as the answer to a multitude of problems, analyzed as cultural in nature by proponents who often pay lip service to Spanish but do not use the language themselves nor live in the large low-income areas where it is spoken. Fortunately, Spanish is more than a symbol of the aspirations of middle-class Chicanos and Latinos seeking upward mobility. It is a sign of the community, a product of the community, a reflection-refraction of the material culture of the community. The term *culture* however has been variously defined, particularly during the period of civil rights protests. In order to understand its relation to language, it will be necessary to analyze the concept itself.

Language may be a sign of material culture but it is clearly not synonymous with culture. Yet in many areas of the world, language serves to determine ethnicity. In Mexico, for example, language is used to determine who classifies as an Indian.[52] "Indian," however, is not simply an ethnic term but rather a socio-economic and linguistic classification of groups who have continued to live "marginally" or in isolated areas. Many of the Latin American Indians are far from marginalized in any real sense as they constitute the entire labor force in the large landed estates of the *hacendados,* especially in the Andean nations, even while continuing to dwell "marginally" in their Indian communities where they retain their culture and language. Other Indians are in fact marginal in the sense that they live in remote jungle or mountain areas with a subsistence economy. These too retain their language and their culture. Limited labor relations mean limited social and linguistic contact with the dominant culture and language.

In the United States acculturation is common to all immigrant groups but social and economic stratification continues to produce different experiential modes for the poor and for minority communities segregated in particular residential areas. It is in the verbal and social interaction produced by these contexts that the links between language, culture and ideology become manifest, for rejection by the larger society produces not only internal strife and self-hate but the seeds for organizational efforts to combat the oppressing forces as well. Given the racist policies of this country, especially within political and labor circles, the Mexican-origin population has historically had to pool its own resources for resistance efforts. Each time that the entire community has had to respond en masse to economic and political oppression, its solidarity has been strengthened and its need for possessing something that is inalienable and strictly Chicano has led to a search for uniqueness in national origin and language. Language and culture have thus been identified with struggle since 1848, but only symbolically, for often the leaders of struggle have been English-dominant Chicanos themselves.

To understand this tie between language, culture, and struggle, we need to define our term "culture" and then review the patterns of struggle since 1848 as well as the cultural responses that have characterized various segments of the community.

Culture has been variously defined. It is said to be the sum of traditions and customs, the language and the life-style of a society. Archaeologists define culture as "an assemblage of associated traits that recur repeatedly."[53] The archaeological picture of a culture is constituted mainly by "traits that reflect social habits and are conditioned by social traditions." For the anthropologist, Childe points out, culture is an even more comprehensive concept:

It comprises all aspects of human behavior that are not innate reflexes or instincts. It is everything that men derive from nature or the sub-human environment. It includes language and logic, religion and philosophy, morality and law, as well as the manufacture and use of tools, clothes, houses and even the selection of food to eat. All this men must learn from their fellows in society.[54]

These rules that men learn from society "belong to the collective tradition, accumulated and preserved by the society into which a human being is born."[55] Following the interactionists' propositions, we could say that these rules are the social codes through which men are socialized in their interaction with family, friends and others. These cultural signs or codes can be studied in a society's religion, customs, dress, diet, manufacture and use of tools, houses, law and morality, but the most significant area is the labor process. In fact when we compare the culture of Mexican immigrants with that of the dominant Anglo population, we often find that differences are tied to relations of production rather than to national origin. Often what we are describing is fundamentally the difference between a highly developed imperialist economy and a dependent economy with limited development. For this reason, the Mexican immigrant who has previously toiled over his *minifundio* without being able to eke out an existence is culturally different as well from the Mexican middle-class professional. The material culture that results from the labor process although primary has to be considered alongside other fields of culture: language, nationality and political allegiance. Those sharing the same material culture, however, do not necessarily speak a single language nor act as a political unit. Childe notes that in Mesopotamia during the third millennium B.C., the culture was homogeneous "not only in tools, weapons, dress, housing and artistic taste but also in religious architecture, burial rites and even script" even though two different languages were spoken and politically the area was divided into a number of autonomous city states fighting against each other.[56] Thus it is possible for Mexicans and U.S. citizens of the same class to share the same culture and speak a different language.

Any discussion of culture must take into consideration that culture is never static; it is constantly in a process of motion, for it is life itself. It is constantly being influenced by material conditions or through contact with other cultures to add particular social traditions which may be useful, retain those which continue to be socially necessary and lose those no longer viable. Often these cultural changes come through political and economic changes. Thus if we were to contrast the culture of the Southwest with that of Mexico or Latin America, we would find much in common, for the dominant "North American culture" has permeated even the most remote corner of Latin America where transistor radios, American missionaries and American products have penetrated. This cultural imperialism however does not completely obliterate differences in habits of thought and action, in institutions and customs, for these cultural differences are obvious and in stark contrast in the very streets of Latin American cities. As it evolves and changes, however, culture never completely loses all traces of previous stages. For example, man's dependence on gods for sustenance or support in previous epochs is not completely eliminated in the twentieth century despite new technology which enables the development of high-yield seed varieties to foment the Green Revolution.[57] The past is always there, even as it fades into a mere vestige, no longer operable, but yet somehow still coloring the beliefs of modern man. Thus, even though it is the labor process in which societies participate that determines their experiences, their values and their ideology, there is always that certain quality that distinguishes one nation from another, even after years of coexistence. That element is history.

Cultural history is the history of economic conditions, of the social forces of production and the technical advances in the instruments of production, as well as the history of the superstructure, of the ideological apparatuses of the state. As Childe has noted:

> The archaeologist's divisions of the prehistoric period into Stone, Bronze, and Iron Ages are not altogether arbitrary. They are based upon the materials used for cutting implements, especially axes, and such implements are among the most important tools of production. Realistic history insists upon their significance in moulding and determining social systems, and economic organization.[58]

Thus the tools and the work of man tell the cultural history of mankind, not only in prehistoric times but in modern times as well. Chicano culture can be told in a study of the production and work of Chicanos, in the many years of hoeing and chopping cotton, in the years of riding the range as *vaqueros,* in the past-to-present toiling in the fruit and vegetable farms and canneries of the Southwest, in the laying of the railroad track, in the sweeping of floors, washing of dishes, digging of ditches, spreading of gravel over highways and in the daily shifts in assembly plants, garment industries and toy factories. It is in this labor that the social being of Chicanos is etched. As the labor has changed, so has the culture. But we cannot forget that culture is also subject to the dominant ideology transmitted by the ruling class through various state institutions: educational, religious, political and intellectual as well as recreational. Yet there is no mechanistic process operating in the transmission of culture, for as Childe has pointed out, changes in culture and tradition can be initiated, controlled or delayed by the conscious and deliberate choice of human beings.[59]

The material cultural history of Chicanos has not been the subject of many studies although some works have appeared on Chicano folklore and Chicano learning styles. A recent and influential article on the culture of Chicanos has been written by Juan Gómez Quiñones: "On Culture."[60] Gómez Quiñones describes three cultures and identities among the population of Mexican descent in the United States. The first is said to be characterized by its adoption of the dominant culture and identity.[61] The second is the transitional group, characterized by its "amalgamated character," and "its brief time of existence," with elements from both cultures and a sub-cultural identity.[62] The third sector is the group of Mexicano culture and identity.[63] As Gómez Quiñones himself states, his continuum has two cultural poles: Mexicano vs. Anglo-American.

Without denying the existence of ethnic and national differences between the two countries, we find that Gómez Quiñones's primary distinction of cultural types along national origin and ethnic lines avoids the issue he raises on the relation between class and culture. What exists in fact is a class antagonism rather than an ethnic continuum. Within each class there are a number of intersecting continua but the only continuum that encompasses both capitalist and worker is the ideological continuum. Differences within the working class are determined by participation in a primary, secondary or tertiary labor sector; income level; occupational category; habituation or resistance to the labor process; and acceptance or rejection of the dominant ideology. These various intersecting continua produce a variety of cultural patterns within the Chicano community, additionally affected by the "culture" of incoming Mexican immigrants. No one has defined precisely what "generalized Mexican culture" is.[64] Often the phrase evokes superficial notions of food, music, charro dress, macho men and legends. Some traditionally mentioned characteristics, like large families, an authoritarian father image and virginal women are in reality the product of rural family units, where children function as farm hands to ensure survival and subsistence and the father functions as foreman to maintain discipline in the field without incurring additional maintenance burdens. As Mexico has urbanized and its unemployed rural workers have migrated by the millions to the cities and the border area, the peasants' contact with the dominant Mexican culture has increased. Arizpe, for example, has found that Indian migrants to Mexico City adapt to social patterns that ensure support. Cultural patterns determining familial ties are closely connected to economic situations:

> a mayor pobreza y marginación de las familias migrantes, mayor su dependencia de los lazos de parentesco; a mayor independencia económica, los grupos domésticos han podido sustituir estos lazos por otros nuevos, de compadrazgo, con los habitantes de la ciudad.[65]

Thus urbanization and migration lead to cultural change for these Indians from the Mazahua region, which is 250 kilometers northwest of Mexico City, in the state of Mexico and bounded by the states of Queretaro and Michoacan.[66] Urban Mexico, on the other hand, is very much influenced by American culture for very objective reasons. Today the United States supplies 62% of Mexico's imports and receives 60% of its exports.[67] The United States also represents 64% of the foreign investments in Mexico. United States corporations control 33% of the 100 largest firms and 35% of the 200 largest. Over 60% of Mexico's loans come from U.S. banks.[68] Mexico's economic dependence on U.S. capital is matched by its consumption of U.S. products from Coca-Cola to Walt Disney comics to General Electric TV sets. The control by U.S. corporations of communication satellites, TV programs, publishing houses, newspapers and popular magazines in Latin America is extensive and well documented.[69] Billions of dollars are spent by U.S. multinationals on Children's TV programs in Latin America, including Mexico. United States cultural imperialism has penetrated even the most remote village in Mexico and Latin America.

The Mexican immigrant is thus not automatically coming from a counter or purely antagonistic culture but in most instances from a culture already controlled and influenced by United States multinational corporations, a culture already permeated by the dominant ideology of the United States. The degree of acculturation of the immigrant is largely determined by his degree of consumption of this ideology through his acquisitional power of cultural goods. The more middle class, the greater the acculturation. The lower the income, the less the acculturation. This phenomenon is repeated in the United States among first-generation immigrants. Consumption of the dominant ideology is thus synonymous with acculturation, a process promoted through the consumption of goods and services according to one's class status, as indicated by Gelvin Stevenson: "In a class society, one's status as worker or capitalist generally determines what and how one consumes and to whom and how one relates personally."[70] One's status as worker is largely, but not entirely, determined by one's paycheck. Income in turn constrains access to commodities and services. Since most Chicanos fall at the lower-income levels, individually their consumption power is small, but as a group, it represents a substantial market for particular goods. As we shall see, efforts are now under way to appeal to the Spanish-speaking consumer through Spanish-language propaganda over the media and on billboards.

Consumption of the dominant ideology however is more than the consumption of commodities. It is the consumption of values and a political perspective. Previous studies of the Chicano community have focused on a vague notion of acculturation, often along culturalist lines rather than as consumption of the dominant ideology. One interesting exception is Santillán, who combines the two and finds two dominant perspectives in Chicano political research and community organization: pluralism and Marxist political economy.[71] Within pluralism, Santillán examines three distinct forms: assimilation, cultural democracy and cultural nationalism.[72] Santillán sees these various perspectives and forms as stages leading to the political goal of self-determination and cultural autonomy.[73] The first group—the assimilationists—"were convinced that total cultural immersion was key to social acceptance into the decision-making process."[74] He quotes the League of United Latin American Citizens' (LULAC) preamble to the Constitution in 1929, which we present below, as reflecting the philosophy of assimilation:

> To develop within the members of our race, the best, purest, and most perfect type of true and loyal citizen of the United States of America. The acquisition of the English language, which is the official language of our country, being necessary for the enjoyment of our rights and privileges . . . we pledge ourselves to learn and speak and teach the same to our children.[75]

This assimilation tendency, according to Santillán, lasted between 1920 and 1950 when cultural democracy appeared as a viable strategy, which he describes as follows:

> The essence of cultural democracy is an attempt to integrate the positive qualities of both the Anglo-American and Mexican cultures in order to create a bilingual, bicultural American citizen whose loyalty is to the U.S.[76]

Among these liberal Chicano groups he places Chicano political associations like the Mexican-American Political Association, the U.S. Hispanic Congressional Caucus and the "Viva Kennedy and Johnson" Clubs of the early sixties. Differences with the assimilationists are presented at the cultural level:

> These groups reject the assimilationist doctrine that ethnic minorities have to sacrifice their culture as a means of acquiring social equality, arguing that on the contrary, ethnic diversity and organization based on it have been instrumental in the distribution of tangible rewards.[77]

Since this perspective did not resolve social inequality, Santillán states, in the mix-sixties Chicanos proceeded on to the "highest and final stage of pluralism": cultural nationalism.[78] Santillán defines this last stage as follows:

> Cultural nationalism as expressed in the last decade rejects Anglo-American culture and social institutions and instead embraces the culture and traditions of Mexico and other Latin American countries. It views the inequality of Chicanos as directly tied to the Anglo-American political and economic system in which Chicanos formulate and carry out their political and social activities, and advocates a separatist philosophy for achieving social equality.[79]

Among these cultural nationalists, Santillán places proponents of *El Plan de Aztlán* (1969) and *El Plan de la Raza Unida* (1967). Santillán notes that these militant Chicanos were in fact reformists and that "their activities legitimized and supported the American political system."[80]

The second major perspective presented by Santillán is the Marxist analysis of Chicanos as a distinct cultural group within the U.S. working class. This perspective he finds in the recent publications of various Chicano writers.

Possibly Santillán's presentation is one of the few that analyzes the various pluralist tendencies as reformist and system-oriented where solutions are sought within the existing socio-economic capitalist structure. Where we disagree however is in his analysis through the concept of stages, his retention of vague culturalist descriptions to distinguish between different pluralist tendencies, his analysis of Marxist thought as a *recent* addition to Chicano political thought and his lack of consideration of utopic elements within the Chicano movement.

The notion of stages denies the presence of various culturalist and political tendencies throughout the history of Chicanos in the United States. Recent research into labor history has demonstrated that struggle against the dominant Anglo society and its Mexican-origin allies began even before 1848. These various tendencies fomenting solidarity or antagonism often found expression in their position towards language but in fact originated from economic and political factors.

The population of Mexican origin residing in the Southwest in 1848 was not one of all landless peasants and wage laborers. A socio-economic and political structure existed with a small segment of the Mexican population in control and in possession of vast extensions of land. These ruling Californios, Hispanos from New Mexico and Tejanos, who allied with the incoming dominant Anglo population, were the first Chicano assimilationists. This assimilation was obviously political although it led to cultural changes. Assimilation has always been seen as a vehicle for upward mobility by those whose economic standing allowed for the possibility—whether real or false—of integration with the new ruling class. Nothing assimilates like wealth. Back in the nineteenth century assimilation was cemented with cattle and land and through intermarriage. Some Chicano political scientists have tended to see assimilation as a later phenomenon but in fact cultural and ideological stances of assimilation date back to 1848.

Resistance to the dominant ideology also occurred throughout the century. Prominent among these acts of resistance was the trade-unionist movement in the Mexican community originating as early as 1900.[81] Twentieth century workers of Mexican origin were always involved in the labor movement, even though they often faced racist tendencies within the labor unions themselves which excluded them and forced them to form independent unions. It was the concentration of workers in particular occupations and the prevailing racism which led to solidarity among the Mexican-origin workers and reinforced their cultural and linguistic ties.

The Movement of the sixties also saw the promotion of Cultural National-ism, particularly among certain segments of Chicano university students, but even this orientation has been present throughout this century. In fact in 1915 in the South of Texas an insurrection of Mexicans broke out with the Proclamation of the Plan de San Diego.[82] These separatists sought to leave the American Union and reunite with Mexico or establish a separate sovereign State. During the first half of this century first-generation Mexican immigrants in the United States continued to see themselves as Mexicans and frequently sought out the Mexican consular offices located throughout the Southwest for redress of abuses against Chicanos and Mexicans in the United States.

The various pluralist positions described by Santillán have all been present throughout the century and are not stages arising out of the failure of previous propositions. In fact even the Marxist analysis has been around since the early part of this century. Socialist labor organizers were active even in the first decade of this century.[83] It is evident that events of the past two decades did not mark a new direction for Chicano political activity since they were only quantitatively but not qualitatively different from previous acts of struggle. The various ideological and cultural positions can in fact be summarized in terms of a continuum with two ideological poles marked as follows: acceptance of the dominant ideology vs. rejection of the dominant ideology. Proponents of one position accept the existing capitalist economic structure and seek to resolve conflicts which arise through reforms, while proponents of the other position see antagonistic and unresolvable class contradictions within the existing system.

The first position responds to the functionalist model of society which stresses harmony and unity in the system. Functionalists propose that "all parts of the social system work together with a sufficient degree of harmony or internal consistency, i.e., without producing persistent conflicts which can neither be resolved nor regulated."[84] Functionalists in fact suggest that the system is able to provide solutions for those problems which arise and produce disharmony; they justify the status quo.

The second position—the dialectical-materialist position—sees conflicts of interest arising between classes. The organization of the oppressed class as a revolutionary element brings about social change and the abolition of every class. It is thus the struggle between two antagonistic classes—the workers and the capitalists—that produces social and political change.

The dominant political position among Chicanos is the functionalist one, where the cause of economic failure is viewed as the result of a lack of opportunities, lack of English-speaking abilities, lack of education and even lack of ambition. Those members of the Mexican-origin population who have generally been called assimilationists, as if the problem were one of culture, are actually not particularly attracted by another culture or language. What moves them to advocate certain measures, like education or acquisition of the English language, is their belief in the harmony of the total structure. Functionalists thus include proponents of education, be it monolingual or bilingual, as the solution to the economic problems of Chicanos. Functionalists also propose the establishment of minority or alternative political parties, like la Raza Unida Party, as increased participation in the political system is seen as the solution. Others propose Brown capitalism or Brown politicians in office as the solution. Those proposing a culturally pluralistic society are also functionalists, for they view the possibility of different cultures functioning as equals within the existing social structure. Even the self-determination position for an autonomous Chicano State within the existing system is a functionalist view. The functionalist position is thus not so much culturally based as ideologically motivated since it looks for solutions within the proposed myths of the dominant ideology.

In the area of language, functionalists, who are advocates of education as the vehicle for social mobility, see the English language as indispensable and as the dominant language of this country. Bilingual education, inasmuch as it facilitates the learning of English and to the degree that it increases student achievement in school, is accepted as a necessary correlate of academic success for limited and non-English-speaking students. Maintaining the Spanish language is thus not in itself the objective; being integrated into the total social picture and sharing significant functions within the existing system is the objective. What about the cultural pluralists? Among educators, linguistic pluralism is synonymous with bilingual-bicultural education. Unfortunately bilingual education legislation has enabled the implementation of transitional rather than maintenance programs; furthermore, school districts are only too willing to establish exit criteria to move students from bilingual classes through meaningless assessment procedures.

In opposition to the functionalists are those who see no solutions within the existing framework. Within this group we find the separatists and the Marxists. Unlike the 1915 separatists in Texas, present-day advocates have only produced mythical utopias of Aztlan. On the other hand, much like the Chicano socialists of the early part of the century, today's Chicano Marxists are involved in trade-unionist movements and occasionally can be found in colleges and universities. In the case of language, Marxists recognize that language is a social product and as such, subject to material conditions; they recognize that labor segmentation, racist policies in employment, housing and education, and social stratification—all produced by the class structure of society—in fact contribute to isolate the community and maintain the minority language.

Resistance to the dominant ideology and culture in the Chicano community has not been revolutionary up till now, nor has it sought real structural change. Resistance in fact has generally been reformist in nature and has advocated social mobility, civil rights, more educational and employment opportunities, more voting rights, more minority educators, more minority students in various fields, more minority elected officials and more bilingual education. Participation in this reformist-oriented struggle has undoubtedly kept the Chicano community active throughout the century and has sharpened analytical tools and raised political consciousness, although its primary goal has been an increase in the number of middle-class Chicanos within the existing system.

Table 1.8 summarizes the various proposals made by functionalists, separatists and Marxists. As is obvious, the problem causes and solutions proposed by functionalists are the very same as those presented by proponents of the dominant ideology.

A review of these culturalist and ideological positions has hopefully explained why the Spanish language has not had the same function here in the Southwest that Catalan has had in Catalonia or Basque in the Basque country or French in Quebec. In the next chapter we will look specifically at the relation between income, education and Spanish language loss. For even though material culture produces the context for language maintenance or loss, there is always the additional factor of ideology. Acceptance of the socio-economic structure and the ideology disseminated by the ruling class essentially means acculturation to the dominant language and culture, habituation to the labor process under capitalism, and consumption of myths and cultural commodities. Thus positions on the Spanish language have to be seen in terms of both material culture and ideology. A consideration of material culture forces us to look at the way people live in order to understand why, where maintenance is strongest, there is often a strong sense of the need to acquire English as a means of moving out of a situation of poverty. In the Chicano community we can find three general types of material culture and two ideological positions. As we have indicated before, the pervading ideological position is functionalist. The types of material culture on the other hand are determined by class status as well as by factors determining the type of social interaction and social relations within which that individual or group participates. The three types are as follows:

1. Urban and Rural Middle Class
2. Urban Low-Income Working Class
3. Rural or Semi-Rural Low-Income Working Class

The urban and rural distinction is significant because it determines, in the lower-income cases, whether interaction is intra-group (within the lingual and national minority population) or inter-group (with other lingual and ethnic groups).

Table 1.8   Cultural-Ideological Perspectives

1. Functionalists—belief in harmony and unity of the system. Problems which arise can be solved within the existing political and economic structure.

Variants:
  a) cultural democrats
  b) assimilationists
  c) cultural pluralists
  d) cultural nationalists
  e) self-determinists

Problem: Lack of socio-economic success

Causes:
1. Deficit Models—focus on victim
   a) lack of language skills
   b) lack of labor skills
   c) lack of education
   d) cultural deprivation
   e) economic deprivation
2. Opportunity Models—focus on reforms
   a) lack of economic opportunity
   b) lack of educational opportunity
   c) lack of recognition of Civil Rights

Solutions:
  1. Acquisition of English Language
  2. Increase in Educational Attainment
  3. Bilingual Education
  4. Compensatory Education
  5. Brown Elected Officials
  6. Brown Capitalists
  7. Brown Political Party: La Raza Unida Party
  8. Brown Landowners: Tierra Amarilla
  9. Cultural Pluralism
  10. Racial Integration
  11. Judicial Decisions on Civil Rights
  12. Civil Rights Legislation
  13. Trade-Unionism
  14. Self-Determination—Autonomous Chicano State within Union
  15. Voting Rights Legislation

2. Separatists—Nationalists—Utopic Model: proposal for establishment of mythic Aztlan state.

Problem: A functionalist analysis which goes beyond proposal for autonomous Chicano State

Solution: Creation of myths and resurgence of Aztec Myths

3. Marxist Analysis:
   Given class antagonisms within capitalism, problems can only be solved through social and political change, i.e., the elimination of capitalism.
   Problem: Class society
   Cause: Capitalist mode of production
   Solution: Revolutionary social and political change

There are undoubtedly a few Chicano capitalists, but they are too few to consider here. The majority of the population, as we have seen, fall at the lower end of the economic scale, although there are now a number of Chicano professionals and highly paid skilled workers whose income allows them to live in primarily Anglo or integrated communities as middle-class consumers. Their work if not completely satisfying, is economically rewarding. These full believers in American democracy and the capitalist system are primarily English speakers. There are of course some middle-class and upper-class Mexicans, who are first-generation residents of the United States and who continue to speak Spanish, but these individuals fast become bilinguals.

On the lower end of the pay scale we must distinguish between urban and rural residents, as life in metropolitan areas is totally different from that of small town rural or semi-rural areas where communal ties are meaningful and long-lasting and there is a great deal more interaction between neighbors of all ages. The concentration and segregation that occurs in small towns in residence and employment create a particular life-style where ties established among family, neighbors, relatives and friends are reflected in the workplace, in recreation, in the church, in the community and in the home. Survival in the United States means that these families acquire the second language—English—but continue to use Spanish in all communal activities. In the urban areas, there is both concentration of Mexican-origin people and integration with other minority groups or low-income whites. People travel longer distances to work, play and shop. Communities are divided by factories, freeways, junkyards, motels, shopping centers and cemeteries. Urbanization dissolves social bonds and as these are dissolved, so are cultural and linguistic ties except in those areas where the concentration of Mexican-origin people is so high that in fact the urban community functions like a small town within a city.

This general review of the social, cultural and economic history of the Chicano community provides the context for a closer look at language use in the Chicano community in terms of the types of bilingualism and the characteristics of the Chicano speakers who continue to maintain the Spanish language.

Notes

1. Magne Oftedal, "What are minorities," *Lingual Minorities in Europe* (Oslo: Det Norske Samlaget, 1969), p. 16.

2. Bjórn Aarseth, "The situation of the Lapps, especially in Norway," *Lingual Minorities in Europe* (Oslo: Det Norske Samlaget, 1969), p. 55.

3. Antony Ward, "European Migratory Labor. A Myth of Development," *Monthly Review,* Vol. 27, No. 7, December 1975, p. 24.

4. Robert Blauner, *Racial Oppression in America* (New York: Harper & Row, 1972), p. 52; see also Mario Barrera, Carlos Muñoz and Charles Ornelas, "The Barrio as an Internal Colony," *People and Politics in Urban Society,* ed. Harlan Hahn (Beverly Hills: Sage Publications, 1972), pp. 465–498; see also Tomás Almaguer, "Toward the Study of Chicano Colonialism," *Aztlán,* Vol. 2, No. 1, Spring 1971, pp. 7–21; see also James Blaut, "Are Puerto Ricans a National Minority," *Monthly Review,* May 1977, pp. 35–55.

5. *Carter's Immigration Policy: Attack on Immigrant Labor.* The North American Congress on Latin America (NACLA) Publication, 1978, p. 4; see also "The New Braceros," NACLA,

Vol. XI, No. 8, November–December 1977, pp. 5–9; see also Samir Amin, "The New International Economic Order," *Monthly Review*, Vol. 29, No. 3, July–August 1977, pp. 1–21.

6. Joshua A. Fishman, "Varieties of Ethnicity and Varieties of Language Consciousness," *Language in Sociocultural Change* (Stanford, Calif.: Stanford University Press, 1972), pp. 179–190.

7. *1976 Britannica Yearbook*, "Rhodesia," (Chicago: Encyclopaedia Britannica, Inc., 1976), p. 619.

8. *1976 Britannica Yearbook*, "South Africa," (Chicago: Encyclopaedia Britannica, Inc., 1976), p. 632.

9. Alberto Escobar, "La Educación Bilingüe en el Perú," *Proceedings of the First Inter-American Conference and Bilingual Education*, eds. Rudolph C. Troike and Nancy Modiano (Arlington, VA: Center for Applied Linguistics, 1975), pp. 32–42.

10. Blaut, p. 38.

11. *Ibid.*

12. John Macnamara, "Success and Failure in the Movement for the Restoration of Irish," *Can Language be Planned*, ed. Joan Rubin and Bjórn H. Jernudd (Hawaii: University Press of Hawaii, 1971), pp. 65–94.

13. Richard C. Edwards, Michael Reich and David Gordon, *Labor Market Segmentation* (Lexington, Mass.: Lexington Books, 1975), pp. xi–xii.

14. Leo Grebler, Joan Moore and Ralph Guzman, *The Mexican-American People* (New York: The Free Press, 1970), p. 51.

15. Edwards, Reich and Gordon, p. xvii.

16. Grebler, p. 52.

17. *Ibid.*, pp. 52–54.

18. Carey McWilliams, *North from Mexico* (New York: Greenwood Press, 1968), p. 52.

19. Gilberto Cárdenas, "United States Immigration Policy Toward Mexico: A Historical Perspective," *Chicano Law Review*, 2, Summer 1975, pp. 68–69.

20. *Ibid.*

21. *Ibid.*, p. 70.

22. *Ibid.*

23. *Ibid.*, pp. 75–77.

24. M. Vic Villalpando, *A Study of the Socioeconomic Impact of Illegal Aliens on the County of San Diego* (San Diego: Human Resources Agency, San Diego County, 1977).

25. *NACLA Report, Attack on Immigrant Labor*, p. 1.

26. "Mexican Oil. Sold Out Game," *NACLA, Report on the Americas*, Vol. XIII, No. 3, May–June 1979, pp. 43–45.

27. *NACLA Report, Attack on Immigrant Labor*, p. 4.

28. *Ibid.*

29. "Las maquiladoras como explotación neocolonial," *Punto Crítico*, No. 25/26, febrero–marzo, 1974, pp. 24–28.

30. *Ibid.*

31. *Ibid.*

32. José Luis Fernández Santisteban, "Algunas consideraciones sobre los programas de industrialización y de comercialización fronteriza, sus efectos y perspectivas (MS presented at Monterrey, Nuevo Leon, Symposium on the Border, January 24–27, 1979).

33. Margo Margulis, "Crecimiento y migración en una ciudad de frontera; Estudio preliminar de Reynosa" (MS presented at Monterrey, Nuevo Leon, Symposium on the Border, January 24–27, 1979).

34. Mónica Claire Gambrill, "Composición y conciencia de la fuerza de trabajo en las maquiladoras" (MS presented at Monterrey, Nuevo Leon, Symposium on the Border, January 24–27, 1979).

35. *Ibid.*

36. *Ibid.*

37. Victor L. Urquidi, "La ciudad subdesarrollada," *Demografía y Economía,* Vol. III, No. 2, 1969, pp. 137–155. Quoted in MS "El crecimiento demográfico y los servicios públicos en las ciudades fronterizas," by Gerónimo Martínez (MS presented at Monterrey, Nuevo Leon, Symposium on the Border, January 24–27, 1979).

38. Jorge Bustamante, "La interacción social en la frontera México-Estados Unidos: Un marco conceptual para la investigación (MS presented at Monterrey, Nuevo Leon, Symposium on the Border, January 24–27, 1979).

39. U.S. Bureau of the Census, *Current Population Reports. Population Characteristics,* Persons of Spanish Origin in the United States: March 1977 (Advance Report)," Series P–20, No. 317, Issued December, 1977.

40. Bustamante.

41. *Ibid.*

42. U.S. Bureau of the Census, "Persons of Spanish Origin: March 1977," report.

43. U.S. Bureau of the Census, *Current Population Reports: Population Characteristics,* "Persons of Spanish Origin in the United States: March 1978," Series P–20, No. 339, Issued June, 1979.

44. *Ibid.*

45. U.S. Bureau of the Census, "Persons of Spanish Origin: March 1977," report.

46. U.S. Bureau of the Census, *Current Population Reports: Population Characteristics,* "Persons of Spanish Origin in the United States," March, 1976, Series P–20, No. 302, Issued November, 1976.

47. U.S. Bureau of the Census, "Persons of Spanish Origin: March 1978," report.

48. U.S. Bureau of the Census, "Persons of Spanish Origin: March 1976," report.

49. *Ibid.*

50. U.S. Bureau of the Census, "Persons of Spanish Origin in the United States: March 1977," report.

51. V. N. Volosinov, *Marxism and the Philosophy of Language* (New York: Seminar Press, 1973), p. 19.

52. Salomón Nahmad, "La Política educativa en regiones interculturales de México," *Proceedings of the First Inter-American Conference on Bilingual Education,* eds. Rudolph C. Troike and Nancy Modiano (Arlington, Virgina: Center for Applied Linguistics, 1975), p. 21.

53. Gordon Childe, *Social Evolution* (London: Watts & Co., 1952), p. 30.

54. *Ibid,* pp. 31–32.

55. *Ibid.*

56. *Ibid.,* p. 39.

57. Errol Black, "Seeds of Destruction," *Monthly Review,* Vol. 31, No. 11, April 1980, pp. 13–23.

58. Childe, *Man Makes Himself* (London: Watts & Co., 1956), p. 8.

59. *Ibid.,* pp. 16–17.

60. Juan Gómez Quiñones, "On Culture," *Revista Chicano-Riqueña,* Ano 5, No. 2, Spring 1977, pp. 29–47.

61. *Ibid.,* p. 39.

62. *Ibid.*

63. *Ibid.*

64. *Ibid.,* p. 35.

65. Lourdes Arizpe, *Migración, Etnicismo y Cambio Económico* (México: El Colegio de México, 1978), p. 165.

66. *Ibid.,* p. 238.

67. Norris Clement, "United States-Mexico Economic Relations: The Role of California" (MS for a seminar organized by the American Friends Service Committee and the Chicano Studies Department, California State University, Los Angeles, November 1977).

68. *Ibid.*

69. Armand Mattelart, *La cultura como empresa multinacional* (México: Serie Popular ERA, 1976).

70. Gelvin Stevenson, "Social Relations of Production and Consumption in the Human Service Occupations," *Monthly Review,* Vol. 28, No. 3, July–August 1976, pp. 78–87.

71. Richard Santillán, "Dialectics of Chicano Political Development," *Appeal to Reason,* Vol. 5, No. 4, Winter 1979–1980, p. 51.

72. *Ibid.,* p. 52.

73. *Ibid.*

74. *Ibid.,* p. 54.

75. *Ibid.*

76. *Ibid.*

77. *Ibid.,* pp. 54–55.

78. *Ibid.,* p. 56.

79. *Ibid.*

80. *Ibid.,* p. 58.

81. Juan Gómez Quiñones y Luis Leobardo Arroyo, *Orígenes del Movimiento Obrero Chicano* (México: Serie Popular ERA, 1978), p. 22.

82. *Ibid.,* p. 19.

83. *Ibid.,* p. 18.

84. Robert Merton, "Toward the Codification of Functional Analysis in Sociology," *Theories and Paradigms in Contemporary Sociology,* ed. R. Serge Denisoff, Orel Callahan, Mark H. Levine (Itasca, Illinois: F. E. Peacock Publisher, Inc., 1974), p. 249.

CHAPTER 2

Chicano Bilingualism:
Participants and Domains

The Mexican-origin population is essentially a bilingual national minority for whom Spanish continues to be either the first or second language. Although a segment of the Chicano population has ceased to function in Spanish, the majority retain some degree of passive or active competence in the language. In this chapter we will explore specific material culture factors determining language shift through available information provided by the Census Bureau, our own survey, and years of observation and participation in this phenomenon. Available statistical data will be analyzed in relation to the types of bilingualism which exist in the Chicano community as we examine how socio-economic factors are leading to particular patterns of social and verbal interaction. Though class is the primary factor which determines the type of social and language contact in our society, other variables like nativity, residence, generation and age are also important. We will begin by looking at the latter first.

LANGUAGE—NATIVITY—ORIGIN

Census statistics for 1970, as we have indicated before, are generally assumed to have been inaccurate in their reports on the Spanish surname and Spanish-origin population. These statistics are currently reported comprehensively for persons of Spanish origin and further subdivided in terms of Mexican, Puerto Rican, Cuban, Central or South American and other Spanish origin. Thus 1970 Census reports on persons of Spanish origin indicated a total of 9 million; 1976 figures, on the other hand, reported 11 million persons of Spanish origin; 1978 statistics indicated 12 million persons. The provisional 1980 count of the Spanish-origin population was 14.6 million, but the Current Population Survey estimates for March 1980 indicated a population of 13.2 million. Unofficial estimates indicated over 19 million persons of Spanish origin. Census Bureau estimates for May 1981 (Table 2.1) indicated the breakdown of "Hispanic subpopulations."[1] Although none of these statistics can be said to be entirely

Table 2.1   Hispanic Subpopulation from
Census Bureau Estimates
for May 1981

Mexican	60%
Puerto Rican	14
Cuban	6
Central or South American	8
Other Spanish	12

Table 2.2   Division of Mexican-origin Population According to Nativity and
Parentage (1970 Census)

		Total Mexican-origin population %
Persons of Mexican origin	4,532,000	100
First generation from Mexico	760,000	17
Second generation from Mexico	1,579,000	35
Third and subsequent generations	2,339,000	48

accurate, the compiled figures in each case show definite proportions in terms of income, residence, education and identification which are highly useful in attempting to characterize the population of Mexican origin in quantitative terms.

Census figures for 1970, for example, allow us to see certain trends in terms of nativity and parentage. Out of the estimated 4.5 million persons of Mexican origin in 1970, about 1.6 million were second generation (persons born in the United States with a parent or parents born outside the United States) and 760,000 were first generation (persons born outside the United States (Table 2.2). Thus in 1970 the Mexican-origin population could be divided into three groups.[2] Statistics are also available on the mother tongue of the total Spanish-origin population as well as of foreign-born Mexican-origin persons and Mexican-origin persons of foreign or mixed parentage in the five Southwestern states. "Mother Tongue" reports in 1970 were based on language spoken in the household during the person's childhood. The most common mother tongue other than English in 1970 was Spanish, reported by 7.8 million.[3] More recent statistics, as we shall see later, are higher. As is to be expected, 1970 statistics indicate a high rate of maintenance in households of first and second-generation persons and a lower rate for persons of third and subsequent generations as indicated in Table 2.3.[4] While 86% (7.8 million) of the total Spanish-origin population (9 million in 1970) reported Spanish as their mother tongue,[5] in the Southwest only about 78% did. Spanish was found to be the household language of most (93.3%) foreign-born Spanish-origin residents and of about 87% of natives of foreign or mixed parentage. Comprehensive statistics for the Spanish-origin population however do not reflect an accurate picture of the Mexican-origin population. Statistics for Chicanos are much higher in both categories as

Table 2.3   Rate of Maintenance of Spanish as Mother Tongue (1970 Census)

	Total population	Reporting Spanish mother tongue	%
Total Spanish surname or Spanish-language population	5,988,155	4,661,801	77.8
Native of native parentage	3,463,015	2,405,327	69.5
Native of foreign or mixed parentage	1,637,042	1,428,236	87.3
Foreign born	888,098	828,238	93.3
Native of foreign or mixed parentage from Mexico	1,320,777	1,255,598	95.1
Foreign born from Mexico	646,252	639,817	99

Table 2.4   Rate of Maintenance of Spanish as Mother Tongue for Puerto Rican and Other American (Non-Mexican) Persons

	Total population	Persons with Spanish mother tongue	%
Born in Puerto Rico	25,718	20,121	78.2
Puerto Rican parentage	25,227	24,573	97.5
Native of foreign or mixed parentage—Other America	77,499	53,829	69.4
Foreign born—Other America	108,729	101,495	93.3

is evident in the lower part of Table 2.3. For first-generation persons of Mexican origin, Spanish was the mother tongue of 99%. A high 95.1% of second-generation Mexican-origin persons also reported Spanish as the mother tongue.

When we compare the 1970 statistics of the Mexican-origin population with those for other Spanish-origin persons, we find a correlation between mother tongue statistics, education and income. The statistics in Table 2.4 appeared in 1970 for Cubans, other Americans (Central and South Americans) and Puerto Ricans.[6] (See Tables 1.6 and 1.7 for education and income comparisons.)

Second generation persons from South and Central America have the lowest proportion for Spanish as the mother tongue. The group's higher educational attainment and income level fall into a pattern of surveys where educational attainment and income correlate. The July 1977 issue of *Current Population Reports* indicates that in 1976 the educational attainment of adult family members had a direct bearing on family income. In general as the educational level increased, so did the family income. The median income for a Spanish-origin family in which the head had less than eight years of school completed was $7,100. Where the head had completed high school, the median income was $12,500; with four years of college or more, the median family income was $20,000.[7]

The correlation of income, education and language is demonstrated as well in studies on Spanish-language media. In his study *Spanish-Language Radio and Chicano Internal Colonialism*, Félix Frank Gutiérrez reports that Spanish-language radio is preferred by lower income Chicanos, by the older and less educated, and by listeners born in Mexico, while higher socio-economic Chicanos prefer English-language radio stations.[8] His report that the Spanish broadcast audience is primarily of lower socio-economic standing serves to reinforce our argument that language maintenance and low economic standing correlate positively.

Nativity, language use and income were also found to be closely related in a study of the viewers of Spanish-language TV in Los Angeles. The researchers López and Enos found a high correlation between nativity and preference for Channel 34 (KMEX), a Spanish-language television station.[9] Of all respondents indicating that they watch this Spanish-language television station 75.5% were Mexican-born.[10] This station preference was also closely tied to use of Spanish at home: those using Spanish predominantly at home listed Channel 34 as their favorite station.[11] These Spanish-language TV viewers were predominantly a low-income group (89.3% earned $10,000 or less) with low educational attainment.[12]

LANGUAGE AND AGE

The relation between nativity and maintenance of Spanish as the usual language appears to be significant in the López and Enos report although about 60% of those respondents born in the United States used some Spanish with their children as well.[13] Here, length of residence in Southern California was not a major factor in determining viewers of Spanish-language TV, since 70% of these had lived in the area for six or more years (5.13% had resided for 19 years or more).[14] Age, however, was found to be significant in this study: the young, more schooled and U.S. born, preferred English language television.[15] Those viewers watching Spanish-language TV were predominantly over 30 years of age; few viewers in the 18–21 age bracket indicated watching Channel 34.[16] It is difficult to be precise on the relation between age and language use where nativity and length of residence have to be taken into account. Surveys generally provide ambiguous information about language use as well. In this particular study, 74.4% of all respondents with children indicated that they spoke at least some Spanish to their children; 25.1% indicated that they spoke Spanish exclusively.[17] In the case of bilingual households it is impossible to determine the functions of each language or the degree of proficiency of the children in the Spanish language with a survey. What was most important here was that a high 35% of those surveyed continue to prefer the Spanish-language media whether they are bilingual or predominantly Spanish speaking.[18]

Although not totally reliable, additional Census Bureau studies on language use are also important to consider since they offer statistics on sample populations. A special Census Bureau study on usual and second languages spoken in the United States indicates that Spanish persists as the usual or second language of a significant number of persons.[19] About 4 million persons (four years old and over) reported Spanish as their usual language. An additional 4.9 million reported Spanish as their second language. In a Spanish-origin population of over 12 million, the proportion is relatively high considering that in the Southwest only about 14% of the Spanish-origin population surveyed by the Census is foreign born and about 27% is of foreign or mixed parentage (second generation).[20] Thus of the total Spanish-origin population approximately 79% reported continued use of the Spanish language. Yet in those same households where Spanish was reported as the usual language, a large number (20%) of persons reported English as their individual language.[21] In these same households where Spanish was the usual household language, 56.6% reported English as their second language.[22] These statistics thus indicate actual bilingualism among approximately three fourths of the persons in households where Spanish is the usual language.

For some linguistic groups surveyed by the Census Bureau, language and age distribution showed some interesting patterns. For example, 44% of those whose usual language is Italian are in the 65 years old and over age bracket, although they constitute only 11% of the total Italian-origin population. Only 5% of persons whose usual language is Italian are of elementary and high school age.[23] For Spanish-language persons, the distribution includes 21% of persons between 6–17 years of age; this age bracket makes up about 30% of the population. In Table 2.5 we correlate population and age statistics with information provided by the Census language report. The Spanish-origin population is a young population with a median age of 27.7 as compared to 29.2 for the total population. The median age for Chicanos and Puerto Ricans is even lower: Mexican-origin population—median age 20.8; Puerto Rican population—20.4 years. These 1977 statistics indicate that about 57.6% of the population of Spanish origin is 18 years old and over; yet this group accounts for 73.1% of the people with Spanish as their usual language. Conversely about 29.9% of the population is between 5 and 17 years of age; interestingly enough this group accounts for 26.9% of the speakers who have Spanish as their usual language.

An additional report for March 1972 indicated that in the Southwest approximately two thirds of the Spanish-origin population reported Spanish as the household language. Statistics here were higher for the Mexican-origin population than for persons of Puerto Rican, Cuban, Central or South American origin. Table 2.6 also indicates that language maintenance is stronger among

Table 2.5   Correlation Between Age and Spanish as Usual Language of Spanish-origin Persons

Spanish-origin population by age: March 1977.[24]		Spanish language as usual language of persons 4 years old and over	
	% of Total		% by Age[25]
Under 5	12.4	4 & 5 yrs.	5.5
5–17	29.9	6–17	21.4
18–24	14.0	18–24	12.5
25–44	26.3	25–44	34.7
45–64	13.2	45–64	18.0
65 & over	4.1	65 & over	7.9

Table 2.6 Persons of Spanish Origin Reporting Spanish Currently Spoken in Home by Age and Type of Spanish Origin, for the Five Southwestern States: March 1972

(Numbers in thousands)

Age	Spanish origin			Mexican origin			Other Spanish origin[1]		
	Total	Reporting Spanish currently spoken in home		Total	Reporting Spanish currently spoken in home		Total	Reporting Spanish currently spoken in home	
		Number	%		Number	%		Number	%
Total	5,429	3,333	63.1	4,549	3,076	67.9	881	458	52.0
Under 5 years	734	195	67.4	622	426	68.3	111	70	63.1
5 and 6 years	282	187	66.3	241	168	69.7	100	60	60.0
7 to 9 years	479	320	66.8	120	279	66.4	58	48	54.3
10 to 13 years	588	372	63.3	500	324	64.8	175	78	44.6
14 to 19 years	736	162	62.8	621	408	65.7	127	55	43.3
20 to 24 years	428	260	60.7	369	236	64.0	109	60	55.0
25 to 34 years	718	130	59.9	592	376	63.5	189	89	32.1
35 to 44 years	608	375	61.7	499	316	63.3			
45 to 54 years	418	283	67.7	344	247	71.8			
55 to 64 years	243	177	72.8	183	146	79.8			
65 years and over	193	172	58.2	137	149	94.9			

[1]Includes persons of Puerto Rican, Cuban, Central or South American, and other Spanish origin.

persons over 45 years of age and weaker among young adults 25–35 years of age.[26]

Thus a significant percentage of younger speakers and young adults of third generation and beyond continue to be bilingual. Only approximately 30% of these Chicanos indicated no longer using Spanish at home.

Statistics for March 1971 (Table 2.7) also indicated that persons of Spanish origin 14 years old and over reporting Spanish currently spoken in the home had a lower level of educational attainment.[27]

Table 2.7   Educational Attainment of Persons of Spanish Origin 14 Years Old and Over Speaking Spanish in the Home

	Total	Median school yrs. completed
Male, 14 years old and over		
Total Spanish origin	2,679,000	9.6
Total reporting Spanish currently spoken in home	1,869,000	8.7
Mexican origin	1,504,000	9.1
Mexican origin reporting Spanish currently spoken in home	1,056,000	8.3
Other Spanish origin	796,000	11.2
Other Spanish origin, reporting Spanish currently spoken in home	491,000	10.4
Female, 14 years old and over		
Total Spanish origin	2,927,000	9.6
Total reporting Spanish currently spoken in home	2,056,000	8.6
Mexican origin	1,534,000	9.1
Mexican origin, reporting Spanish currently spoken in home	1,100,000	8.2
Other Spanish origin	911,000	11.6
Other Spanish origin, reporting Spanish currently spoken in home	549,000	10.3

This Census report also indicates a higher proportion of Mexican-origin persons reporting Spanish as the household language. The Other-Spanish-origin population not only had a lower rate of maintenance of Spanish language as the household language but also a higher level of educational attainment. Interestingly, even those Other-Spanish-origin persons reporting Spanish as the usual language had a higher educational attainment than either of the Mexican-origin groups.

All of these statistics indicate that both language maintenance and language loss have taken place among the Spanish-origin population. Retention of Spanish is highest among the older population, the foreign born and natives of foreign or mixed parentage, but maintenance is still fairly strong among the younger generations although it is here where the shift to English as the usual language appears to be occurring. Retention of Spanish is also more evident among the Mexican-origin population than among persons of South and Central

American origin. The Mexican-origin population, as we indicated earlier, has a lower economic standing and a comparatively lower educational attainment. Thus although several factors appear to correlate positively, the two principal factors present in Spanish language maintenance are foreign nativity and income, i.e., class.

Comparable information is now being made available through *La Red/The Net*, where one can find preliminary findings of the 1979 Chicano Survey directed by Carlos Arce. In its April 1981 issue, *La Red* published some of the findings on Chicano language patterns in terms of frequency of use of Spanish and English with particular family members. The June 1981 issue provides figures on the language of the interview and the proficiency of the interviewee as indicated by his/her stated ability to function in either language in given domains. (*La Red* is the monthly newsletter of the National Chicano Research Network at the University of Michigan.)

Studies indicating strong Spanish language maintenance among second generation residents and the foreign born have been corroborated by our own small-scale survey among Chicano students at UCSD. Although survey instruments can offer some information on attitudes and self-assessment of language use in particular domains and with particular addressees, they never indicate with any degree of precision what actually takes place in verbal interaction. They can only serve to provide a general idea of what speakers think is taking place or what they would like to think is taking place when they interact with other Chicanos. For this reason future research will require ample recording of Chicanos in various domains with different addressees where language patterns can be studied in relation to different functions and as expressed through different speech acts and events. Still these surveys do provide some insights into the attitudes of Chicano students towards their own language use and language choice.

In a survey of 28 Chicano students in a UCSD class, we found four generations of students which included (1) those born in Mexico (first generation in the United States), (2) those born in the United States, with parents and grandparents born in Mexico (second generation), (3) those born in the United States with one parent born in Mexico and one in the United States and the grandparents in Mexico (mixed parentage: second–third generation), (4) those born in the United States with native-born parents and foreign-born grandparents (third generation) and (5) those born in the United States with parents and at least one set of grandparents born in the United States (fourth generation). In doing the survey we were particularly interested in a self-appraisal of language dominance and the relation of language dominance to generation, language dominance of parents, area of residence (rural or urban), type of residential area (segregated or integrated) as well as ethnic composition of high school and language used in various domains.

The six students who were first generation in the United States all grew up in an urban community which was predominantly Chicano. All classified themselves as bilingual: four as bilingual, dominant in Spanish and two as bilingual, equally proficient in both languages. The parents of the balanced bilinguals were both bilingual, dominant in Spanish while the parents of the Spanish dominant students were monolinguals in Spanish. For all of these first-generation bilinguals, Spanish is primarily the language of the home and the neighborhood and English, the language of work and the classroom. With friends and young Chicanos, these first-generation students indicated that they used both English and Spanish. All of the students entered elementary school as Spanish monolinguals but by the time they were in high school they considered themselves to be bilingual. These students indicated that they wrote letters home in Spanish, listened to radio broadcasts in Spanish but read materials in English only.

The five second-generation Chicanos (those born in the United States with foreign-born parents) entered school as either monolingual in Spanish or bilingual, dominant in Spanish. By the time they were in high school, the original monolinguals felt that they were bilingual, dominant in Spanish, while the original bilinguals considered themselves bilingual, dominant in English. The language of the child upon entering school depended on the mother's language. In cases where the mother was said to be monolingual in Spanish, the students entered school as monolinguals and where she was bilingual, they also classified themselves as bilingual. Thus the mother determined the home linguistic setting, although our own observation over the years has indicated that siblings can often determine the home language as well. There was one exception to the early monolingual student findings. In this particular survey we included the instructor of the class, a Chicano from Lubbock, Texas. Although his mother was monolingual in Spanish and he too was monolingual upon entering school, he considered himself to have been bilingual, dominant in English by the time he was in high school, as he was one of three or four Chicanos in the entire school system. His school setting thus determined his dominance in English. After doing undergraduate and graduate work in Spanish literature, this professor now considers himself to be bilingual, dominant in Spanish and prefers to do his teaching and writing in the Spanish language. Thus one's linguistic setting and training as well as one's career objectives and political stance can greatly alter language choice.

Eight of the students were second generation on one side of the family and third generation on the other. Of the eight, six had fathers born in the United States and mothers born in Mexico. Two had mothers born in the United States and fathers born in Mexico. Of these eight students, seven indicated that they were bilingual dominant in English. In all of these cases the students' mothers, regardless of nativity, were bilingual. The only student who classified himself as bilingual dominant in Spanish indicated that his mother was monolingual in Spanish. Of the seven students classifying themselves as English-dominant bilinguals, four entered elementary school as Spanish monolinguals, but by the time they were in high school their dominance was in English. Two of these students were already dominant in English by the time they entered school and one entered school as a monolingual in English. The one student who classified himself as bilingual dominant in Spanish was also bilingual upon entering school. This particular student appears to participate in domains where Spanish is the usual language, as he indicated Spanish use for home, neighborhood, friends, relatives and even younger Chicanos. The other students, those dominant in English, indicated that they used a combination of both languages for most domains except work (which was always English) and home, which in most cases called for a combination of both languages but in three cases was strictly a Spanish domain.

Among the five students who were third generation (native-born with native parents and foreign-born grandparents), three no longer considered themselves as native speakers of Spanish. Of these three, two indicated they were monolingual in English, despite the fact that both knew some Spanish. Of the five students, three considered themselves bilingual, dominant in English. For all of the five, English is the primary language of communication in all domains. Three indicated that as the years go by they forget their Spanish while two indicated that they learn more Spanish. In all but one of these cases, the mother was bilingual. The student with the monolingual Spanish-speaking mother entered school as a monolingual as well, but by the time he was in high school he considered himself to be bilingual, dominant in English. Of the other four students, three entered school as English-dominant bilinguals and one as an English monolingual. These third generation students socialized primarily with English-speaking friends in English-language domains and their parents had some college education.

Of the fourth generation students, those born in the United States with native-born parents and grandparents, all four classified themselves as bilingual, dominant in English. Only one of these students considered himself to be a native speaker of Spanish. Two of the students entered school as English monolinguals and one as a bilingual, dominant in English. The one student who considered himself to be a native speaker of Spanish entered school as a Spanish monolingual but became dominant in English by the time he was in high school. On the other hand, the two English monolinguals were bilingual by the time they were in high school. Thus peer pressure could be an important factor to consider, but judging from the language choices indicated for the different domains, we have to assume that these fourth-generation students function primarily in the English language.

If these 28 students are indicative of the general trend among Chicanos, then each succeeding generation tends to shift more and more to English. Thus whereas most first generation students become or remain bilingual, dominant in Spanish, those of the third and fourth generations are primarily bilingual, dominant in English or English monolinguals. The fact that UCSD is in San Diego, California, a border city, with a small Chicano student population (about 5% of total student population) coming from the San Diego area, Imperial

Table 2.8   Sociolinguistic Survey of 81 Chicano Students. Information gathered by Toscano, Hernández and Ortiz.

Generation	Total number of students	Income bracket	
		Under $15,000	Under $10,111
First—Foreign-born	30	87%	50%
Second—Native-born Parents: foreign-born	13	92	77
Second–Third—Native-born Parents: one native; one foreign	17	88	53
Third—Native-born Parents: Native-born	21	86	48

County and the Los Angeles area, led us to expect a strong cross-generational maintenance of Spanish among the students. The results with this small sampling however corroborate commonly expressed impressions of California Chicanos when compared to those from Texas, i.e., California Chicano students are much more English dominant than Texas Chicanos. This study was later replicated by three UCSD students: Ricardo Toscano, Víctor Hernández and María C. Ortiz.[28] Their report, presented as a term project for a Third World Studies course on bilingualism, confirmed our initial findings. This extended study involved 81 UCSD Chicano students, who were subsequently subdivided into four groups. Table 2.8 summarizes some of their findings.

In the Toscano-Hernández-Ortiz survey we again find that the number of English monolinguals increases significantly with third-generation students. Bilinguals dominant in English are present as early as the first generation but become the majority by the second generation. Only a third of the third-generation students continue to use some Spanish in the home and already a third consider themselves monolingual in English. The income statistics were gathered to see whether income and occupation were significant variables but in this case, all of the Chicano students, whether first or third generation, were concentrated in the lower-income brackets, with 50% or more making under $10,000. Thus an increase in the number of years or generations of residence in the United States would indicate an eventual loss of bilingualism.

These findings are corroborated by the work of Eduardo Hernández-Chávez who has found that "a growing body of evidence" demonstrates "that Spanish speaking communities are shifting dramatically to English":

> In general, studies of language use are beginning to show very clearly that third generation Mexican Americans—and in urban areas even second generation speakers—are following the familiar pattern of other non-English languages in the United States. The first generation acquires a limited amount of English in adulthood, the second generation becomes bilingual, and the third generation shifts to English.[29]

Although our research indicates that years of residence or generations in the

Table 2.8 (continued)

Home Language			Self Assessment of Language Proficiency			
			Bilingual			
Spanish	English	Both	Dominant in Spanish	Dominant in English	Balanced Bilingual	English Monolingual
57%	13%	27%	50%	30%	13%	—
30	30	40	15	62	15	8
24	29	47	12	65	6	18
0	66	33	5	62	0	33

United States are not the only factors to be considered and that in fact, fourth-generation Chicanos who have been socially marginalized in rural areas are very much like second-generation Chicanos in urban areas in terms of Spanish-language use, there is undoubtedly a strong correlation between generation group and language maintenance or loss.

What we in fact have here are individuals at different stages of the bilingual process, whether their position is determined by generation, residence in urban or rural areas, or socio-economic factors, all of which allow an increase or decrease of contact with other Spanish-speaking persons. These various bilinguals can be classified according to language proficiency in both languages, use of language for particular functions, in particular domains and with particular addressees, frequency of use of both languages, types of shifts from one language to another and attitudes towards the two languages. On a community level, these various factors pointing to different tendencies in language use combine to form different types or composites of bilinguals, as we shall see in the next section.

BILINGUALISM AND LANGUAGE DOMAINS

In a society where Spanish has been relegated to a subordinate position by the dominant language, the future of bilingualism lies with the continued presence of a Spanish-speaking population not yet totally assimilated to the English language, i.e., with the continued presence of first-generation Mexican immigrants in areas of Chicano concentration. The social and economic factors determining the functions of the two languages and the domains within which they are used also determine the status of the two languages and the survival or extinction of the subordinate language. In the Southwest, where a significant number of Chicanos are bilingual, there are various types of bilingualism which reflect the particular historical conditions which produce them. Glyn Lewis has described four types of bilingualism in terms of language functions and sociolinguistic contacts. Since these four types reflect existing types of bilingualism in the Southwest, they will be briefly summarized below:

1. *Stable bilingualism* is characterized by the "geographically contiguous co-existence of linguistic groups." In this case, "the bilinguals resort indifferently to either language in most situations."[30]
2. *Dynamic bilingualism* is typical among people "on the move socially and geographically." In this case, "social mobility, role differentiation and appropriation of different languages for those roles prepare the ground for assimilation."
3. *Transitional bilingualism* begins when "two or more languages assume overlapping functions," a situation which inevitably leads to the exclusive use of one language for those functions.[31]
4. *Vestigial bilingualism* is marked by "almost complete assimilation, where bilingualism is vestigial and often only symbolic, characterizing a small and diminishing minority."[32]

A form of stable bilingualism exists along the U.S.-Mexican border for a segment of the Chicano (and sometimes non-Chicano) population. Here it is easy to find business and local government employees who are equally proficient in both languages. Radio and television stations as well as all sorts of written materials are equally available in both languages and residents travel daily from one side of the border to the other for shopping, entertainment, work and other business. Figure 2.1 reflects the existence of two stable language groups.

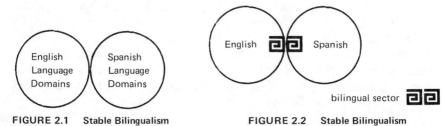

FIGURE 2.1   Stable Bilingualism   FIGURE 2.2   Stable Bilingualism

In areas of stable bilingualism, there are domains where both languages may be used. For example, in the commercial area, both English and Spanish may function without altering the stability of the two language communities. Thus it is not uncommon for an American tourist to be addressed in English while browsing through the wares exhibited outside Mexican curio shops. The large number of Mexicans shopping in American shopping centers in border cities also require a bilingual sales staff. This particular dimension can be exemplified in Figure 2.2, where each circle represents a lingual community and the checkered rectangle within represents a shared domain. Thus within a situation of stable bilingualism there may be dimensions where either language can be used without introducing radical social and linguistic consequences. Were one language to begin assuming functions within the domains of another, then dynamic bilingualism would have set in.

For the immigrant, dynamic bilingualism begins when participation in English-dominant domains leads to the acquisition of a second language in order to function satisfactorily. It is of course possible to survive in the Southwest as a Spanish monolingual by restricting one's activities to areas of strong Mexican-origin concentration. Cases of Spanish monolingualism are frequent among recent immigrants and older first-generation Chicanos, but school and occupation force most persons of Mexican-origin to learn the second language. Survival often depends on learning English.

Even among residents of rural or segregated barrios where the minority population is segregated from the dominant language community for informal and intimate functions, dynamic bilingualism is triggered in formal or occupational domains where workers and school children must shift from Spanish to English. Often it takes crossing the proverbial railroad tracks, a main thoroughfare or the like to enter a different lingual community. Thus we may have home, neighborhood and recreational domains totally in the minority language while school, government and employment are in the dominant language. These cases of initial diglossia often pave the way for transitional bilingualism:

Chicano Domains	Shared	Anglo Domains
Home	Work	Home
Barrio	School	Neighborhood
Recreation	Government	Recreation
Spanish	English	English

Under dynamic bilingualism, which is often a latter development for earlier stable-bilingual communities and a stepping stone for transitional bilingualism, overlapping begins to occur among previously exclusively one-language domains, as in Figure 2.3. Often within a generation one of the languages (the minority) may be totally displaced by the other (the dominant), particularly

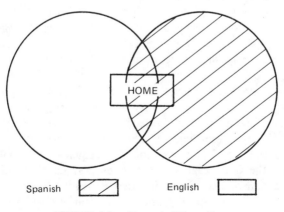

Spanish English

FIGURE 2.3   Dynamic Bilingualism

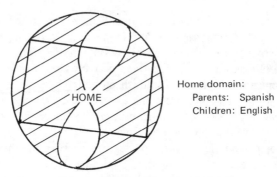

Home domain:
    Parents: Spanish
    Children: English

FIGURE 2.4   Transitional Bilingualism

among the younger members of the population, to the point where the minority language may be limited to the parent role or to specific speech acts within the home domain, as shown in Figure 2.4. In these cases the child may have receptive competence in the minority language. This shift constitutes transitional bilingualism.

Vestigial bilingualism is the case for a large number of fourth, fifth, and sixth-generation Chicanos who have assimilated completely to the English language but still retain a few words or expressions as ethnic markers. Of course, vestigial bilingualism can occur as easily in the second generation under particular social conditions or whenever the Spanish speaker is severed from a Spanish-speaking base through long-distance migration.

For Chicanos in the Southwest, bilingualism is primarily dynamic and Spanish proficiency is primarily oral rather than literate. For here, despite the existence of bilingualism, all prestigious social roles and functions are English-language domains. Few formal domains call for the use of Spanish. With the exception of New Mexico, all of the Southwestern states have English as the sole official language. Admission to statehood of the Southwestern territory brought the institution of language requirements making knowledge of English a requisite for voting, serving on juries, conducting official business and acquiring an education. Only New Mexico with a population in 1850 of about 50% Spanish speakers preserved Spanish as one of its official languages through constitutional provisions.[33] Today the language policy of this country, that is, the requirement of English proficiency and literacy for various formal functions, is beginning to be addressed as a violation of the Civil Rights of language minority populations. The Voting Rights Act of 1975, for example, extended the previous Voting Act and placed a permanent ban on English literacy qualifications for voting and specifically provided for the protection of the voting rights of members of language minorities.[34] The Supreme Court in its Lau Decision also recognized the rights of linguistic minorities to equal educational opportunities by ruling that the Civil Rights Act of 1964 forbade discrimination among students on account of race or national origin and prohibited as well the denial of meaningful and effective participation in educational programs offered by school districts on the basis of inability to speak and understand the English language.[35] This decision, in part, has led to federal and state funding and provisions for the implementation of bilingual education for limited and non-English-speaking students, an important issue in itself, and at the same time has served to focus attention on other language restrictions. English proficiency, for example, is still an educational requirement in the Southwest. With the institution of examinations to test the academic proficiencies of high school students as a requisite for graduation in some states (like California), the notion of distinguishing between minimal academic achievement (i.e., the acquisition of academic skills) and English-language proficiency is already being discussed among Spanish-speaking educators and lawyers. Recognition of language discrimination in voting and education has thus set the stage for a recognition of language rights in other areas.

Since the Voting Rights Act was extended and expanded in 1975, Texas and California have enacted laws (presently being challenged) providing for voting materials and information in languages other than English. In legal proceedings, English is the language used although most courts allow for the use of interpreters and translators. Greenfield and Kates have documented how literacy requirements for placement on grand juries and English proficiency have worked against the participation of the Mexican-origin population on juries.[36] Since most states only require that jurors be qualified voters, the Voting Rights Act may alleviate juror discrimination to some extent. In other official cases, as in the application for motor-vehicle licenses and documentation, the material is generally available in Spanish as well as other languages besides English. In the case of federal jurors, however, Congressional policy provides for the disqualification of a person to be a federal juror if he is "unable to read, write and understand the English language with proficiency sufficient to fill out satisfactorily the juror qualification form" and/or is "unable to speak the English language (28 USC 1865)."[37] Naturalization as a citizen of the United States also requires that the candidate demonstrate "an understanding of the English language, including an ability to read, write, and speak words in ordinary usage in the English language (* USC 1423)."[38]

The issue of language choice and language rights has been addressed by Reynaldo Macías. He finds that "the Constitution and federal law do not provide for, nor guarantee, language choice or language rights directly or explicitly." Macías points out that only where language is part of a national-origin classification, as in the case of the Lau Decision, does language discrimination constitute the basis for claiming infringement of fundamental rights.[39] Given recent statements by President Reagan of the United States on bilingual education as "UnAmerican" and Senator Hayakawa's bid to make English the national language of the land, progress on the recognition of language choice as a civil right will probably be thwarted in the near future. Stressing that competing in English should be the first priority for all non-English-speaking students, President Reagan declared in a speech to the

National League of Cities that "it is absolutely wrong and against American concepts to have a bilingual education program that is now openly, admittedly dedicated to preserving their native language and never getting them adequate in English so they can go out into the job market and participate."[40] His clear distortion of the goals of bilingual education, where acquisition of the English language is in fact the goal of transitional programs and one of the goals of maintenance programs, was an attack on bilingual education and an expression of disregard for the educational and language rights of minorities. The constitutional amendment (SJR 72, April 27, 1981) proposed by Senator Hayakawa making English the official language of proceedings and documents is one more example of this conservative wave intent on denying national minorities their language rights.[41]

Although legally there may be little or no support for the maintenance of minority languages, at the functional level, the future of Spanish will depend on the speakers themselves and their ability to maintain significant functions for the Spanish language. Given the use of English for most formal functions, Spanish has survived primarily as the familiar language. There are, however, several formal domains where Spanish is the usual language. Among these are Chicano churches, Chicano newspapers and Spanish-language radio and TV stations. Most Protestant churches in the barrios conduct services and Sunday school in Spanish. Materials, Bibles and hymnals are almost always in Spanish, published in either Spain or Latin America. In recent years Sunday school classes for the younger children or teenagers have been introducing English-language materials. Yet all church-related activities, whether prayers, hymns, dinners, meetings and sermons, are in Spanish. It is also possible to find numerous local newspapers in Spanish throughout the Chicano communities of the Southwest, particularly in the major cities and along the Mexican border. In many cases residents along the border buy and read Mexican newspapers daily to the point where San Diego advertisements for the recruitment of minority candidates to be highway police officers were published in a Tijuana, Mexico, newspaper, according to an interview on TV Channel 8. Chicano newspapers are generally totally in Spanish but sometimes they are bilingual with Spanish translations of most English articles.

Materials with a Chicano appeal whether in health, religion, education or politics are also often distributed in Spanish. Most consumer propaganda is in English, with spot announcements in Spanish on English-language television once in a while. The existence however of a Spanish-speaking market is already attracting Spanish-language billboards throughout the Southwest as is evident in Spanish advertising of beer, hamburgers and airlines. The *Los Angeles Times* indicates that Spanish-language advertising is increasing as business becomes aware of a Hispanic Market.[42] Estimates for Los Angeles and Orange counties point to 2.7 million people with a spendable income in the two-county area at nearly three billion dollars. The Spanish-language media are busy convincing business of the existence of a sizeable Hispanic market and of the need to sell in the Spanish language. A Los Angeles Spanish-language station (KWKW) administrator summed up the sales pitch as follows:

> "The Spanish-speaking represent a market within a market. Yes, they listen to Anglo radio and yes, they watch Anglo TV. But you don't SELL them in a foreign language. The marketers of any products must deal with Hispanics in Spanish or his competitors will. It's that simple."[43]

The media which have a great deal of impact in the barrios are the Spanish-language radio stations. In Los Angeles, 1972 ratings, for example, indicate that a Spanish-language radio station had the second largest audience of women between 18 and 49 during the early morning and late afternoon.[44] Today, although these radio stations have to compete with "As the World Turns," "Guiding Light" and other soap operas during the late morning and noon hours, barrio women are turning on their Spanish language radios early in the morning, shifting to TV and then back again. Gutiérrez' study on Spanish-language radio divides these stations into primary (those broadcasting 50% or more of their programming in Spanish) and secondary stations. Gutiérrez found that 11% of the 485 Spanish language stations were primary and 425 (88%) were secondary.[45] Texas and California account for 64% of all primary Spanish-language stations and 30% of all Spanish-language stations.[46] These two states presently comprise 49% of the Spanish-origin population in the country.[47] Over half (about 58%) of the Spanish-origin population resides in the Southwestern states (California, Texas, Colorado, New Mexico and Arizona) where approximately 49% of all Spanish-language stations can be found as indicated in Table 2.9.

Table 2.9   Correlation of Census Bureau: Percent Distribution of Persons of Spanish Origin by Residence in Selected States: March 1976,[48] with Gutiérrez' Spanish-language Radio Stations Statistics.[49]

State	Percent of Spanish origin population	Total stations	Number primary stations
Texas	20	93	17
California	29	82	18
Arizona, Colorado and New Mexico	9	65	11
New York	15	18	2
Remainder of U.S.	27	227	7
Total		485	55

As we can see from these statistics, about 84% of all primary stations are based in the Southwest. Border areas in California, Texas and Arizona are also served by 35 Mexican Spanish-language radio stations. These stations serve Chicano audiences living in San Diego, Calexico, Yuma, Nogales, El Paso, Brownsville, McAllen, Del Rio, Laredo, Eagle Pass and their surrounding areas.[50] It is precisely in these areas where stable bilingualism is possible. Gutiérrez' study also notes that most Spanish-language radio stations in the

United States are "heavily dependent on personnel who were raised, educated and had their first broadcasting experience in a Latin American country and then migrated to the United States."[51] This use of foreign-born and educated announcers reflects a bias against local popular Spanish varieties and has meant that the formal language used for broadcasting is generally a standard variety of Spanish, primarily Mexican. Some stations, however, do feature local announcers, community businessmen and public officials who broadcast their announcements or commercials in the local varieties of Spanish.

Another important formal domain to consider is that of literature. Within the last two decades, a number of Chicano literary works, published primarily by Chicano publishing companies and aimed generally at a Chicano university and college readership, have appeared. Although earlier Chicano novels were published in English (*Pocho,* 1959, 2d ed. 1970[52] and *Chicano,* 1969),[53] it is the Spanish-language novels by Tomás Rivera (*. . . y no se lo tragó la tierra*),[54] Miguel Méndez (*Peregrinos de Aztlán,* 1974)[55] and Rolando Hinojosa (*Generaciones y Semblanzas,* 1976)[56] which are the major literary works in Chicano literature. The major poets, however, like Alurista, Tino Villanueva, José Montoya, Sergio Elizondo and Raúl Salinas, write in both Spanish and English, often code-switching in the literary act itself. That the major novelists should write in Spanish about a Chicano reality within a small-town, rural and border setting, however, is understandable given the context of the Chicano population during the first half of the twentieth century. Interestingly enough it is only after urbanization and occupational mobility as well as increased educational attainment that Chicano novel production has been possible.

BILINGUAL EDUCATION

The other formal domain where Spanish is beginning to be used is the school. After more than a century of suppressing the Spanish language in the schools of the Southwest, federal and state legislation finally recognized what UNESCO specialists in 1951 determined to be fundamental: that every effort be made to provide education in the mother tongue.[57] Although instruction in the mother tongue is not a new nor revolutionary idea in the Southwest, the mandate for bilingual education has provided a great deal of controversy and antagonism. At the present time, efforts are under way at the state and federal levels to eliminate subsidized bilingual education and substitute instead second language instruction. When one considers the low educational attainment of Hispanics under policies of English submersion, it seems illogical but, given the discriminatory policies of this country, not surprising to find that the dominant group is more concerned with budgetary matters and with ensuring job tenure for English monolingual teachers than with facilitating the acquisition of academic skills by lingual minority students. Bilingual education has become such a complex matter that it is often impossible to separate instructional objectives from political and economic considerations or even problems of implementation.

Bilingual education was established in this country as a transitional program, that is, as a means of facilitating the acquisition of English language skills without retarding the student in his acquisition of conceptual skills. Yet despite the ultimate language shift objectives, these federally and state funded programs have permitted the Spanish language, both standard and local varieties, to be used as a medium of instruction in hundreds of schools throughout the Southwest. According to the Office of Bilingual Education, 565 programs, serving an estimated 295,000 students in 64 languages, are currently benefitting from federally funded bilingual demonstration grants. About 80% of these projects are in Spanish.[58] The possible role of bilingual education in the maintenance of the Spanish language can only be understood after an analysis of the phenomenon itself within the present social, economic and political context, for the formulation of language-related directives in education are related to an entire political scheme established to maintain the existing conditions and modes of production by placating dissident and disaffected minorities who might threaten, as Sweezy puts it, "to disrupt the whole social order."[59] Policy formulations have to be studied then in terms of the objectives of those creating and disseminating them, in terms of the conditions under which they are to be interpreted and implemented, and in terms of the possibilities for infusing these programs with meaningful social content. In this case what was established as yet another remedial education program has generated a great deal of cultural, linguistic and political awareness and contradictions, primarily for those seeking change within the existing system. In the case of some administrative personnel in education, efforts have been totally channeled towards legislation, funding, and personal advancement within newly created bilingual education hierarchies. The need to compromise with the dominant society eventually also leads to watered-down versions of cognitive and linguistic objectives, loss of initial gains in education, and cancellation of previous goals. It is in this light then that we will look at the objectives and implications of bilingual education.

The primary objective of bilingual education, first legislated in 1968, is to remedy the low achievement levels and high drop-out rates among language minority students by promoting the development of a student's cognitive skills in his native language while he is in the process of mastering the English language. Once this student has acquired a locally determined proficiency in English, he is exited out of bilingual education programs and placed in regular classes where English is the sole medium of instruction. The creation and implementation of bilingual education can be explained from a structural-functionalist theoretical base, as discussed by Christina Bratt Paulston. She places this theory within the "equilibrium" paradigm where concern lies with "maintaining society in an equilibrium through the harmonious relationship of the social components" and through "smooth, cumulative change."[60] This theoretical model, recognizing the low-income level of limited English-speaking students and their low scholastic achievement, ascribes lack of socio-economic success to "unequal opportunity" and scholastic failure to poor English language skills. The solution to inequality is found within the existing structures. Where academic achievement and merit are seen to be the causal variables affecting socio-economic success, the school and compensatory educational programs like bilingual education function as intervening variables.[61] By increasing educational opportunity, the school maintains *merit* as the determining factor, as it seemingly allows those with the *potential* for meritorious achievement (i.e., those who can qualify) the chance to succeed.[62]

The structural-functionalist model fails to recognize that political institutions are created and established for the sole purpose of maintaining existing social and economic stratification. As Carnoy has pointed out, the poor generally buy this myth of social mobility through equal educational opportunity.[63] Schools however must be seen as lower-level institutions established for the purpose of disseminating the ideology of the ruling class.[64] As Althusser notes, "the church has been replaced today in its role as the dominant Ideological State Apparatus by the School."[65] The educational apparatus is "the dominant ideological state apparatus in Capitalist social formations," he adds, because it has access to "children from every class" from "infant school age and then for years, the years in which the child is most 'vulnerable'," and it ejects these children "into production" at different levels and for different roles in the existing class society with an inculcated ideology which allows the ruling class to reproduce the relations of production necessary in capitalist society, that is, "the relations of exploited to exploiter and exploiter to exploited."[66]

The whole educational apparatus can be more specifically examined in terms of what Sweezy calls the three levels of politics involved in carrying out educational policy: the national ruling class, the local ruling class and the ghetto or minority community.[67] The structural-functionalist model described by Paulston, falls into the realm of the national ruling class, which Sweezy describes as "prepared to promote programs, including educational reforms, calculated to pacify the ghetto and reduce the danger which it presents to order and security."[68] At the same time, the national ruling class seeks to create and foster a minority elite, "which it can deal with and, if possible, manipulate."[69] Support for these compensatory programs is available from the big corporations behind the national ruling class. As Sweezy explains, "the major foundations [like Ford and Rockefeller foundations] are national ruling class institutions *par excellence,* devoted to finding solutions to problems of the capitalist system as a whole on both the national and international levels."[70] It is this interest in maintaining a state of equilibrium which explains the support of educational reforms, like bilingual education, by the national ruling class:

> The national ruling class does not want to abolish the ghetto, and it certainly has no intention of changing the basic class structure and socializing role of the public school system. It simply wants to make these institutions of a racist capitalist society less intolerable and in the process of doing so it will seek to capture, ideologically and politically, as large a part of the ghetto community as it can. Ultimately, therefore, the aim of the national ruling class is to make the ghetto community into a willing accomplice of its own oppression and exploitation.[71]

Whatever the plans at the federal level, these compensatory educational reforms eventually have to be implemented at the local level. It is here then that opposition to these programs is more evident, as was obvious in the *E. Cintrón et al. vs. Brentwood Union Free School District et al.* decision in which a New York federal district court ruled that "where compliance with both federal and state regulations is an impossibility, the state enactments must give way." The court ordered the district to hire qualified and experienced personnel to staff bilingual programs, thereby overriding state regulations which required staff decisions to be based on seniority rather than program requirements.[72]

In light of separatist action taken by the majority French population in Quebec, opponents of the preservation of minority languages and cultures in this country, like U.S. Senator S. I. Hayakawa, are speaking out against the use of bilingual education programs to accomplish these linguistic and cultural ends.[73] In 1978 a *Chicago Tribune* editorial accused bilingual education employees of trying "to develop and enlarge a non-English enclave within the public schools."[74] The "empire builders" were said to want a "maximum number of pupils for a maximum length of time," retaining students in programs when they were ready for instruction in English. Media coverage of Mexican undocumented workers and projections that the Spanish-speaking minority will soon become the largest minority in this country have created fears of Mexican hordes invading English-dominant domains and threatening the existent power structures. Even the *New York Times* warned in an editorial on bilingual education that "the present encouragement given to making such enclaves permanent, in the mistaken view that they are an expression of positive pluralism, points the road to cultural, economic and political divisiveness."[75] The reason given for the warning is "that political splinter groups within the Spanish-speaking community, and among educators, are misinterpreting the goals of bilingual education in New York as a means of creating a Spanish-speaking power base."[76] What these newspapers reflect is concern at the state and local levels, where minority blocs could determine the outcome of elections, that Spanish speakers may yet gain political power.

Legislation proposed under the Reagan administration would in fact eliminate federal government involvement in education by proposing that federal programs providing grants for disadvantaged students and migrant education now be replaced by state programs. State legislatures would receive federal monies and determine how these would be allocated in the individual areas, thereby ensuring state control of education.[77] These proposed changes represent a dramatic shift and augur badly for the continuation of minority-oriented programs, for education would now be left strictly to the designs of state legislatures. And, as Sweezy has explained, it is the national ruling class which in the past has favored educational reforms, not the local or state-wide ruling class.

Opponents of bilingual education have sought to influence federal policy-making, as has been evident in congressional hearings on the renewal of the Bilingual Act, and in the American Institute for Research (AIR) report on Title VII programs,[78] suggesting that bilingual education does not have a significant impact on student achievement. The Noel Epstein articles for *The Washington*

Post, disseminating the AIR report, also questioned the validity of federal support for minority language and culture maintenance.[79] Sweezy explains this type of opposition as follows:

> The local ruling class wants to keep the ghetto as, so to speak, a profitable asset. And since the present educational system is one of the principal means of preserving the existing pattern of neighborhood and racial relations, the local ruling class and its supporters naturally reject or sabotage all efforts at educational reform. Their chief instrument in this negative and destructive enterprise is the educational "establishment". . . .[80]

Major opposition to bilingual education has thus been concentrated at the district and local school level where legal punitive measures in the past, like loss of federal funding for non-compliance with federal guidelines, have had to be exerted. Proposals to eliminate this federal leverage may lead to the gradual phasing out of these programs. Opposition has also come from teacher organizations and unions threatened by laws requiring teacher certification in bilingual education prior to participating in programs addressed at students of limited English-language proficiency. As a result, it has become necessary to include a "self-destruct" measure in the legislation of states like California, where provisions for exiting students from such programs are being developed, to assure the public that these programs are in fact transitional. It is at the local level, then, that federal programs, like bilingual education tend to be neutralized as to effective application and implementation.

The impact of local action or inaction on these educational programs has been discussed by Henry Levin, who provides some interesting information on Title I projects. Levin reports on an Office of Education study based on data obtained from Title I projects through 1970 which indicated that there was "no evidence that states were closing the achievement gap between advantaged and disadvantaged children." The continuation of these programs, however, is profitable to the local school districts, as Levin indicates:

> In summary, although there is a great deal of evidence that Title I money has helped the local taxpayer and school-district employees, there is little evidence that it has substantially improved the educational outcomes for disadvantaged children. . . . Stated more strongly, educational personnel will *always* benefit from the expenditure of additional money on the schooling of disadvantaged youngsters, but only *rarely* will the children themselves benefit. (italic in original)[81]

The failure of these programs is not the result of faulty academic goals, for conceptual development is absolutely indispensable and possible to attain at the highest levels, whatever the socio-economic status of the child. What Levin is discussing is the political factor involved which ensures that these programs will succeed in failing a certain percentage of students. His findings on compensatory programs could well be applied to bilingual education when he states:

> In short, the failure of additional funding to improve educational outcomes is not a technical failure of the schooling process as much as it is a technical by-product of the political process. This diagnosis is consistent with the view that so-called compensatory education has not failed; it has never been tried. Nor is it likely to be tried.[82]

Bilingual education is often not tried, simply simulated, often disguised as thirty minutes of English-as-a-Second Language or even nonexistent in so-called "bilingual" classrooms.

As in the case of compensatory education programs, bilingual education has created a local and state-wide group of employees which profit from the implementation of these programs, just as all other personnel in education profit from any given educational program, whether for majority or minority students. Education is a big business in this country. In the case of bilingual education, the difference is the creation of a *minority* "academic elite" who manage and administer these programs for the local educational establishment. Our concern here would be that the new elite not end up serving the interests of the local ruling class, to the detriment of bilingual students, simply to maintain their positions and status. Problems arise when bilingual directors fail to oppose the hiring of noncertified and/or nonqualified bilingual teachers, the use of untrained teacher aides to do all instruction in Spanish, the neglect of the curriculum in the first language, the farce of language assessment with inadequate instruments merely to meet district and state requirements, the nondevelopment of students' basic skills, the nonassessment of students' basic skills in their first language, the crowding of over 35 students with various levels of proficiency in English and often from various language groups in one classroom with one teacher, and the continual acceptance of English as a Second Language programs as substitutes for bilingual education.

All too often the genuinely concerned educator who seeks to introduce change through educational reforms which serve the needs of the students, which promote the development of cognitive and communicative skills, and which provide the students with skills for critical thinking, will find himself/herself frustrated by indifferent, budget-minded and ignorant school administrators and boards. The efforts of dedicated educators, although commendable, fail because of the nature itself of educational institutions within the superstructure. The contradictory role of teachers seeking social change through educational reforms has been pessimistically analyzed by Althusser, who declares that "those teachers who, in dreadful conditions, attempt to turn the few weapons they can find in the history and learning they 'teach' against the ideology, the system and the practices in which they are trapped," are rare. Althusser notes that most teachers do not even suspect their role as part of the Ideological State Apparatus.[83]

The basic socio-economic contradictions arising within a capitalist economy do not then disappear with an increase in educational opportunity. As C. B. Paulston states: "Because formal education is dependent on the dominant economic and political institutions, it cannot be a primary agent of social transformations."[84] This latter analysis falls under her Conflict Model paradigm which recognizes social factors or inequity as a cause for school failure. But Paulston's proposed Conflict Model eventually leads her back to a consideration of school and bilingual education as intervening variables which can lead to scholastic achievement and social integration. Thus in Paulston's model, as in the functionalist one, large scale reforms are presented as viable ways of maximizing equity and achieving social equality. Yet, where reality points to continued labor segmentation and residential as well as occupational segregation, bilingual education can only be an attempt at showing good faith, one which does not in any way threaten the class structure of this society nor threaten to eliminate inequity.

The school, as an educational ideological apparatus, however, embodies its contradictions, like the rest of society. When the church was the dominant ideological state apparatus, ideological struggle was concentrated in anti-clerical and anti-religious struggles. Today ideological struggle can occur within the school, especially now that contradictions begin to affect the larger population as well. Education has become a critical issue in the United States where the illiteracy rate is deemed to be three times higher than that of the Soviet Union.[85] According to United Nations reports, two million Americans of at least normal intelligence were illiterate in 1970.[86] Another report indicates that 30 million adult Americans are functional illiterates.[87] This crisis is not necessarily an "organic crisis," in Gramsci's terms, which can disrupt the whole class structure of this society. It is important nonetheless to note the crisis and observe the increasing reaction against "unsuccessful" programs in education.

Although bilingual education may not serve to "maximize equity in the distribution of wealth, goods and services," as postulated by the proponents of the Conflict Model,[88] it is important to recognize its effect on language shift. Where socio-economic stratification determines language maintenance or shift, bilingual education and schools in general function as intervening variables capable of facilitating the acquisition of the English language through predominantly transitional bilingual education models and of disseminating the dominant ideology of social integration, acculturation and English monolingualism.

At a psychological and human development level, opposition to instruction in the language of the child is incomprehensible. Those who question the effectiveness of bilingual-bicultural education generally confuse implementation and administration of particular programs with the linguistic and cognitive basis for these programs. What is generally forgotten in the chauvinistic rhetoric against bilingual education is that language development, as a part of human development, proceeds through several stages in childhood until the adolescent reaches a formal stage in his linguistic and cognitive development which allows him to conceptualize and deal with abstractions. Research has shown that students who are not allowed to develop cognitively in their primary language have a low academic achievement[89] even though superficial language assessment limited to a descriptive function of language may indicate fluency in the second language. Here in the Southwest, teachers working with Mexican children who have received several years of instruction in Mexico prior to their immigration find that these children have no serious academic problems in school and can achieve at grade level while acquiring the English language. Unfortunately, these achieving non- and limited-English-speaking students are often placed in remedial or compensatory education classes way below their cognitive level where they are bored and their intellectual growth is stunted. Some teachers and administrators seem to think that lack of English proficiency is synonymous with poor cognitive skills.

The pressing problem at the moment however is that of children who have immigrated before starting school and native Chicano students who are monolingual in Spanish or even bilingual. These children have not had the advantage of intensive instruction in Spanish to develop their basic skills: nor is public school instruction allowing them to develop cognitive skills nor to develop a broad range of language functions in either language. As tax-paying and productive members of society, the parents of these children have the legal right to demand the type of instruction currently guaranteed to middle and upper class pupils for full linguistic, cognitive and social development. In view of available research, the implementation of bilingual instruction stressing cognitive development throughout the public school curriculum could be a reform in the right direction. It may seem contradictory to first point out that schools are set up to ensure the academic failure of a significant segment of the population, that is, to maintain the *status quo,* and then to suggest that bilingual education, stressing cognitive and linguistic development in both languages could be a step in the right direction. The struggle for a literate population equipped with critical and analytical skills however is always a step in the right direction, for it facilitates political consciousness and has the potential of leading the group to seek political and economic change.

Institutional support for the use of a nondominant language can often be mere tokenism if the social and economic conditions fostering language maintenance are not present. Support of transitional programs, or of Spanish as simply a supplemental language, paves the way for language shift and eventual language loss. As long as the dominant society preserves significant functions, especially the literacy function, solely for English, Spanish will be primarily the *home* language of first-generation and sometimes second-generation persons of Spanish origin.

LANGUAGE CHOICE

There are several factors affecting language choice but the most significant is the dominant ideology in this country. The individualism, social mobility and assimilation myths created by American society are fully espoused by optimistic incoming immigrants. Like new converts, they perceive education and the acquisition of the English language as the keys to a prosperous future. In many cases first-generation parents reject bilingual education programs for their children since instruction in the primary language is seen as a retardant in the process of assimilating into the mainstream. For these same reasons, parents who themselves experienced difficulty in primary schools as monolingual Spanish speakers often address their children only in English, retaining their Spanish for use with older relatives or with spouses. The community thus develops a dual set of intra-group verbal exchanges: those with the young who are assigned the feature of "high potential" (that is, those who are seen as potentially forming a part of dominant society) and those with older members of the community who are associated with lower-income brackets and classified as belonging to the subordinate culture. Although specific acts of language choice can only be understood in terms of concrete situations and interlocutors, a hierarchical factor determined by standing on a socio-economic scale operates in determining language shifts in social-verbal interaction. This interrelation between verbal forms and forms of communication as determined by social factors will become more evident in our chapter on code-switching, where language shifts in mid discourse are sometimes shown to rely on type of speech act and its ideological content.

Second- and third-generation Chicanos, however, develop varying attitudes towards language shift. These Chicanos, who are fluent English speakers, have remained locked in the lower-wage levels of the occupation scale, unable to move out of older housing units, and lacking the many modern conveniences and facilities advertised on TV. The myth of English acquisition as the vehicle for upward mobility begins to fade. At this point, the imposed residential and economic segregation can trigger a negation of the negative context, resulting in a positive social value as an ingredient for solidarity. This mechanism of defense serves to unite the community, at a rhetorical level ("¡Que viva la raza!" "¡Somos pura raza!") at the outset, but sometimes it figures in social and political struggles leading to demonstrations ("Raza sí, Migra no"), school walkouts, labor strikes ("¡Que viva la huelga!"), anti-war demonstrations and anti-immigration policies punitive to the immigrant ("¡Chale con el plan de Carter!"). At this level, then, use of the minority language is seen as a sign of loyalty to the group. From the evidence we have seen, language loyalty is widespread among those who reside in low-income areas with a high concentration of Chicanos, although it is also here where persons interested in social mobility and assimilation prefer shifting to English. Those who resent the dominant culture or who have developed anti-gringo attitudes as a result of the constant expressions of racial discrimination in this society will often cling to their Spanish as their sole inalienable possession. In public schools where the use of Spanish was for many years prohibited, the more rebellious or more resentful-of-discrimination students delighted in persisting with their Spanish on the playground or in the bathrooms, especially if an Anglo teacher was around. The use of Spanish thus becomes a sign of defiance and group solidarity. For others, on the other hand, Spanish is the language to be spoken when no one else can hear, when it is safe to do so. In all of these cases, Spanish has been marked as the subordinate language, reflecting the subordinate socio-economic position of the speakers and the sign of stigma that they wish to avoid or from which they wish to disassociate themselves.

Since the beginning of the twentieth century, for those first-generation Chicanos who had received instruction in Mexico and were aware of the historical context of land appropriation by Anglo-Americans, housing and educational segregation, and violation of human rights, the Spanish language was a vehicle for protest in the community, in the local Spanish-language newspapers, in the *comités patrióticos* and in the Mexican Masonic lodges. In Texas, the notion of "la colonia mexicana" as a distinctive entity carried with it not only cultural pride but linguistic pride as well.

For all of these groups, the Spanish language conveyed ties to the community. For this reason, desires to escape conditions of poverty led many to reject their language and their national origin until the Civil Rights Movement of the sixties and seventies, which provoked a social crisis but allowed the expression of "ethnic pride." And when, thanks to the media, being a minority became "beautiful," the inoculation[90] permeated other cultural spheres as well to the same distorted degree. The myth of acceptability never brought any significant changes to minority ghettos and barrios but it did accompany certain surface changes, like the institution of war on poverty programs and in 1968, bilingual education. As a consequence, minority issues and minority language questions were rendered innocuous. Knowing another language is now touted as an attractive commodity for foreign-service work and for employment with international banks, multinational corporations and even the CIA. It is then no surprise that the President of the United States himself recommended the acquisition of foreign languages and in fact in 1978 established National Foreign Language Week.[91] There has been little change however in the status or functions of minority languages in this country.

SUMMARY: LANGUAGE USE

In the Southwest Spanish is primarily an informal, oral language which predominates in areas of strong Chicano concentration. It is the most obvious sign of cultural adhesion, the code to resort to in the presence of English-speaking Others, the language of home, barrio, the inalienable possession. As we indicated earlier, forced concentration of population can lead to loyalty to the group and a recognition of the milieu within which the group functions as an intimate part of their lives. The language used for interaction in this environment assumes then the features assigned to the community of speakers and the barrio or community within which it occurs. Since these are generally marked as "subordinate," the language also assumes the same status. Its designation as "language of culture" is not however the case for all Chicanos. As we have seen, many Chicanos are dominant English speakers. For these non-bilingual Chicanos, culture and language are distinctively separate matters and not interconnected. If culture is the sum of experiences and traditions held in common by a group of people, one can find different "cultures" within the Chicano population, determined by socio-economic class, residence in urban or rural areas, residence in barrios or integrated communities, generation in the United States, and nativity. Spanish is closely tied to culture for the low-income, first and second-generation, working-class Chicanos in town barrios. For them Spanish is still the language of restaurants, filling stations, small grocery stores, bakeries, *tortillerías*, parks and community centers. In urbanized barrios adjacent to industrial zones, traversed by innumerable freeways, the language bonds are weakened. English becomes the language of the Anglo-owned supermarkets, the shopping centers, the drugstores, the white-bread bakeries, the filling stations, the community clinics and the fast-food drive-ins. Border towns and cities are more likely to maintain a stable bilingual situation where both languages can function in the same domain. Residents of rural areas with greater isolation and less contact with the English-speaking community have been shown to retain Spanish to a greater extent and for more generations.[92]

The relation between language, class and ideology is thus complex and creates conditions rife with contradictions. These conditions are not only present within the community but outside it as well. Even a consideration of the language situation in the Southwest, as if it were some sort of unit, forces us to consider the varied economic development of the Southwestern states with varying rates of urbanization and industrialization. Thus it is impossible to talk about Chicanos of the Southwest as if they were a homogeneous entity. A second-generation Chicano from Texas may still reflect a rural background, whereas a California Chicano of second generation will probably be an urban ghetto or barrio resident. Social and linguistic contact with English monolinguals also varies among Chicanos even though labor segmentation has ensured the concentration of the Spanish-speaking population in low-wage jobs, low-rent residential areas with minimum, often subservient or official contact with the dominant English-speaking society. The occupational shifts of this century, converting Chicanos into an urban blue-collar and service-worker population, has undoubtedly increased contact with English speakers in factories and the service sector, reducing thereby interactional segregation. The linguistic picture of the Southwest is thus as complex as the occupational, economic and social situation.

To the degree then that Chicanos have been isolated or set apart, economically and socially, they have maintained ample use of their Spanish-language varieties. To the degree that they have been incorporated into English-dominant employment categories and moved up the income scale, they have been acculturated, probably moved out of the barrio and into integrated communities and lost significant use of the Spanish language, with almost exclusive use of the English language. Thus incorporation into the urban, industrial sector has had social, cultural and linguistic ramifications for the Chicano community.

In the figures that follow we will try to summarize the domains, both formal and informal, within which the Spanish language functions in relation to the English language. Most of these have been previously discussed, except for the domain of Recreation. Towns and cities with large concentrations of Chicanos generally have several spots where the Spanish-speaking population congregates. For men, it may be the cantina, the pool hall or the barber shop. The whole family, on the other hand, may be found at the Mexican Film Theatre, at church bingos, at the park, or at the local dance hall on Friday or Saturday night where most Chicano bands today play a combination of Mexican, Chicano and American Pop Music.

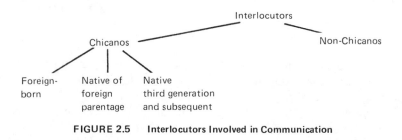

FIGURE 2.5   Interlocutors Involved in Communication

In analyzing the use of Spanish in the Southwest there are a number of factors that have to be considered. In any communicative act we have to deal with the Sender and Receiver of the Message. We could first break down the communication in terms of interlocutors involved as shown in Figure 2.5. It is important to distinguish between participants since use of Southwest varieties of Spanish is generally an intra-group activity limited to exchanges with other Chicanos. The communicative act must also be analyzed in terms of the context within which the participants interact. The primary distinction is determined by area of residence and occupation (Figure 2.6). Rural residents tend to be more isolated than metropolitan dwellers and for that reason, there is more retention of Spanish among working-class Chicano rural residents, but not necessarily among middle-class rural residents whom we have found to reside in integrated or predominantly Anglo neighborhoods. Urban dwellers would also have to be further subdivided into metropolitan and non-metropolitan residents, as well as in terms of residence in segregated and integrated quarters. Of the Mexican-origin population 80% reside in metropolitan areas,[93] like Los Angeles, where one can usually find large centers or districts of Mexican-origin concentration. Within the cities, occupational categories and income are the primary factors determining residence. It is important to remember that segregation in a metropolitan area is often more a predominance of certain groups rather than a total isolation of one group.

FIGURE 2.6   Context of Communicative Acts

FIGURE 2.7   Domains Governed by Spanish

Segregated barrios in non-metropolitan areas, however, are quite different. Here there are several domains that are primarily, if not entirely, governed by Spanish, as in the community domains in Figure 2.7.

The graph of language use in particular domains takes into consideration all the various surveys examined previously on the relation between economic standing, language use and language preferences as manifested in choice of radio station or television channel. The domains incorporate both formal and informal contexts:

Informal:	Home	Neighborhood	Recreation
Formal:	Work	Government	Media

Speakers are divided in terms of class and nativity:

Class:	Middle class (urban and rural)
	Urban working class
	Rural working class
Nativity:	First generation (foreign-born)
	Second generation (native-born with foreign-born parents)
	Third generation (native-born with native-born parents)

The usual language is stated as English, Spanish or Bilingual. The term bilingual indicates that both languages function in this domain for the population although in some cases evidence indicates that one or the other predominates. In some bilingual-home situations, for example, parents will address their children in Spanish but the latter will respond only in English. Table 2.10 thus summarizes what we have indicated in Chapters 1 and 2: middle class Chicanos participate primarily in English-language domains although first and second-generation speakers may retain some use of Spanish in the home. Since all first-generation speakers regardless of class were found to make some use of Spanish-language media and since recreation is an intimate domain where native-language use predominates, we have marked these as bilingual domains for first-generation middle-class speakers. Thereafter all middle class domains would be English-language domains.

In the case of the working class, we distinguished between rural and urban workers to indicate the maintenance of Spanish to some degree in all rural

Table 2.10   Chicano Language Use

Nativity Generation	Middle class			Working class Rural			Urban		
	1	2	3	1	2	3	1	2	3
Domains									
Home	S	B	E	S	B	B	S	B	E
Neighborhood	E	E	E	S	B	B	B	B	B
Recreation	B	E	E	B	B	B	B	B	E
Work	E	E	E	B	B	B	B	E	E
Media	B	E	E	B	B	B	B	B	E
Government	E	E	E	E	E	E	E	E	E

S = Spanish   E = English   B = Bilingual

domains except government, which is always entirely in English. Work in rural areas can be bilingual and even Spanish dominant in areas like agricultural work. First-generation rural workers also retain Spanish in the home and prefer Spanish-language media. For urban Chicanos, bilingualism is the rule in informal and intimate situations except for third-generation speakers who function primarily in English in all domains. Their neighborhood may continue to be bilingual, however. First-generation urban workers are generally found in occupational categories of strong minority concentration; for this reason work for first-generation Chicanos will probably be a bilingual domain.

This general picture of language use in the Chicano community can differ for specific individuals in the presence of other variables, like physical distance from other Chicano bilinguals. Thus a second-generation Chicano may live in an English-language community where there are no bilinguals. In this case, English will be the language of the community. Most Chicano working-class families, however, reside in integrated communities or areas of strong Chicano concentration where Spanish continues to function alongside English. It is also possible for English-dominant or English-monolingual Chicanos from middle class communities to seek out recreational activities in bilingual or Spanish-speaking lower-income Chicano barrios.

What is not evident from a chart outlining domains where both English and Spanish are likely to occur is the relation between the designated variables. The single most outstanding variable appears to be social and linguistic contact; thus, the more contact with the English-speaking community, the more likelihood there is of bilingualism or monolingualism in English. Social contact, as we noted earlier, may take various forms. The greater the social distance and the more limited the contact with English institutions, the more probability that Spanish will retain intimate and informal functions. The greater the contact with the English-speaking community, the greater the degree of language shift to English. Social contact is of course determined by the class factor, by the labor process and the relations of production. Participation in the labor process with a

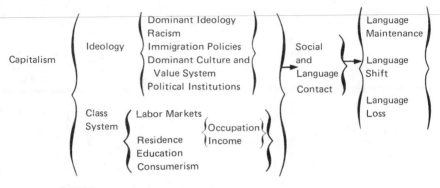

FIGURE 2.8   Relation Between Variables Determining Language Use

given income and occupation in turn determines the area of residence, the people with whom one socializes, educational goals, consumption of commodities and ideology, all factors which determine one's continued use or non-use of the Spanish language. We could then present the various variables as in Figure 2.8. Thus the mode of production gives rise to particular social and labor relations which ultimately determine language choice.

This then is a general picture of the socio-economic and socio-linguistic situation of Chicanos. It is under these contradictory and complex conditions that the question of language policy in the Southwest is being addressed.

Language is a social as well as a linguistic phenomenon and as such must be seen as a communicative force which, although a product of social and cultural history, can also be instrumental in effecting changes in the historical development of culture and society. As a semiotic instrument it can either foment linguistic, cultural and political resistance to forces of oppression or inhibit development of a revolutionary consciousness and facilitate co-optation. The contradictory nature of language and cultural consciousness must be kept in mind. Where languages assume strictly ethnic, racial or cultural dimensions, they can serve as negative divisive ingredients against efforts to organize workers along class line. Here language, like culture, could serve to polarize and alienate the various ethnic groups involved rather than resolve contradictions and reduce differences. If language planning merely serves the opportunistic aspirations of members of the middle class who aspire to leading positions facilitated by interests in these language questions, then it is a reactionary self-serving manipulation of the whole affair. It is only when language planning serves as a corollary of cultural and political resistance against oppressive conditions that organization around language loyalty can be seen as a positive force. For if upon analysis we find that a significant number of the speakers of a particular language are members of a particular class, as is the case with Spanish-speaking Chicanos, then language choice could be said to reflect class identity in addition to cultural identity. It is in view of this correlation between

economic oppression and language maintenance that we can speak of preservation of the Spanish language as a sign of both class identification and political
resistance to mainstream ideology. As a class code it would serve to politicize
the Chicano population. At present however no massive efforts to organize
around language questions have been initiated in the Mexican-origin community. Nevertheless, given the existing social and economic conditions the
continued presence of the Spanish language in the Southwest stands as a sign of
both cultural and class identity.

Notes

1. U.S. Bureau of the Census, *Current Population Reports: Special Studies,* "Population of
the United States: Trends and Prospects: 1950–1990." Series P-23, No. 49, Issued May 1974.
2. *Ibid.*
3. U.S. Bureau of the Census, *1970 Census of the Population: Persons of Spanish Surname,*
PC (2)-10, Issued July 1973.
4. *Ibid.*
5. U.S. Bureau of the Census, "Population of the United States, Trends and Prospects," p. 91.
6. *Ibid.,* p. 93.
7. U.S. Bureau of the Census, *Current Population Reports,* "Persons of Spanish Origin: March
1976," Series P-20, No. 310, Issued July 1977.
8. Félix Frank Gutiérrez, *Spanish-Language Radio and Chicano Internal Colonialism* (Ann
Arbor, Michigan: University Microfilm International, 1978), p. 45.
9. Ronald W. López and Darryl D. Enos, "Spanish Language-Only Television in Los Angeles
County," *Aztlán,* Vol. 4, No. 2, Fall 1973, p. 298.
10. *Ibid.,* p. 309.
11. *Ibid.,* p. 298.
12. *Ibid.,* p. 309.
13. *Ibid.,* p. 290.
14. *Ibid.,* p. 309.
15. *Ibid.*
16. *Ibid.*
17. *Ibid.,* p. 290.
18. *Ibid.,* p. 298.
19. U.S. Bureau of the Census, *Current Population Reports: Special Studies,* "Language
Usage in the United States: July 1975 (Advance report)," Series P-23, No. 60 (Revised).
20. U.S. Bureau of the Census, *1970 Census of the Population: Persons of Spanish Origin.*
21. U.S. Bureau of the Census, "Language Usage in the United States."
22. *Ibid.*
23. *Ibid.*
24. U.S. Bureau of the Census, *Current Population Reports: Population Characteristics,*
"Persons of Spanish Origin in the United States: March 1977 (Advance report)," Series P-20, No.
317, Issued December 1977.
25. U.S. Bureau of the Census, "Language Usage in the United States."
26. U.S. Bureau of the Census, *Current Population Reports,* "Persons of Spanish Origin,"
March 1972, Series P-20.
27. U.S. Bureau of the Census, *Current Population Reports,"* Persons of Spanish Origin,"
March 1971, Series P-20.
28. Ricardo Toscano, Víctor Hernández and María C. Ortiz, "A Study of Bilingualism of
UCSD Students" (Term paper presented for TWS 135, UCSD, June 12, 1976).

29. Eduardo Hernández-Chávez, "Language Maintenance, Bilingual Education and Philosophies of Bilingualism in the United States," *International Dimensions of Bilingual Education,* ed. James E. Alatis (Washington, D.C.: Georgetown University Press, 1978), p. 527.

30. Glyn Lewis, *Multilingualism in the Soviet Union* (The Hague: Mouton, 1972), p. 275.

31. *Ibid.,* p. 276.

32. *Ibid.,* p. 277.

33. U.S. Commission on Civil Rights, *The Excluded Student Educational Practice Affecting Mexican Americans in the Southwest,* Report No. 3, May 1972.

34. Steven A. Grant, "Language Policy—the United States," *Modern Language Association: Profession,* 1978, p. 40.

35. U.S. Commission on Civil Rights, *A Better Chance to Learn: Bilingual-Bicultural Education,* Publication 51, May 1975, p. 207.

36. Gary A. Greenfield and Don B. Kates, "Mexican Americans, Racial Discrimination, and the Civil Rights Act," *California Law Review,* Vol. 63:662, p. 726.

37. Grant, p. 34.

38. *Ibid.*

39. Reynaldo F. Macías, "Language Choice and Human Rights in the United States," *Language in Public Life,* ed. James E. Alatis and G. Richard Tucker (Washington, D.C.: Georgetown University Press, 1979), p. 94.

40. "Reagan Says Schools Distort Bilingual Idea," *Los Angeles Times,* Late Final, March 2, 1981, Part I, p. 1.

41. "SJR 72 Constitutional Amendment—English—National Language," *Congressional Index,* April 27, 1981, p. 16,504. Published by Commerce Clearing House.

42. "Hispanic Market Awaits Right Salesman," *Los Angeles Times,* Outlook Section, July 23, 1978, p. 1.

43. *Ibid.,* p. 2.

44. Gutiérrez, p. 48.

45. *Ibid.,* p. 70.

46. *Ibid.*

47. U.S. Bureau of the Census, "Persons of Spanish Origin: March 1976."

48. *Ibid.*

49. Gutiérrez, pp. 72–73.

50. *Ibid.,* p. 67.

51. *Ibid.,* p. 52.

52. José Antonio Villarreal, *Pocho* (New York: Doubleday, 1959).

53. Richard Vázquez, *Chicano* (New York: Doubleday, 1969).

54. Tomás Rivera, . . . *y no se lo tragó la tierra* (Berkeley: Quinto Sol Publications, 1971).

55. Miguel Méndez, *Peregrinos de Aztlán* (Tucson: Peregrinos Press, 1974).

56. Rolando Hinojosa, *Generaciones y Semblanzas* (Berkeley: Justa Publications, 1976).

57. "Report of the UNESCO Meeting of Specialists, 1951," *Readings in the Sociology of Language,* ed. Joshua A. Fishman (The Hague: Mouton, 1972), p. 688–716.

58. San Diego Lau Center. 1979 Information provided by Director.

59. Paul M. Sweezy, "Afterword: The Implications of Community Control," in *Schools against Children. The Case for Community Control,* ed. Annette T. Rubenstein (New York: Monthly Review Press, 1970), pp. 284–293.

60. Christina Bratt Paulston. "Theoretical Perspectives on Bilingual Education" (Working Papers in Bilingualism, No. 13, Department of General Linguistics, University of Pittsburgh, PA, 1968).

61. *Ibid.*

62. *Ibid.*

63. Martin Carnoy, *La educacion como imperialismo cultural* (México: Siglo veintiuno, 1974), p. 15.

64. Hughes Portelli, *Gramsci y el bloque histórico* (México: Siglo Veintiuno, 1973), p. 111.

65. Louis Althusser, "Ideology and Ideological State Apparatuses," *Lenin and Philosophy and Other Essays* (New York: Monthly Review Press, 1971), p. 155.

66. *Ibid.*

67. Sweezy, p. 285.

68. *Ibid.*, p. 291.

69. *Ibid.*, p. 292.

70. *Ibid.*

71. *Ibid.*, p. 293.

72. California Department of Education, Bilingual Bicultural Education Section, "Analysis of 1978 *Elis Cintrón* Decisions," 1978.

73. *San Diego Tribune*, "Bilingual," Editorial Page, Wednesday, August 30, 1978.

74. "Bilingual Education Ineffective," quoted in *U.S. Congressional Record*, E 2767, May 23, 1978.

75. "Bilingual Danger," *New York Times*, Editorial, November 22, 1976.

76. *Ibid.*

77. Lee May, "Plan to Replace School Aid Program Unveiled," *Los Angeles Times*, Morning Final, April 30, 1981, Part I, p. 1.

78. "USOE Bilingual Education Evaluation Found Invalid," quoted in *U.S. Congressional Record*, E 3736, July 13, 1978.

79. Noel Epstein, *Language, Ethnicity and the Schools* (The George Washington University, 1978).

80. Sweezy, p. 290.

81. Henry M. Levin, "The Economic Implications of Mastery Learning," in *The Limits of Educational Reform*, ed. Martin Carnoy and Henry M. Levin (New York: Longman, 1976), p. 191.

82. *Ibid.*, p. 192.

83. Althusser, p. 157.

84. Paulston, p. 31.

85. "The Miseducation of Millions: The Alarming Rise of Functional Illiteracy in America," *U.S. Congressional Record*, S 14837, September 8, 1978.

86. *Ibid.*

87. *Ibid.*

88. Paulston, p. 45.

89. Tove Skutnabb-Kangas, *Language in the Process of Cultural Assimilation and Structural Incorporation of Linguistic Minorities.* (Rosslyn, Virginia: National Clearinghouse for Bilingual Education, 1979).

90. Roland Barthes, *Mythologies* (New York: Hill and Wang, 1972).

91. "National Foreign Language Week," *U.S. Congressional Record*, March 1978, E. 1359.

92. R. M. Thompston, "Language Loyalty in Austin, Texas" (Ph.D. dissertation, University of Texas at Austin, 1971).

93. U.S. Bureau of the Census, "Persons of Spanish Origin in the U.S.: March 1977."

CHAPTER 3

Theoretical Assumptions

Language itself is just as much the product of a community as in another respect it is the existence of the community: it is, as it were, the communal being speaking for itself.
— *Karl Marx,* Precapitalist Economic Formations

The study of Chicano bilingualism is necessarily a study of a speech community within its particular historical context, where given communication patterns have resulted from particular types of social interaction, including interaction with a second language group. Since it is social contact which determines language contact, a study of bilingualism in the United States requires above all a historical analysis of social relations in this country which have fostered social contact or distance and have thereby created conditions favoring language loss, language maintenance or convergence among particular speakers. Since language is a social product, our study necessarily began by examining the context within which Chicano bilingualism occurs and by analyzing those processes which have determined the functions of particular communal codes and styles of speaking.

THEORETICAL ASSUMPTIONS: DISCOURSE

A study of bilingual speech is necessarily a study of social interaction, since verbal communication is both social and linguistic interaction. As Labov has stated, conversation is a "means that people use to deal with one another." He adds: "The great bulk of human face-to-face interaction is verbal; but unless linguistic interaction is viewed as a subspecies of the larger category it is bound to be misunderstood."[1] Our basic proposition then is that language is a social product used for social interaction. As linguists and sociologists have studied symbolic interaction, they have come to distinguish between *what is said* and *what is done,*[2] between locutionary and illocutionary acts (Austin),[3] between utterance acts, propositional acts and illocutionary acts (Searle),[4] between utterances and Actions (Labov)[5] and between Text and Functions (Halliday).[6]

These classifications recall the traditional division of language into three separate components (Morris)[7]: Syntactic, Semantic and Pragmatic. What is evident is that sociolinguists today distinguish between the linguistic aspect or form of language and its functional use within particular situations. Following the Saussurean analysis of signs, we could postulate a tripartite division as in Figure 3.1.

FIGURE 3.1   Division of Sign

This particular segmentation however would not suffice for a study of language in its interactional function as a social process, in which language is action rather than form, but would merely see function as an additional linguistic component. Function refers to the *process* within which signs operate and is therefore a separate level. In fact Labov seems to see a surface-deep structure analogy in his consideration of the relation between utterances and abstract speech actions:

> The central innovation of our own approach is the view that sequencing rules operate within abstract speech actions and that they often are arranged in a complex hierarchy. There are no necessary connections between utterances at the surface level, though sequencing patterns may take such surface structures into account.[8]

The distinction being made is that of the old *langue* and *parole* (competence and performance) model which allows us to distinguish between actual production and an underlying system. But there is also a difference. Here the focus is on discourse, that is, on the social component of language, on the pragmatic component. Thus discourse itself is seen to have an underlying form: abstract speech actions, and a surface form: utterances at the exchange level.[9] This concept of a hierarchical organization is useful in a study of conversation where it is evident that we are faced with two levels of production: linguistic and social. These of course are interconnected. What is significant here is that the social component is seen as underlying the actual speech production. We can now consider a verbal exchange not only at the linguistic level but as a social process, a social act through symbols. We can now focus on the verbal production as a social performance and deal not with sentences but with discourse.

Discourse analysis makes a fundamental distinction between *what is said* and *what is done*. *What is said* refers to the actual surface utterances while *what is done* refers to the function of the discourse. These functions can be expressed in terms of hierarchical structures of speech actions which could be said to generate particular speech acts through sequencing rules:

> Sequencing rules do not appear to relate words, sentences and other linguistic forms, but rather form the connection between abstract actions such as requests, compliments, challenges and defenses. Thus sequencing rules presuppose another set of relations, those between the words spoken and the actions being performed.[10]

Discourse encompasses both *what is said* and *what is done* at the level of exchange. The conversation or discourse studied makes up the *text*. The term *text,* however, has been variously used. Labov, for example, uses the word *text* to refer to the discourse occurring during several tape-recorded therapeutic sessions. But it is not always synonymous with discourse. In fact the terms *text* and *utterance* often have different meanings in the works of different linguists and philosophers of language. Coulthard contrasts *sentences* and *utterances* as well as *text* and *discourse*:

> Sentences combine to form *texts* and the relation between sentences are aspects of grammatical *cohesion*; utterances combine to form *discourse* and the relation between them are aspects of discourse *coherence.*[11]

Here the term *text* is limited to instances of usage in decontextualized data, while utterances are seen to perform social acts in particular contexts of use.[12] Halliday, on the other hand, defines text as a semantic unit: "The unity that it has is a unit of meaning in context, a texture that expresses the fact that it relates as a whole to the environment in which it is placed."[13] He further adds that

> Being a semantic unit, a text is realized in the form of sentences, and this is how the relation of text to sentences can best be interpreted.
>
> Any piece of language that is operational, functioning as a unity in some context of situation, constitutes a text. It may be spoken or written, in any style or genre, and involving any number of active participants. It will usually display a form of consistency that is defined by the concept of register: a consistency in the meaning styles or types of semantic configuration which embody its relation to its environment.[14]

Given these various concepts of text, which in fact share a fundamental distinction made between utterances and sentences, we can now pinpoint the use of the term. Text for us is equivalent to speech event (Hymes), to verbal interaction (Labov) and to Halliday's semantic and functional unit. As Halliday indicates, a text can be oral or written. Thus a novel, a poem and a conversation function as texts.

Of primary importance then is the fact that texts do not exist in isolation; a text is always context-dependent for a conversation takes place within a specific situation. As we said earlier, the text itself functions not only as linguistic acts but as manifestations of social interaction. Verbal communication can thus be studied as an expression-form of social relations where the communicative act itself reflects social contact, social distance, control, subordination, rejection, acceptance, solidarity or social fragmentation. At this level we must consider the relation between the interlocutors as well as their position and status. Communication as a social act is itself connected to other social phenomena which affect it, modify it and change its social meaning. This primary social level will be discussed further later on. In Figure 3.2 we designate the levels of a semiotic system where verbal communication serves as an expression-form of social relations, whose content is the social interaction itself. The social interactional content will of course continue to be mapped onto the content of the actual verbal production at every level; although we will now concentrate on

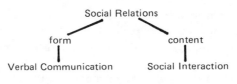

FIGURE 3.2

verbal interaction, it is important to remember that it is only one manifestation of social interaction and that all the components of the verbal interaction have to be seen in the context of social relations.

The actual verbal communication, which we will designate as *text*, has several levels of organization. Like all semiotic systems, it may be analyzed in terms of expression and content, and following Hjemslev's model, these may themselves be subdivided into form and substance in Figure 3.3[15] The text

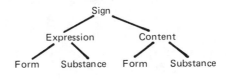

FIGURE 3.3   Levels of Organization in
Verbal Communication

itself then has two principal components: on the one hand it is oral or written production; on the other it is social production, a communicative act. Let us assume that the text is a conversation. In its expression-form we are dealing with the linguistic code. In its content form, we are dealing with the conversation as social interaction or with the text as text (Figure 3.4). We could then conceive of

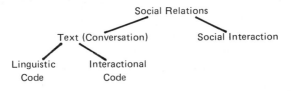

FIGURE 3.4

a hierarchical arrangement of these two components where the left branch is always more surface and the right branch more underlying or a deeper structure, where in effect the content determines the form.[16] A hierarchical vertical arrangement does not capture the inseparability, the interconnection of these various components, but at least a branching tree can facilitate analysis.

A conversation—the text—is thus an expression and an act of social intercourse. Its expression component is inseparable from its interactional component but for the sake of analysis we will represent the form and content of the two codes—linguistic and social—through a branching tree. At the linguistic level we have the grammatical and suprasegmental elements as well as the semantic units which make up the linguistic sign system. The social aspect of the text is reflected in the complex cultural units which make up the substance of the linguistic signs. The particular denotations and connotations of the linguistic sign are of course conditioned by the entire interactional context. At the text-as-interaction level, we are dealing with discourse. As conversational discourse, the text can be subdivided into interactional form (the utterances) and content (the interactional functions). Figure 3.5 shows the various levels of a text. The

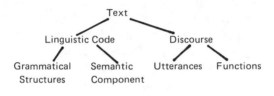

FIGURE 3.5   Text Levels

utterances are the exchanges or *turns* which may involve more than one speech act or *move*.[17] The most important aspect of discourse analysis is its formulation of meaning in terms of functions. The concept of function has been particularly useful in the analysis of literary and anthropological texts (e.g., Propp, Bremond, Levi-Strauss, Greimas).[18] In linguistics the study of functions has been central in the work of Halliday and Labov, who calls these functions abstract speech Actions. Our presentation borrows extensively from Halliday and Labov but differs in the overall formulation and the ultimate social and political implications we will propose.

The analysis of functions is related to that of speech events and speech acts.[19] What we are calling text here—the conversation—would be a speech event composed of smaller units, the speech acts. These acts, which consist of utterances, have a particular function within the speech event. Hymes has exemplified these functional units in English as follows:

> In general the relation between sentence forms and speech acts is of the kind just mentioned: a sentence, interrogative in form, may be now a request, now a command, now a statement; a request may be manifested by a sentence that is now interrogative, now imperative in form.[20]

A speech act then, although it has a grammatical form, derives its meaning from its function which is, in turn, determined by the speech community's rules of interpretation. Labov, although defining a speech act as "an action carried out by means of speech,"[21] sees a more complex division than that traditionally made between sentences and speech acts:

> a common characteristic of the more philosophical approach to speech acts is the absence of any treatment of the more abstract types of social interaction, which go beyond the linguistic structure. We find that the crucial actions in establishing coherence of sequencing in conversation are not such speech acts as requests and assertions, but rather challenges, defenses, and retreats, which have to do with the status of the participants, their rights and obligations, and their changing relationships in terms of social organization.[22]

Although Labov's primary division in the therapeutic discourse is between utterances (*what is said*) and Actions (*what is done*), he has in the words quoted above synthesized the problem for us. Acts like requests and assertions are in fact linguistic in nature; more abstract actions like challenges and retreats are interactional or social in nature. Consider the following exchange between two persons, one of whom (A) has been home all day while the other (B) has just gotten home from work at the office:

A: — Hi, Hon. How'd it go today?
B: — Shit, it's hot in here!

B's utterance could be analyzed grammatically as an exclamatory sentence and interactionally as a speech act where a request is made for turning on the air conditioner, opening the windows or opening the door, according to the situation. On another level, however, this sentence may function as a complaint (Can't you even keep the place cool?) and as a rejection of A (I don't know why I came home. You never do anything right.) We therefore actually have three levels: a grammatical one, a speech act and a social function (or as proposed by Labov, a more abstract Action):

	Grammatical	Speech act	Function
B.	Declarative sentence	Request	Complaint/Rejection

It appears then that there are different types of functions. If we equate *utterance* with *turn* and if shifts in speech acts constitute shifts in *moves,* we can then reflect the correspondence between the functional units of the utterance and the moves as in Figure 3.6. Two types of functions are apparent: those that

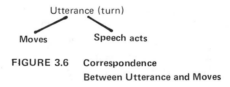

FIGURE 3.6   Correspondence
Between Utterance and Moves

constitute the utterance and are called speech acts and those whose higher node is the discourse itself and which specify the function of the entire utterance as an abstract social Action (Figure 3.7). The abstract functions or Actions on the right branch are of course mapped on to the utterance as specific speech acts.

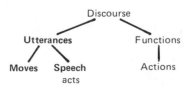

FIGURE 3.7   Types of Functions

Halliday has proposed three general functions of language: ideational, interpersonal and textual. The ideational function is further subdivided into an experiential and a logical function. What is particularly interesting is his presentation of these functions as separate components at the semantic level:

> Broadly speaking, ideational meanings reflect the field of social action, interpersonal meanings reflect the tenor of social relationships, and textual meanings reflect the mode of operation of the language within the situation. But it is at the lower level, that is in the grammatical realization that these functional components are made manifest in the linguistic structure.[23]

Halliday sees these various components as being mapped onto the output, the syntagm, with each component generating either constituent-like structures, prosodic features, and coherence, periodicity and texture.[24] We see Halliday's various semantic components as elements not within a general semantic level from which they feed into the lexico-grammatical level (syntagm) and on to the phonological level but rather as semantic elements which correspond to various levels of the semiotic system of the text and which reflect the various functions of the text: text as social interaction, text as utterances in a verbal exchange, text as reference and text as a proposition. In the end all of these semantic or functional elements are mapped onto the content of the linguistic form, as indicated by Halliday. But it is important to distinguish between the different types of functions and the hierarchy which develops if we are to find the fundamental functions from which all other functions derive.

Let us begin by taking Halliday's functions and placing them within their various levels. His ideational function is both referential and logical. As discussed by Searle, all utterances are *propositional acts* as well as *illocutionary acts.*[25] Utterances are said to perform propositional acts when they refer to (designate) a certain object and predicate (state a proposition) something about that object. This function we would place within the linguistic code. Halliday's interpersonal function is Jakobson's emotive function and Hymes "socio-expressive" function.[26] Since this function sees language as action, is speaker-and-hearer-oriented, and concerned with the communication process itself, we will place it within the Discourse Function level. His third Function, the textual, is concerned with the organization of the text as a relevant and cohesive message which fits in with other texts and within a context. This function which focuses on the text we would also place at the Discourse level. Thus Halliday's functions, although all abstractly presented, in fact fall at different levels of the hierarchy of functions.

Another approach for classifying functions has been presented by Hymes who categorizes them according to the component of the communicative act that they focus on.[27]

> Focus on the addresser or sender
> Focus on the addressee
> Focus on channels
> Focus on codes
> Focus on settings

Focus on message-form
Focus on the event
Focus on the topic

These recall Jakobson's functions which relate the communication model to function according to focus as well (Figure 3.8).[28] The classification of functions

context		referential
message		poetic
addresser_____addressee	emotive_____conative
. contact	phatic
code	metalingual

FIGURE 3.8   Jakobson's Functions

according to focus is valuable in that it allows us to go a step further. As we study these descriptions we find that some deal with the transmission of signs and others with the process of production itself. Those dealing with transmission can be further subdivided into those concerned with the channel and mode of transmission and those concerned with the codes used for the transmission. The production of the signs also falls at two levels. The focus of the production may be the meaning of the interaction itself within a particular context involving particular participants, the meaning of particular utterances or the meaning of particular sentences. We can now locate these functions by focus within their particular levels (Figure 3.9). In all of these cases, it is the Discourse functions

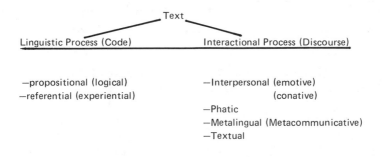

Text

Linguistic Process (Code)   Interactional Process (Discourse)

—propositional (logical)   —Interpersonal (emotive)
—referential (experiential)   (conative)
                                      —Phatic
                                      —Metalingual (Metacommunicative)
                                      —Textual

FIGURE 3.9   Location of Functions According to Focus

which are mapped onto the linguistic structures to produce a functional hierarchy that will be exemplified in the exchange below:

A: — Ahí vienen los literatontos. (Here come the literary-fools.)
B: — Orale, ése; ¿qué se trae? ¿Comiste gallo? (Hey, man, what's with you? Did you eat rooster?)

The first utterance is basically an insult used to challenge a group of individuals who are just arriving at the scene. What A is saying is basically: "You guys in literature (or "You writers" or "You literary critics" or "You guys at the University") are fools." He is thus making an assertion through a declarative sentence. The statement would be construed as a challenge within particular circles where the term *literatontos* has been coined through a Chicano literary newsletter to refer to literary critics, sometimes in jest, sometimes sarcastically, generally derogatorily. It is the social and political positions of A and B which determine whether the assertion is taken as an in-group joke or whether it is perceived as insulting bait which if accepted requires a retort. It is B's response that clarifies the position of the two participants.

If we were to analyze this first utterance, we would find several functions operating at different levels. We can see that there is action at the interactional level where A challenges B's group. The challenge could come through an insult, through a purely physical act like giving them the finger or standing in their way, or even through another type of speech act, like a denial or questioning of a person's statements. At the same time, through this statement or declarative sentence, A asserts his opinion of B's group. In this particular case the function of the declarative sentence is to make an assertion. We can see then two main levels, a linguistic-semantic level and a social-semantic level as indicated in Table 3.1. The form of the social semantic level we call a speech act and the content, a Function (or Action).

Table 3.1   Levels of A's sentence

	Linguistic-semantic		Social-semantic	
	Form	Content	Form	Content
A.	Declarative sentence	Assertion	Insult	Challenge

B's response consists of three moves. The first move takes the form of a semi-greeting, a vocative to draw the attention of A. The style however is colloquial, in-group style, and serves as an equalizer of positions that pretends to erase the distinction between A's "*we*" and "*you,* the literatontos." B then sees himself as A's equal and neither wants to appear as a pedantic scholar from the university nor as someone who does not fit in the inner Chicano circle. In reality he is saying, "Hold it right there, brother." B, however, does not want to be seen as inferior either; so he asks A for clarification. The question here would at first glance appear to be a request for information but actually it functions much like the English "What's bugging you?" or "What's your problem?" when the actual intention is the assertion: "I see you have a problem." The question also says: "I hear you loud and clear. I know where you're coming from." In effect the question is actually B's acknowledgment of A's insult and an assertion of B's general opinion of A as a man with a grudge or an ax to grind. His third move is again in question form but the utterance functions like an assertion: "You're an s.o.b." In interactional terms, B is returning the insult and challenging A to make more out of it. His retaliation, however, has left him open to several possible moves on A's part, as he has used a popular rural crack, probably from Texas, which an urban Chicano from California could spring upon for attack. Were A to pounce on use of this style, however, he would be diametrically opposed to his initial stance, where he tried to show up B's group as snobs and fools. We can now summarize our functional analysis for this exchange (Table 3.2). The

Table 3.2   Functional Analysis of the Exchange Between A and B

	Text			
	Linguistic		Social-interactional	
	Form	Content	Speech act	Function
A.	Declarative sentence	Assertion	Insult	Challenge
B.	Exclamation	Recognition	Greeting	Reading of challenge and restraining action
	Question	Request/Assertion	Acknowledgment	Acceptance of challenge
	Question	Assertion	Insult	Retaliation through a challenge

functional analysis of this exchange with its expansions and propositions à la Labov clearly indicates that it is impossible to determine the function of utterances without knowledge of the social context. A statement that can be analyzed context-free as an assertion or a request is obviously being examined from a linguistic rather than an interactional perspective; conversation on the other hand occurs in specific situations with particular participants whose socio-economic and political background is fundamental in determining the interactional meaning of discourse. Even an analysis of styles of discourse requires knowledge not only of the varieties spoken in various areas but also knowledge for interpreting the implications of shifts from one style to another in discourse. Discourse is fundamentally a social product and as such must be studied within its social context. In fact verbal interaction, as we saw before, is only one manifestation of social interaction and for this reason is constantly affected and molded by other types of social interaction. The analysis of discourse in terms of abstract social Actions or Functions requires a thorough knowledge of the fundamental social processes in society. And, as we all know, the basic form of social interaction in modern history is the labor process.

THEORETICAL ASSUMPTIONS: SOCIAL INTERACTION AND THE LABOR PROCESS

As Labov has indicated, the analysis of conversation provides insights into the ways in which members of a society organize their social interaction. It is this relationship between verbal interaction and other forms of social interaction which determines the mode of interaction, the mode of argument and the mode of expression. Labov has analyzed these modes in terms of directness and indirection.[29] Since both the dimensions of power and solidarity can call for degrees of indirection, where both requests to superiors or conversation among intimate equals can elicit indirection, it would be preferable to focus not on directness or indirection but on the underlying sets of social relations which will relate *what is said* to *what is done* and will determine the underlying functions of discourse.

To speak of dimensions of power and solidarity is to speak of the social organization of society, the status of the participants, their positions and roles and their relationships. Within a capitalist system, dimensions of power create a hierarchical class organization which is determined by particular relations of production operating within that economic system. Where the productive process creates class differences, social stratification leads to antagonistic class relations and conflicting class interests. It is the capitalist labor process, where one class is the owner of the means of production and the other class has only its labor power to sell, which creates conflictive relations between classes, conditions relations between individuals and communities, and determines the degree and type of social contact or distance and ultimately particular modes of interaction, argument and expression. Figure 3.10 reflects these relations.

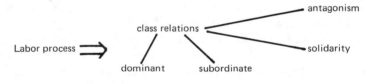

FIGURE 3.10   Class Relations

Since this study focuses on the relation between social interaction and verbal interaction in the Chicano community, it is crucial to identify the dimensions of power and solidarity which operate within that community. As we have seen, relations in the Southwest between the Mexican-origin community and the dominant Anglo population have been conflictive since before 1848. These relations did not simply arise out of the domination and appropriation of Mexican territory in 1848. Conflictive relations between the two language communities arose as a result of the two groups' status and participation within the capitalist labor process, a process which creates class antagonisms.

These social conflicts are indicative of the contradictions within the economic structure which, like all phenomena, is constantly in motion and in the process of change. Of particular intrest for this study are those changes which brought about the division of labor into various skill-based categories, an increased industrialization leading to shifts from labor-intensive to capital-intensive industries, the emergence of a dual labor market and the results of extensive labor unionization in the Southwest. These economic changes, although quantitative in nature, affect and alter social relations, not only between the dominant and subordinate groups but even within a particular group, as economic changes often allow for some degree of social mobility. Our task then necessarily required a historical analysis of changes in the labor process which produced changes in the social existence of the Mexican-origin population and affected social relations between this population and the Anglo population.

A discussion of material conditions determining social organization cannot however fail to consider the various political, legal and religious processes which also emerge. The labor process as it develops gives rise to a number of additional processes which in themselves affect and alter social relations and affect the way we think (social consciousness) and the way we see ourselves and others. These processes form what is commonly called the *superstructure*, which conditions social, political and intellectual life and produces different forms of social consciousness (Figure 3.11). There is no mechanistic

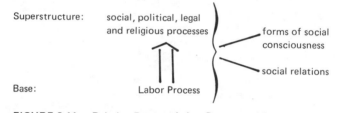

FIGURE 3.11   Relation Between Labor Process and Superstructure Process

correspondence between the labor process and social relations nor between the base and the superstructure since all affect social existence. All of these elements are in fact interconnected and interdependent, for although the labor process is basic, all of these processes affect each other reciprocally and dialectically (Figure 3.12). In their interaction they condition a community's

FIGURE 3.12   Relation Between Processes

social existence. But even though material conditions determine social being, it is also true that men are capable of changing circumstances.

These general theoretical propositions of the structure of society assume particular form in the case of the Chicano community, a language and ethnic minority, primarily working class population within a capitalist system. A study of these various processes in their interconnection allows us to explore the circumstances within which social intercourse and verbal communication take place in Chicano communities. Language choice and language use are thus the result of structural (labor process), cultural (social process) and individual processes. Of these the structural factors determining class status and occupation are the primary forces setting a community in motion and determining the specific circumstances which lead to social contact or distance, particular types of social interaction, and ultimately to particular modes of discourse and expression. These processes have a hierarchical organization which we can illustrate through a branching tree (Figure 3.13), with the right-

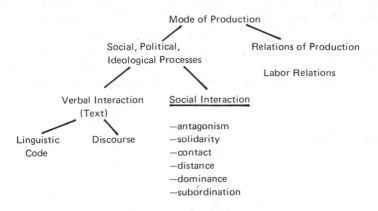

FIGURE 3.13   Organization of Processes

most branches representing the deepest structures and processes. In a right to left direction the right branches are mapped in succeeding order on to the leftward branches and ultimately and cumulatively on to the left-most branch which represents the surface structures used in verbal interaction.

Thus, a study of bilingualism and the maintenance or loss of a minority language in the speech of a community is not only a study of discourse but a study as well of the social organization of the community itself, for language is a social and linguistic product, as it were, "the communal being speaking for itself."

THEORY AND METHODOLOGY

In a fall, 1979, issue of *The New York Review of Books*, Stephen Toulmin reviews three English editions of the Russian psychologist Vygotsky's work in which he notes that Soviet and American psychologists have drifted apart. In contrast to the integrative Soviet approach, the behavioral sciences in the United States "have proliferated into dozens of highly specialized, and largely noninteracting, subdisciplines; ... behavioral scientists have organized their research on the principle that the more narrowly and sharply defined a question can be, the more 'scientific' it is."[30]

In the field of sociolinguistics as well we often tend towards fragmented studies that focus exclusively on componential analyses pairing criterial features to verbal labels or towards studies that appear thoroughly scientific by their incorporation of probability theory in the quantitative analysis of linguistic variation, producing results which are applicable only in restricted or "standard" instances. At the risk of being called eclectic, we propose that the bilingualism of Chicanos be analyzed through the methods used in various disciplines, whenever these enable us to capture a more integrated picture which takes into consideration the numerous interdependent factors and contradictions within our social and linguistic situation. At the same time, although recognizing the importance of survey or interview analyses, we would like to suggest that we need to direct our efforts toward the area of discourse analysis where specific varieties and alternations are studied in the context of the specific circumstances of verbal interaction and where the objective is not simply tabulating occurrences in terms of one or two criterial features but rather interpreting the meaning of discourse. An integrative approach would allow us to consider methods used in semiotics, literary analysis, linguistics and sociolinguistics as well as consider theoretical models and research findings in history, sociology and economics in order to more fully analyze the bilingualism of Chicanos.

The methodology employed for this study is in fact inseparable from the theoretical perspectives that have been discussed. The Marxist economic model, for example, allows us to discuss verbal interaction within a broad context where relations between text and context, between participants, and between sign and referent are examined as reflections of stratified social relations determined by a specific economic structure. The economic model thus allows us to locate the unit of analysis in the social structure without negating the importance of the individual in social interaction.

The particular role of the individual within a social structure has been the focus of symbolic interactionists and ethnomethodologists. The interactionist sees human beings as orienting themselves, learning, thinking, communicating and acting through symbols whose meaning is subject to change.[31] Problems arise with this approach however when the individual's interpretation of this symbolic interaction is considered more important than reality itself, i.e., the symbol becomes more meaningful than the referent itself.[32] Ethnomethodologists, on the other hand, although also concerned with social rules, norms and meanings, propose the study of daily interaction in natural field settings. Garfinkle has described ethnomethodology as "an organizational study of a member's knowledge of his ordinary affairs, of his own organized enterprises, where that knowledge is treated by us as part of the same setting that it also makes orderable."[33] Obviously both interactionists and ethnomethodologists seek to discover and describe the organizational rules or codes that operate under particular circumstances in society. Although it is true that within given contexts there are rules and procedures which serve as the basis for daily interaction and which in fact determine practices, it is also true that the larger societal structure with its economic and social stratification, its racism and its value system forces and continually reinforces certain organizational procedures.

These two theoretical perspectives with their study of interaction complement the traditional perspective of discourse analysis which concentrates on discovering rules operating in verbal interaction. Moreover both propose a variety of methods of observation to discover the organizational rules or symbolic systems operating and the process of interpretation taking place among interactants.[34] Ethnomethodologists additionally favor the documentary method of analysis where observations are classified on the basis of construct models of daily interaction. Construct models are inevitable and useful in the analysis of observed phenomena as long as they recognize the role of force in creating and maintaining a given social order with its particular norms and rules. Other theoretical perspectives have also been useful in analyzing our subject matter. Functionalist sociology which emphasizes social harmony and the stability and persistence of social forms has been particularly helpful in an analysis of cultural perspectives. Conflict theory, on the other hand, directs us toward a study of the relation betwen class and ideology and between class conflicts and social change, thereby enabling us to formulate social relations within the total society and within one particular class in terms of solidarity, harmony, antagonisms, conflict, dominance and subordination. An analysis of these conflicts and contradictions enables us to discover and postulate underlying functions of discourse.

Although the Marxist model has provided the basic propositions which enable us to formulate the relation between verbal interaction and social interaction in the Chicano community, methodologically we have proceeded along interactionist lines with taped interviews, taped family conversations, two small surveys and a lifetime of participant-observations. The analysis of the material itself is highly colored by linguistic conventions, sociolinguistic notions and formulations, and semiotic notations. The three language-related areas could be subsumed under semiotics, since linguistics in fact focuses on the expression-forms of sign systems in communication while sociolinguistics in its analysis of discourse focuses on the interactional aspects of communication. Since semiotics deals with all sign systems, whether they be linguistic or socio-cultural, and with the analysis of signs in relation to other sign systems, it is the semiotic approach which has allowed us to represent the inseparability of social and verbal interaction and the interconnection of discourse and linguistic codes. A semiotic model also directs us toward a holistic consideration of the process of communication, that is, both in terms of the transmission (encoding) and the reception (decoding) of information. Semiotic theory is thus a correlate of communication theory. And since human communication and the transmission of meaning cannot be understood outside of a social context, these processes must be studied within the realm of sociolinguistics as well. To further explain our approach to this study we will look briefly at semiotic theory and at two trends within sociolinguistics.

Semiotics, the science of sign systems, has generally been an idealist formulation, concerned primarily, although not exclusively, with the analysis and classification of logical and linguistic symbolic systems. Linguists like Hjemslev have noted that "in general, a language is independent of any specific purpose,"[35] and that "linguistics must attempt to grasp language, not as a conglomerate of non-linguistic (e.g., physical, physiological, psychological, logical, sociological) phenomena but as a self-sufficient totality, a structure *sui generis*."[36] In opposition to those who consider that language must be studied as an ideal form stand other semioticians, like Vološinov, who sees the sign as "an arena of the class struggle."[37] For Vološinov, verbal signs are ideological signs as well:

> Every sign is subject to the criteria of ideological evaluation (i.e., whether it is true, false, correct, fair, good, etc.). The domain of ideology coincides with the domain of signs. They equate with one another. Wherever a sign is present, ideology is present too. *Everything ideological possesses semiotic value.*[38] (italics in original text)

For Vološinov a semiotic analysis involves a study of the form of the utterance, its content or theme and the form of communication, embodying what sociolinguists call *domain, speech events* and *acts*. All of these are presented in relation to social factors:

> Production relations and the sociopolitical order shaped by those relations determine the full range of verbal contacts between people, all the forms and means of their verbal communication—at work, in political life, in ideological creativity. In turn, from the conditions, forms and types of verbal communication derive not only the forms but also the themes of speech performances.[39]

This materialist and dialectical approach has not however been the case for most proponents of the field of semiotics.

In fact the field of semiotics has reflected the current ideological trends prevalent within a given historical period. Where ontological concerns during the Greek period led to an idealist philosophy of language which posited the "idea" as *a priori*, modern concern for the application of scientific methods of analysis, particularly those of mathematics and logic, has led to studies focusing on the logical form of language. Language in fact becomes a veritable prison house which mediates between us and reality, which is constantly changing. Since the meaning of language is also constantly changing, according to contextual conditions and social conventions, there are only two possible alternatives: either one studies language as a social sign system or as a logical sign system. The first deals with language as a social activity, the second with abstract logical entities. Sociolinguistics deals with language as a social sign system. Structuralists and transformationalists have dealt with language primarily as a logical sign system. In both cases language is seen as rule-governed activity, but in the latter case, language is analyzed as having both a superficial and an underlying structure. Grammar is thus the formal representation of verbal mental processes.

Saussure, the father of structuralism, is the modern proponent of the field of semiology. Saussure analyzed language as a system of signs.[40] Although he spoke of language as a social institution, he is best remembered for his concern with analyzing the constitutive parts of a sign, for his distinction between *langue* (the system of language) and *parole* (speech), and between diachronic (historic—extending through time) and synchronic (limited to a particular time period) analyses and for his synchronic systematization of language.[41] The sign itself he analyzed in terms of *signifier* and *signified*, that is, in terms of expression and meaning.[42] Although Saussure saw language as the form of thought,[43] he also saw language as "a form and not a substance,"[44] that is, as a mediating form combining sound and meaning.[45] As in the case of Hjemslev, Saussure wished to distinguish the field of linguistics from related or subordinate ideas of study. Hjemslev's further expansion of Saussurean ideas led to his scheme proposing that all semiotic systems are based on properties of functions and terminal functives designated as *expression* and *content* and further subdivided into *form* and *substance*.[46] This scheme was particularly useful for our analysis as it allowed us to distinguish not only between the form and substance of content and expression at the linguistic and interactional levels, but also the form and substance of macrostructures as well.

Although cognizant of public discourse, these two linguists were more concerned with a systematization of language structures than with the process of verbal interaction and the exchange of messages and signs. Sebeok has designated the latter as being the subject matter of semiotics.[47] Most philosophers and linguists have studied language as inner discourse from an ontological or epistemological perspective, seeking either to prove the existence of an absolute being, to postulate the existence of innate ideas or transcendental schemes or to explain the origin of knowledge in terms of solipsistic perceptions and thoughts. As technology has advanced, so have ideas about language and sign systems, but these advances have been primarily at the formal level.

A philosopher who was keenly interested in the interpretation of signs was Charles Sanders Peirce, considered to be the founder of semiotics. Peirce developed a theory of signs based on mathematical logic and common experience. What is central to his theory is the concept of mediation of "thirdness" between a sign and its interpreter, an effect he called "an interpretant."[48] This phenomenological approach, which he termed *phaneroscopy*,[49] led him to a formulation which distinguished three kinds of signs: icon, index and symbol, three kinds of meaning: feeling, action and habits, and three kinds of interpretants: the immediate, the dynamical and the final.[50] Signs could be further classified as Qualisigns, Sinsigns or Legisigns. This division of signs, which led to a classification of 66 different kinds,[51] was quite theoretical but metaphysical in nature. The reality corresponding to the mental ideas (or *phanerons*)[52] behind all signs, that is, the truth or falsity of these signs, did not concern him. His notion of sign as "Something which stands to somebody for something in some respect or capacity,"[53] and of interpretation as "the collective total . . . in any sense present to the mind"[54] was strictly mentalist rather than social.

Peirce's ideas were further developed by Charles W. Morris, whose orientation, however, was primarily pragmatic and behavioristic. Morris proposed dividing semiotics into three subordinate branches: syntactics (the relation between combinations of signs within a language), semantics (the relation of signs to their designata and to the objects denoted), and pragmatics (the relation of signs to their users).[55] Later, however, Morris modified his behavioristic classification of signs to one based on different aspects of meaning, of "modes of signifying," which posited different kinds of signs, different modes of signifying and different types of discourse.[56] These semiotic classificatory systems share many features with current sociolinguistic analyses of speech acts and functions.

The work of these semioticians provides us with useful tools for analyzing language as a sign system. The semiotic formulation allows us to consider (1) codes in terms of expression and content, (2) the whole process of the transmission of codes which involves the channel, the message source (addresser-speaker or writer), the addressee, storage units, noise or the nonlinguistic components in transmission, and (3) both encoding and decoding. A semiotic approach also allows us to study meaning and the process involved in different levels of signification. Using binary features or various meaning relations, signs can be analyzed in terms of semantic features or semantic fields. This method allows for an analysis of cultural units or socio-semantic features providing denotative or connotative levels of meaning within different content areas or fields covering the "whole of culture," to use Eco's words.[57] A semiotic approach thus involves a study of both the transmission of codes (the communicative process) and the interpretation of codes (the process of signification.)

If we accept Eco's proposition of studying all cultural processes as processes of communication with an underlying system of signification, we can see the relation of semiotics to sociolinguistics. Briefly stated, sociolinguistics is concerned with a study of those extralinguistic factors which affect the production of language. Since language is both a formal and social sign system, it has to be studied in terms of all the surrounding phenomena which affect language. Fishman has distinguished two major sociolinguistic orientations: Micro-sociolinguistics and Macro-sociolinguistics.[58]

Micro-sociolinguists are concerned with immediate elements within the speech process: language variety, repertoire, topic, situation, role, speech acts and speech events, to name a few. Macro-sociolinguists, on the other hand, are interested in major socio-economic constructs which create the social constraints which are continually operating upon language. Macro-sociolinguists thus deal with major realities like nation, social class, formal institutions, societal domains, demographic data, nationalism, colonization, standardization procedures in developing nations, and ideology. Thus, while one set of sociolinguists deals with the immediate elements in the communicative act (addresser, addressee, code, subcode, content and channel), another is concerned with social, economic and political structures which maintain certain modes of production and certain relations of production. These, it is clear, determine the type of social and linguistic contact in a given linguistic community, the type of language planning and policies that are formulated and implemented, the degree of language maintenance and language shift and the stratification of language varieties along class and racial lines. It is the major social and economic structures that determine more immediate factors like the roles a speaker may play, the codes to which he has accessibility, the situations within which he can interact verbally, and his whole culture which makes up the content of his speech.

Here again sociolinguistics provides important tools for the analysis of verbal interaction but even these have at times been used in reactionary ways. Sociolinguistic proposals have included the whole hypothesis of verbal deficiencies to explain the low achievement in schools of working-class children in England or Black children in the United States. Fortunately other sociolinguists like Labov have refuted the Bernstein Deficit Hypothesis through a Language Variability model which demonstrates the complexity and logic of all language varieties and the varied functions which all have. Labov's studies have demonstrated the bias behind models which posit classificatory systems that distinguish between "elaborated" and "restricted" codes and the desire to blame the victim rather than the school or society for school problems.[59]

Recent studies in sociolinguistics have been primarily quantitative studies in which particular forms or responses are elicited. The researcher attempts to determine the factor or factors responsible for a particular frequency of use, and to describe the phenomenon through variable rules that account for the frequency percentage. Proponents of variable rules in linguistics differ on their willingness to integrate variable rules into linguistic theory. The concept that speakers' knowledge about language varieties and use frequency is part of human linguistic competence has led to assertions and counter-arguments about what constitutes a speaker's knowledge of (1) precise percentages of application, (2) the probability of application, (3) a hierarchy of constraints which favor a variable rule and (4) the relative weight of environmental factors leading to application of a rule.[60]

Although probability theory offers insights into the range of linguistic variation and change of a given community, these types of studies, by their nature, are limited by the particular survey or interview situation artificially created to assess application of a particular variable rule. Assume, for example, that a linguist visits a predetermined number of Chicano families in West Texas and notes the use of the subjunctive forms *vuélvanos* and *siéntanos*. If these and only these appear, the interviewer would have to assume that these forms were not variable but were produced through obligatory rules of the language. Were he to extend this sample and interview a larger number of families, he could find alternations between *vuélvanos, vuélvamos* and *volvamos*. The linguist could then provide frequency percentages and seek to identify the semantic or social or demographic factors which contribute to the application of particular morphological rules. The notion of probability that particular rules would be applied in particular socially determined environments would give the study a "scientific look" and presumably provide conventional usage, but the findings would be questionable given another set of sociolinguistic assumptions and considerations as well as a different set of informants from the same community. Perhaps the variable rule was triggered not by nativity or residence but by speech act, presence of a non-Chicano interviewer, topic, relationships, or any number of other factors not taken into consideration. Since it is impossible to recreate the exact same situation in each home, in each specific case, there would certainly be a number of circumstantial features present which the linguist would have to consider. In each case the meaning of particular rule applications would be subject to the context of use.

The frequency of application of particular variable rules can only be specified in terms of a particular text within a given situation. When we go beyond a particular verbal interaction and attempt to describe group patterns, we can only speak of optional rules which account for utterances that are possible in a language or variety. Given the numerous possibilities within communication of producing a given number of variants, the task of sociolinguistics should be to enable analysis of meaning—of denotations and connotations—within a given text. At most, sets of rules to be provided should enable the analyst to identify and determine the sort of speech act with which he/she is confronted.[61] And finally, as Cicourel has stated, to be able to systematize sets of contextual constraints which account for the alternation patterns between the linguistic items so that one can extract a particular reading from a given text requires an interpretative competence on the part of the analyst himself.[62]

Verbal interaction in the Chicano community has generally been studied from a linguistic or micro-sociolinguistic perspective. The approach taken in this work, however, has been influenced by studies of language shift and language maintenance in other parts of the world and throughout history. In many cases we found language shift to be a result of military conquest and economic control of a population. It was especially interesting to see the language situations in the Third World, where policy reflects the effects of conquest, colonization, independence and neo-colonialism. The migratory labor situations in Europe and Africa provided new insights into the relation between language and migration and the linguistic implications of an international labor force. Glyn Lewis's work on multilingualism in the Soviet Union was particularly useful in relating language shift to demographic factors.[63]

Our formulation of different postulates is highly tinged with the style provided by linguistic conventions. The branching trees are everywhere. From sociolinguistics we have borrowed the focus on both micro and macro-structural considerations. In the area of semiotics we have been influenced by Eco's and Barthes's work on levels of signification,[64] and particularly by Eco's analysis of content in terms of interacting semantic fields. In conjunction with demographic, historical and economic studies, these semiotic and sociolinguistic approaches allowed for the postulation of variables giving rise to particular mediating elements which affect communication in the Chicano community.

This particular integrative approach offers new insights into Chicano bilingualism which have not previously been formulated in this light. A brief survey of previous research in Spanish linguistics and Chicano Spanish might better clarify our position. This brief presentation is not meant to be an exhaustive review of the literature since that is not the objective of this study. We merely wish to indicate previous directions in these fields.

REVIEW OF STUDIES ON THE SPANISH LANGUAGE AND CHICANO SPANISH

A study of Spanish-language use in the United States is necessarily a study of language choice in the context of socio-economic developments, as we have indicated. The impact of large-scale historical processes on patterns of language choice is evident not only in variation in Spanish-language use but also in the distribution of old and new Spanish-language variants. The components to be analyzed in a study of language variation and language use could be summarized as in Figure 3.14. As we shall see, each component has attracted several studies

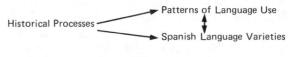
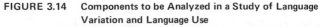

FIGURE 3.14   Components to be Analyzed in a Study of Language Variation and Language Use

and some studies have been characterized by taking all of these components into consideration. The studies have reflected various schools of linguistic theory and analysis. Some studies are part of the traditional field of Spanish linguistics; some form part of American sociolinguistic research and studies. Since we have looked already at the general sociolinguistic framework, it will be necessary to look briefly at previous work in Spanish linguistics in order to place Chicano-language studies within the context of other Spanish-language research.

Historical processes and their impact on the Spanish language have attracted numerous studies which have dealt with language change during periods of major social transformation, as for example: the Arabic invasion of the Spanish peninsula which lasted for eight centuries (771–1492), the expulsion of Sephardic Jews from Spain in the fifteenth century, the Spanish colonization of the Americas and the arrival of Southern European immigrants to the Americas. Spanish linguistic studies documenting these periods of linguistic change have generally been descriptive in nature and characterized by the inclusion of large inventories of lexical and morphological variants which have been retained from past centuries or incorporated through language contact with other language groups. Some of these studies have concentrated on establishing the roots of particular lexical items, tracing them back to Arabic, Germanic, Celtic, Basque, Greek, Quechua or Nahuatl forms. A few studies, like Rosenblat's exhaustive compendium of information on the indigenous populations of America from the fifteenth to the twentieth centuries, have focused primarily on historical processes.[65] Studies like that of Shirley Brice Heath on the language policy in Mexico from colonial times to independence have also dealt with historical processes and their effect on language choice in Mexico.[66]

Following historical trends in linguistic theory and analysis, Spanish linguistic studies could be subdivided into three different types primarily, with the fourth type a more recent addition:
   a) philological studies
   b) dialectological studies
   c) structuralist studies
   d) sociolinguistic studies
Philological studies have been comparative and historical in nature, concerned with the evolution of Spanish from Vulgar Latin and with rule variations which distinguish Spanish from other Romance languages. The work of Menéndez-Pidal,[67] Lapesa,[68] Iordan,[69] Lausberg,[70] and García de Diego[71] are good examples of philological work. Out of this concern for linguistic borrowing and variation arose interest in detailed studies of dialectal varieties. Both philological and dialectal studies can be characterized as "taxonomic" works as their main focus is the tabulation of inventories of phonological and morphosyntactic elements and their distribution.

Thus, Latin American dialectology has been primarily descriptive and taxonomic and characterized by a concentration on studies dealing with phonology and phonetics. The work of Matluck,[72] Boyd-Bowman,[73] Lope-Blanch,[74] Navarro-Tomás,[75] Zamora Vicente,[76] and López Morales,[77] to name a few, has been concerned overwhelmingly with sound variants, particularly with liquid, sibilant, fricative, affricate and vocalic variants. Some studies have focused on tracing the Andalusian, indigenous or African roots of particular sound patterns, morphological variants or lexical forms. The work of Amado Alonso,[78] Canfield,[79] Malmberg,[80] Clavijero,[81] and López Morales[82] are good examples of these studies. Other linguists have simply presented inventories and distributions of particular forms, whether syntactic, lexical, phonetic or morphological, as evidenced by the work of Resnick,[83] Kany,[84] Moreno de Alba,[85] and Gobello.[86] English interference in the Spanish of America has also been the topic of some articles, particularly those concerned with the Spanish of Puerto Rico and the Southwest of the United States. The studies of Pérez Salas[87] and Granda Gutiérrez[88] have focused on cases of interference in Puerto Rican Spanish.

Structuralist studies analyze language as system and focus on an analysis of the general structure of language. In the United States structuralist studies have been primarily taxonomic and descriptive. In Europe, on the other hand, structuralist studies, while not eliminating the descriptive component, have sought to posit underlying structures, especially for the philological component, following the work of Trubetzkoy, Jakobson, Saussure and Hjemslev. The best example here is the work of Emilio Alarcos Llorach,[89] although it is true that structuralist notions of analysis are evident in the work of many other linguists previously mentioned as philologists or dialectologists, like Amado Alonso. Structuralism and communicative theory are the bases of more recent work in semantics and semiotics. The work of several semioticians is now available in Spanish translation, as are the Spanish language works of Díaz Guerrero,[90] Baldinger,[91] Bobes Naves,[92] and Luis Prieto.[93]

Sociolinguistic studies concerned with patterns of language use are beginning to appear in Spanish, particularly in the area of bilingualism. Concern in Spain for regional autonomy and for gaining official status for Catalan and Basque, for example, have increased interest in bilingualism and sociolinguistic studies. The work of Ninyoles[94] and the appearance of an anthology on *bilingüismo* and *biculturalismo* in Spain are good examples of this new trend.[95] In Latin America, the work of American sociolinguists like Hymes, Gumperz, Labov and Fishman is beginning to have an impact and has led to studies like those of Catalina Weinerman on the use of second person pronouns,[96] the anthology of Garvin and Lastra de Suarez,[97] the theoretical analysis by Rona,[98] the analysis of multilingualism by Uribe Villegas,[99] the work on bilingual education for indigenous populations by Georgina Paulín de Siade,[100] the work on sound patterns in Mexico City by Perissinotto[101] and the work by Beatriz Lavandera on *cocoliche* in Argentina.[102]

These references obviously do not include all publications on Spanish linguistics, but they do point to certain trends in the area which are reflected in the study of Chicano Spanish. In the presentation which follows we will point to particular trends within the field of Spanish-language studies in the Southwest. For a review of a broader corpus of bibliographic material we suggest the work of Fernando Peñalosa (*Chicano Sociolinguistics. A brief introduction*)[103] and the review by Berk-Seligson ("A Sociolinguistic View of the Mexican-American Speech Community").[104] Though neither is exhaustive, both works review an ample segment of the literature on Chicano Spanish to provide readers with a general idea of available works on the verbal interaction of Chicanos.

Studies on Chicano Spanish or on Chicano verbal interaction have also been characterized by focusing primarily on a description of varieties themselves. A few have summarized historical processes and some have explored language usage among different generations within a family and in rural areas. A few surveys have sought to determine language preference and attitudes, but most studies have been descriptive in nature, isolating linguistic data to demonstrate the presence of particular variants. Increasingly, masters and doctoral theses and dissertations influenced by the work of Fishman, Gumperz and Labov and related to bilingual education are being produced in universities of the Southwest. A few studies on the acquisition of language among Chicano children have also appeared.

The larger body of studies has dealt with the lexicon, focusing primarily on loanwords or archaisms. Espinosa's studies from the early twentieth century, following the peninsular philological tradition, documented loans from English, Spanish archaisms and "voces indígenas."[105] In the last few years several glossaries or lexical studies have appeared, with a few concentrating on *caló*.[106] This variety, called *caló, chuco* or *pachuco*, has attracted the interest of several researchers who have invariably treated it as the secret language of alienated youth, delinquents or criminals.[107] Present interest in the pachuco, arising in part from the Valdéz *Zoot Suiter* theater hit and subsequent films, has led to a certain mythicizing of this figure and his code by the media and by Chicano cultural works. New analyses of this phenomenon are only now beginning to be published.[108]

Another group of studies on Chicano Spanish has recorded the presence of numerous phonetic variants, frequent in the popular Spanish varieties of Mexico, the rest of Latin America, and Spain.[109] These studies generally document the laxing or loss of fricatives in Southwest Spanish, the diphthongization of *hiatos*, the reduction of diphthongs, the simplification of consonant clusters and other phonetic changes like aphaeresis, epenthesis, metathesis, apocope, syncope and lateralization.[110] In the area of morphology, only a few studies have dealt with verb, pronoun and noun variants.[111] A few of the studies have sought to give an overview of the varieties found within the repertoire of given communities, either from a grammatical point of view or a sociolinguistic point of view.[112]

The phenomenon which attracted the most recent interest is that of code-switching. It has been analyzed from a descriptive-linguistic perspective, from a socio-linguistic perspective, from socio-psycholinguistic perspectives, from a cultural perspective and from a semantic perspective.[113] Perhaps the most prominent study is the work of Gumperz and Hernández-Chavez which accounts for Chicano code-switching in terms of ethnic identity, attitudes, solidarity and confidentiality.[114] Studies of code-switching in poetry add another dimension to analyses of code-switching functions, although linguistic constraints present in conversational discourse do not always hold in the literary act.

Most of the studies on Chicano Spanish have been, then, in the area of descriptive linguistics, whether the description utilized transformational grammar conventions or philological, taxonomic conventions. In the area of sociolinguistics, the best known study of a Mexican-origin community is probably that of George C. Barker, whose research in Tucson, Arizona, identified five social groups, four types of bilinguals and four fields of interpersonal relations: the field of intimate or familiar relations, the field of informal relations, the field of formal relations, and the field of Anglo-Mexican relations.[115] This study completed in the mid forties concerns a small urban center 65 miles from the Mexican border. The author discovered that several generations of Mexican-origin families retained Spanish for intimate and familial relations although not in interaction with Anglos. Given the acceleration of urbanization since then in Arizona and an increase in educational attainment along with occupational mobility for persons of second, third and fourth generation, we would probably find some changes in language patterns in Tucson today, but Barker's study stands as the first attempt to analyze language use patterns in terms of social and family relations.

Since Barker's study, other sociolinguistic studies have appeared, analyzing the variables which trigger the use of particular language variants. Most of these studies prefer to focus on what we consider micro-sociolinguistic constraints, by-products of large-scale historical processes, with a few exceptions.[116] It is our premise that studies of Chicano discourse must be seen in light of a macro-sociohistorical framework. Although those of us who have been born and raised in Chicano communities of the Southwest are natural carriers of a store of information—social, economic and linguistic—it is nevertheless necessary to substantiate observations through empirical research, through the gathering of taped discourse and even through surveys. Sociolinguistic studies require an integrative approach, which pools data from various fields of study and studies them in their interrelation and in their effect on verbal interaction. Otherwise we are left with meaningless quantitative studies, giving us proportions and numerous statistics indicating the number of times a particular variant appeared in the speech of one group or another.

Thus, rather than three different types of studies, we need studies that treat language interaction in the Chicano community as a whole and analyze the effect of historical processes on patterns of language use and on Spanish-language change. Only by studying the relations among these elements from a sociolinguistic and semiotic perspective can we understand the type of organization and adaptation that has taken place in the verbal interaction of Chicanos.

To summarize, our study on Chicano verbal interaction has tapped several sources as well as several methodologies and theoretical perspectives. Census statistics, however unreliable, are one source that we have used for general information on a sample of the population. We have not only considered economic and sociological studies of the Southwest but have also resorted to newspaper articles collected through the years on immigration, migrant families, labor unions, housing problems, Chicano gangs and other related items. The latter provide us with tiny bits of information which fit in with the more general and broader studies which we cite. Large-scale studies, for example, may indicate that in the Los Angeles area the Hispanic population is increasing rapidly but a small feature story on "Rent Control in El Monte"[117] offers substantive evidence of strong first-generation Mexican-origin concentration in low-income areas where Spanish is the usual language.

In our attempt to establish the various cultural-historical conditions under which Chicanos interact with each other and other groups, we did not, however, eliminate the text, that is, the discourse, within and upon which these conditions operate. An integrative approach has thus required that we borrow from different fields, all of which contribute essential information to a study of Chicano communication: history, economics, sociology, sociolinguistics, semiotics and linguistics.

Notes

1. William Labov and David Fanshel, *Therapeutic Discourse* (New York: Academic Press, 1977), p. 30.

2. *Ibid.,* p. 67.

3. J. L. Austin, "How to Do Things with Words," in *Readings in the Philosophy of Language,* eds. J. F. Rosenberg and C. Travis (Englewood Cliffs, N.J.: Prentice Hall, Inc., 1971), p. 562.

4. John R. Searle, *Speech Acts. An Essay in the Philosophy of Language* (Cambridge: University Press, 1969), p. 23.

5. Labov, p. 350.

6. M. A. K. Halliday and Ruqaiya Hasan, *Cohesion in English* (Hong Kong: Longman, 1976).

7. Charles Morris, *Foundations of the Theory of Signs*, Vol. 1, No. 2 (Chicago: University of Chicago Press, 1975), p. 8.

8. Labov, p. 350.

9. *Ibid.,* pp. 25 and 350.

10. *Ibid.,* p. 25.

11. Malcolm Coulthard, *An Introduction to Discourse Analysis* (Hong Kong: Longman, 1977), p. 10.

12. *Ibid.,* p. 9.

13. Halliday, p. 293.

14. *Ibid.,* pp. 293–294.

15. Louis Hjemslev, *Prolegomena to a Theory of Language* (Madison: University of Wisconsin Press, 1963), pp. 47–55.

16. Bertolt Brecht, "El formalismo y las formas," *Estética y Marxismo*, Tomo 1, ed. Adolfo Sánchez Vázquez (Mexico: Ediciones Era, 1975), p. 232.

17. Coulthard, p. 106.

18. Jonathan Culler, *Structuralist Poetics. Structuralism, Linguistics and the Study of Literature* (Ithaca, N.Y.: Cornell University Press, 1976).

19. Dell Hymes, *Foundations in Sociolinguistics. An Ethnographic Approach* (Philadelphia: University of Pennsylvania Press, 1974), p. 53.

20. *Ibid.*

21. Labov, p. 59.

22. *Ibid.*

23. Halliday, "Modes of meaning and modes of expression: types of grammatical structure and their determination by different semantic functions," *Function and Context in Linguistic Analysis,* ed. D. J. Allerton, Edward Corney and David Holdcroft (Cambridge: Cambridge University Press, 1979), p. 78.

24. *Ibid.,* p. 79.

25. Searle, p. 24.

26. Halliday, 1979, p. 60.

27. Hymes, pp. 22–23.

28. Robert Scholes, *Structuralism in Literature. An Introduction* (New Haven: Yale University Press, 1974), pp. 24–25.

29. Labov, p. 68.

30. Stephen Toulmin, "The Mozart of Psychology," *The New York Review of Books,* September 28, 1978, p. 55.

31. Arnold M. Rose, "A Summary of Symbolic Interaction Theory," in *Theories and Paradigms in Contemporary Sociology,* eds. R. Serge Denisoff, Orel Callahan and Mark H. Levine (Itasca, Ill.: F. E. Peacock Publishers, Inc., 1974), pp. 139–149.

32. Normal K. Denzin, "Symbolic Interactionism and Ethnomethodology," *Theories and Paradigms in Contemporary Sociology*, ed. Denisoff, Callahan and Levine (Itasca, Ill.: Peacock Publishers, Inc., 1974), p. 153.

33. Harold Garfinkel, "The Origins of the Term 'Ethnomethodology'," *Ethnomethodology,* ed. Roy Turner (Middlessex, England: Penguin Education, 1975), p. 18.

34. Denzin, pp. 157–158.

35. Thomas A. Sebeok, *Contribution to the Doctrine of Signs* (Bloomington: Indiana University, 1976), p. 20.

36. Hjemslev, pp. 5–6.

37. V. N. Vološinov, *Marxism and the Philosophy of Language* (New York: Seminar Press, 1973), p. 23.

38. *Ibid.,* p. 10.

39. *Ibid.,* p. 19.

40. Ferdinand de Saussure, *Course in General Linguistics* (New York: McGraw-Hill Book Co., 1966), p. 16.

41. *Ibid.,* p. 15.

42. *Ibid.,* p. 65.

43. *Ibid.,* p. 112.

44. *Ibid.,* p. 122.

45. *Ibid.,* p. 113.

46. Hjemslev, p. 52.

47. Sebeok, p. 1.

48. John J. Fitzgerald, *Peirce's Theory of Signs as Foundations for Pragmatism* (The Hague: Mouton & Co., 1966), p. 11.

49. *Ibid.,* p. 25.

50. *Ibid.,* p. 76.

51. Sebeok, p. 7.

52. Fitzgerald, p. 26.

53. *Ibid.,* p. 42.

54. *Ibid.,* p. 79.

55. Charles Morris, *Foundations of the Theory of Signs* (Chicago: The University of Chicago Press, 1975), p. 8.

56. Charles Morris, *Signs, Languages and Behavior* (New York: George Braziller, Inc., 1946), pp. 123–152.

57. Umberto Eco, *A Theory of Semiotics* (Bloomington: Indiana University Press, 1976), p. 22.

58. Joshua A. Fishman, *Sociolinguistics, a Brief Introduction* (Rowley, Mass.: Newbury House Publishers, 1971), pp. 37–56.

59. Norbert Dittmar, *A Critical Survey of Sociolinguistics* (New York: St. Martin's Press, 1976), pp. 102–126.

60. Ralph W. Fasold, "Language Variation and Linguistic Competence," *Linguistic Variation*, ed. David Sankoff (New York: Academic Press, 1978), pp. 85–87.

61. Anthony Wootten, *Dilemmas of Discourse* (London: George Allen & Unwin Ltd., 1975), p. 47.

62. Aaron V. Cicourel, *Cognitive Sociology. Language and Meaning in Social Interaction* (New York: The Free Press, 1974), p. 56.

63. Glyn Lewis, *Multilingualism in the Soviet Union* (The Hague: Mouton, 1972).

64. Roland Barthes, *S/Z* (New York: Hill and Wang, 1974).

65. Angel Rosenblat, *La población indígena y el mestizaje en América, I y II* (Buenos Aires: Editorial Nova, 1954).

66. Shirley Brice Heath, *Telling Tongues* (New York: Teachers College Press, 1972).

67. R. Menéndez-Pidal, *Manual de Gramática Histórica Española* (Madrid: Espasa-Calpe, S.A., 1962).

68. Rafael Lapesa, *Historia de la Lengua Española* (Madrid: Escelicer, S.A., 1965).

69. Iorgu Iordan, *Lingüística Románica* (Madrid: Ediciones Alcalá, 1967).

70. Heinrich Lausberg, *Lingüística Románica, Tomos I y II* (Madrid: Editorial Gredos, 1966).

71. Vicente García de Diego, *Gramática Histórica Española* (Madrid: Editorial Gredos, 1970).

72. Peter Boyd-Bowman, "La pérdida de vocales átonas en la altiplanicie mexicana," *Nueva Revista de Filología Hispánica*, 6 (1952), pp. 138–140.

74. Juan Lope-Blanch, "Hispanic Dialectology," *Current Trends in Linguistics*, ed. T. A. Sebeok, Vol. 4 (The Hague: Mouton, 1968).

75. Tomás Navarro Tomás, *El español en Puerto Rico* (Río Piedras: Universidad de Puerto Rico, 1948).

76. Alonso Zamora Vicente, "Rehilamiento porteño," *Filología* 1, 1949, pp. 5–22.

77. Humberto López-Morales, "El español de Cuba: Situación bibliográfica," *Revista de Filología Española*, 51, Maddrid: 1968, pp. 111–137.

78. Amado Alonso, *Estudios Lingüísticos. Temas Hispanoamericanos* (Madrid: Editorial Gredos, 1961).

79. Lincoln Canfield, *La pronunciación del español en América* (Bogotá: Instituto Caro y Cuervo, 1962).

80. Bertil Malmberg, *La América hispanohablante* (Madrid: Ediciones ISTMA, 1966).

81. Francisco Xavier Clavijero, *Reglas de la lengua mexicana con un vocabulario* (Mexico: UNAM, Instituto de Investigaciones Históricas, 1974).

82. López Morales, "El español de Cuba."

83. Melvyn C. Resnick, *Phonological Variants and Dialect Identification in Latin American Spanish* (The Hague: Mouton, 1975).

84. Charles E. Kany, *Sintaxis hispanoamericana* (Madrid: Editorial Gredos, 1969).

85. José G. Moreno de Alba, *Valores de las Formas Verbales en el Español de México* (Mexico: UNAM, 1978).

86. José Gobello, *Vieja y Nueva Lunfardía* (Buenos Aires: Editorial Freeland, 1963).

87. Paulino Pérez Salas, *Interferencia lingüística del inglés en el español hablado en Puerto Rico* (Hato Rey, P.R.: Inter American University Press, 1973).

88. Germán de Granda Gutiérrez, *Transculturación e interferencia lingüística en el Puerto Rico contemporáneo (1898–1968)* (Bogotá: Instituto Caro y Cuervo, 1968).

89. Emilio Alarcos Llorach, *Fonología Española* (Madrid: Editorial Gredos, 1965).

90. Rogelio Díaz Guerrero y Miguel Salas, *El diferencial semántico del idioma español* (Mexico: Editorial Trillas, 1975).

91. Kurt Baldinger, *Teoría Semántica. Hacia una semántica moderna* (Madrid: Ediciones Alcalá, 1970).

92. María del Carmen Bobes Naves, *La semiótica como teoría lingüística* (Madrid: Editorial Gredos, 1973).

93. Luis J. Prieto, *Principes de Noologie* (The Hague: Mouton & Co., 1964); see also Luis J. Prieto, *Estudios de Lingüística y Semiología Generales* (Mexico: Editorial Neuva Imagen, 1977).

94. Rafael Ll. Ninyoles, *Idioma y Poder Social* (Madrid: Editorial Tecnos, 1972).

95. *Bilingüismo y Biculturalismo* (Barcelona, España: Ediciones CEAC, 1978).

96. Catalina Weinerman, *Sociolingüística de la forma pronominal* (Mexico: Editorial Trillas, 1976).

97. Paul L. Garvin y Yolanda Lastra de Suárez, eds. *Antología de Estudios de Etnolingüística y Sociolingüística* (Mexico: UNAM, Instituto de Investigaciones Antropológicas, 1974).

98. José Pedro Rona, "La concepción estructural de la sociolingüística," in *Antología de Estudios de Etnolingüística y Sociolingüística,* ed. Garvin and Lastra de Suárez (Mexico: UNAM, 1974).

99. Oscar Uribe Villegas, *Situaciones de multilingüismo en el mundo* (Mexico: UNAM, 1972).

100. Georgina Paulín de Siade, *Los indígenas bilingües de México frente a la castellani-zación* (Mexico: UNAM, Instituto de Investigaciones Sociales, 1974).

101. Giorgio Sabino Antonio Perissinotto, *Fonología del español hablado en la Ciudad de México. Ensayo de un método sociolingüístico* (Mexico: El Colegio de México, 1975).

102. Beatriz Lavandera, "The variable component in bilingual performance," in *International Dimensions of Bilingual Education,* ed. James E. Alatis (Washington, D.C.: Georgetown University Press, 1978), pp. 391–409.

103. Fernando Peñalosa, *Chicano Sociolinguistics. A Brief Introduction* (Rowley, Mass.: Newbury House, 1980).

104. Susan Berk-Seligson, "A Sociolinguistic View of the Mexican-American Speech Community: A Review of the Literature," *Latin American Research Review,* Vol. XV, No. 2, 1980.

105. Aurelio Espinosa, "Problemas lexicográficos del español del sudoeste," in *El lenguaje de los Chicanos,* ed. Eduardo Hernández-Chávez, Andrew D. Cohen and Anthony F. Beltramo (Arlington, Va.: Center for Applied Linguistics, 1975); see also Jacob Ornstein, "The Archaic and the Modern in the Spanish of New Mexico," *El Lenguaje de los Chicanos,* pp. 6–12; see also Jerry Craddock, "Lexical Analysis of Southwest Spanish," *Studies in Southwest Spanish,* ed. J. D. Bowen and Jacob Ornstein (Rowley, Mass.: Newbury House, 1976), pp. 45–70; see also Gilberto Cerda, Berta Cabeza and Julieta Farías, *Vocabulario español de Texas* (Austin: University of Texas Press, 1953).

106. George Carpenter Barker, *Pachuco* (Tucson: The University of Arizona Press, 1974); see also Dagoberto Fuentes and José A. López, *Barrio Language Dictionary. First Dictionary of Caló* (La Puente, Calif.: El Barrio Publications, 1974); see also José Gonzales Hernández, *Chicano Dictionary,* n.p., 1970.

107. Lurline Coltharp, *The Tongue of the Triliones: A Linguistic Study of a Criminal Argot* (University, Ala.: University of Alabama Press, 1965).

108. Lauro Flores, "La Dualidad del Pachuco," *Revista Chicano-Riqueña,* Año VI, No. 4, Otoño, 1978, pp. 51–58.

109. Espinosa, "Studies in New Mexican Spanish," *Bulletin, University of New Mexico,* Vol. I, No. 2, December 1909; see also Daniel Cárdenas, "Mexican Spanish," *El Lenguaje de los Chicanos,* pp. 1–5.

110. Rosaura Sánchez, "Nuestra Circunstancia Lingüística," *Voices,* 1973, pp. 420–449.

111. Fritz G. Hensey, "Toward a Grammatical Analysis of Southwest Spanish," *Studies in Southwest Spanish,* ed. J. Donald Bowen and Jacob Ornstein (Rowley, Mass.: Newbury House Publishers, 1976), pp. 29–44; see also J. Donald Bowen, "Structural Analysis of the Verb System in New Mexican Spanish," *Studies in Southwest Spanish,* ed. J. Donald Bowen and Jacob Ornstein (Rowley, Mass.: Newbury House Publishers, 1976), pp. 93–124; see also Rosaura Sánchez, "Nuestra Circunstancia Lingüística"; see also Rosaura Sánchez, "A generative study of two Spanish dialects" (dissertation, University of Texas at Austin, 1974).

112. Lucía Elías-Olivares, "Ways of speaking in a Chicano speech community" (dissertation, University of Texas at Austin, 1975); see also Rosaura Sánchez, "Spanish Codes in the Southwest," *Modern Chicano Writers,* eds. Joseph Sommers and Tomás Ybarra-Frausto (Englewood Cliffs, N.J.: Prentice-Hall, Inc., 1979).

113. Guadalupe Valdés Fallis, "Social Interaction and Code-Switching Patterns: A Case Study of Spanish/English Alternation," *Bilingualism in the Bicentennial and Beyond,* eds. Gary D. Keller, Richard V. Teschner and Silvia Viera (New York: Bilingual Press, 1976), pp. 53–85; see

also Rogelio Reyes, "Language Mixing in Chicano Bilingual Speech," *Studies in Southwest Spanish,* eds. J. Donald Bowen and Jacob Ornstein (Rowley, Mass.: Newbury House Publishers, 1976), pp. 183–188; see also Rodolfo Jacobson, "The Social Implications of Intra-Sentential Code-Switching," *New Directions in Chicano Scholarship,* eds. Ricardo Romo and Raymund Paredes (San Diego: Chicano Studies, UCSD, 1978); see also Rosaura Sánchez, "Chicano Code-Switching," *SWALLOW IV: Linguistics and Education* (San Diego: San Diego State University, Institute for Cultural Pluralism, 1976); see also Guadalupe Valdés-Fallis, "Code-Switching in Bilingual Chicano Poetry," *Southwest Languages and Linguistics in Educational Perspectives,* eds. Harvey Cantoni and M. F. Heiser (San Diego: San Diego State University, 1975), pp. 145–170.

114. John J. Gumperz and Eduardo Hernández-Chávez, "Cognitive Aspects of Bilingual Communication," *El Lenguaje de los Chicanos,* pp. 154–163.

115. George C. Barker, *Social Functions of Language in a Mexican American Community* (Tucson: University of Arizona Press, 1972).

116. See Peñalosa, *Chicano Sociolinguistics,* for other examples.

117. "Rent Control in El Monte," *Los Angeles Times,* March 1979, View, pp. 1, 16 and 17.

CHAPTER 4

The Spanish of Chicanos

This chapter will describe some of the major characteristics of the Spanish of the Southwest as well as analyze samples of Southwestern Spanish discourse in terms of stylistic shifts. Code-switching, a process in which two languages converge in the same utterance or exchange, is also a characteristic of Southwest Spanish. Because of its frequency and importance, we will devote the next chapter solely to it.

Since sociolinguists, linguists and educators continue to wonder about the linguistic status of Chicano Spanish, we will present data demonstrating that the Spanish varieties spoken in the Southwest are authentic Spanish varieties, sharing features of peninsular and Latin American Spanish. The phonological, syntactic, morphological and semantic rules that we find in Spanish varieties of the Southwest are not unique to Chicano Spanish. The phonetic and morphological variants that we will describe are found in the popular Spanish varieties of all the Spanish-speaking world. Given the social stratification in Latin America, Spain and the United States, it may also be possible to describe Spanish varieties in the rest of the Spanish-speaking world in terms of class, ideology, nativity and residence, as we will seek to do here and in the following chapter, for those factors which affect and determine type of social interaction also determine type of verbal interaction.

The fact that the rules and forms to be described in Chicano Spanish varieties are not unique to the Spanish of the Southwest will not however stop us from labeling these varieties as Chicano Spanish. Can one speak of Cuban Spanish if sibilant aspiration and loss, nasalization of vowels, lateralization of vibrants or velarization of final nasals can be found in the Spanish of other Latin American countries beyond the Caribbean area? Can one speak or write of the language of a particular area if the features of the language varieties spoken in that country are not unique to that area? It would be absurd to dismiss all the hundreds of dialectological studies of the Spanish of Argentina, Chile, Peru, Ecuador, Mexico or wherever on the basis of their concentration on features of a particular province, city or country, without specific recognition, for example, that laxing of fricatives also occurs in a neighboring nation and even in one two thousand miles away.

The other extreme would be to think that the Spanish of a particular area, for example the Southwest, is different from that of any other area. As we shall see, this is not the case, as rule differences found here are present in the Spanish of the rest of the Spanish-speaking world. In fact all variants occurring within Chicano Spanish can be explained within the rules of Spanish grammar and are not the result of English interference or convergence.

Descriptive studies of the Spanish of the Southwest, like most dialectological studies of peninsular or Latin American Spanish, have sought to account for the presence of particular variants. A compilation by Melvyn C. Resnick of studies on phonological variants in Latin American Spanish is particularly interesting in its inclusion of contradictory reports in the cases of particular phonological phenomena.[1] Thus what for one author is a rare variant, for another may be the predominant, general or "sometimes" form; there is also disagreement on whether particular forms are to be classified as "cultas" or "vulgar" or rural or urban. The problem lies partly in seeking to identify an area by one particular variant. Given the mobility of modern urbanized societies and the forced migration that results from disparities in development, it is difficult to find a homogeneous society that uses one single widespread form. The real source of the problem can be traced to earlier studies concerned with noting the appearance of particular variants rather than with their function in the discourse of particular individuals and in particular contexts. These same difficulties have arisen in studies on Chicano Spanish when attempts have been made to identify varieties by states in an attempt to ascribe a particular feature to one state. Despite some general patterns of immigration from Northeastern Mexico to Texas and from Northwestern Mexico to California, one is just as likely to find immigrants from Puebla in Texas as in California. In fact the border states often serve only as way stations for immigrants on their way to Chicago, Minneapolis or Seattle. Available statistics on the origin of migrants in border Mexican towns indicate the presence of many regional varieties of Spanish in the Spanish of the Southwest, because Chicano Spanish is first and foremost Mexican Spanish with a number of lexical borrowings from English.

As we have indicated in previous chapters, there are three principal cultural groups within the Chicano communities of the Southwest with varying patterns of socialization and consequently of language maintenance and shift. Since social interaction and verbal interaction are interconnected, the various Spanish varieties of the Southwest can be analyzed in terms of the linguistic process as well as the interactional process within which they are used. In the area of the social-interactional process we must consider the characteristics of the speakers, the context of communication and the socio-semantic objectives of the communicative act. These various categories can be further subdivided as follows:

1. Characteristics of the Participants:
   Material Culture
   a) Middle class
   b) Urban working class
   c) Rural working class
   Roles
   a) Dominant
   b) Subordinate
   c) Equals
   Generation
   a) First generation—Foreign-born
   b) Second generation—Native-born
   c) Third and subsequent generations
   Residence
   a) Urban
   b) Rural
   Age
   a) Children
   b) Adolescents and young adults
   c) Older adults
   Relation to Dominant Ideology
   a) Resistant
   b) Acceptant, proponent
   c) Habituated, passive
2. Context of Communication:
   Fields of Discourse
   a) Formal
   b) Informal
   c) Intimate
   d) Familiar
   Circles
   a) Inter-group
   b) Intra-group
   c) Intra-sub-group

The characteristics of the speakers in terms of class, generation, roles, residence and age were discussed in previous chapters. In the area of ideology we have indicated that the prevalent perspective is functionalist, that is, there is full acceptance of the existing socio-economic structure and faith in its power to resolve whatever conflicts arise. There are nonetheless resisters who, whether from a political awareness or a defense mechanism, adopt an antagonistic attitude to the dominant culture, language and sometimes to the Anglo population as well. Then there is the habituated group of individuals who, although passively accepting, are so involved in a struggle for survival that for them activities like questioning the system or defending it are irrelevant issues.

These positions assume an expression-form when shifts to Spanish signify opposition or retreat from the dominant culture and ideology.

Fields of discourse are analyzed in terms of the degree of formality. The formal style can be further subdivided into Broadcasting Style, Academic Style, Interview Style or other styles, depending on the context. The informal style is the Everyday Style in which speakers of all classes engage but not necessarily with the same varieties. This everyday style is differentiated from two other informal styles: intimate and familiar. An Intimate Style allows the speaker to engage in verbal activities that are not felt to be subject to public criticism. This Intimate Style is synonymous with Family Style. It becomes important to distinguish both Informal and Intimate from Familiar in order to account for the style used in peer situations where informality rather than intimacy reigns. In a familiar-informal situation particular roles, especially among young adults and adolescents, lead to an intra-sub-group style characterized by adherence to the sub-group's linguistic norms in order to express adhesion to the sub-group itself. Thus the interaction can also be categorized according to the composition of the participating group and the participants' affiliation: inter-group, intra-group and intra-sub-group.

Linguistically, then, we are postulating three principal Spanish varieties in the Southwest with subcodes within each code:

> *Chicano Spanish Varieties of the Southwest*
> a) standard Spanish
> b) popular urban Spanish
> c) popular rural Spanish

Although there is a large Latin American contingent in the Southwest, our study focuses on the Spanish varieties spoken by people of Mexican origin. Thus "standard" refers to the standard Mexican Spanish spoken by middle-class Mexican radio announcers and professionals, who have immigrated to the United States. More specifically it is the Spanish spoken by educated individuals who have received formal instruction in the Spanish language, where Spanish has been the medium of instruction. If this generalized notion of what constitutes standard Mexican Spanish is vague, it is in part the result of a lack of definitive statements on what constitutes "standard Mexican Spanish" in the various Mexican regions. Once these linguistic studies are available, we might be able to pinpoint whether the standard operating in the Southwest is the standard of Mexico City or that of Jalisco, Sonora, Coahuila or Chihuahua. In what follows we will attempt to describe general features of the two popular varieties, contrasting these with a postulated "Mexican Standard" based on the Spanish of Mexican radio announcers transmitting from Los Angeles over XPRS (Radio Exprés), XEGM (Radio 95, La Grande) and KLVE.

These three varieties differ in terms of grammatical rules, with a great deal of rule simplification occurring in the popular codes. Rule differences occur at the phonological, morphosyntactic and lexical levels. These Spanish codes and their subcodes could be said to constitute a community continuum, ranging from a standard variety to the popular variety with the greatest number of morphosyntactic rule differences. All of these rules, as we said before, are Spanish rules and could be found in the grammars of Spanish varieties from other countries. It is possible for one speaker to have full command of the entire range of varieties contained within the continuum, but it appears that a number of external factors in fact determine one's position and range along the continuum and one's accessibility to particular varieties.

Before discussing this continuum further, we would like to note that there are norms for each Spanish code, that their use is dictated by both social and linguistic norms. Standardization codifies a particular type of norm; here the dominant group or class in society creates and dictates the official norm. Where there is no specific language academy, official norms are established and disseminated by the state apparatuses: schools, colleges and universities, government agencies, churches, intellectual centers and of course, the media (radio, TV, newspapers, journals, publications, etc.). Where the dominant class is not Spanish-speaking, Spanish norms are borrowed from some accepted model: *la Academia Española* or *la academia mexicana.* Yet, it is important to recognize that given the particular historical context of the Mexican-origin population in the United States, oftentimes Spanish-language publications and radio transmissions reflect the popular varieties of speakers and writers who have received no formal training in Spanish. Thus within formal domains, more than one norm may function. Thus what functions as a formal style may not be necessarily verbalized in the standard variety.

The presence of various norms for different segments of the population make shifting between Spanish varieties indispensable. Interaction at different levels with different Chicanos requires a repertoire that includes several codes and several styles of speaking. Much has been written about the fact that no one is monodialectal, that all have a repertoire consisting of several varieties from one or more languages. Our study of factors triggering particular shifts indicates that although it is true that each individual's repertoire contains more than one variety or mode of expression, there are particular types of shifts across code borders that do not occur in the absence of certain social conditions. In analyzing a large corpus of taped material where shifts in languages and styles accompanied by shifts in topics and speech acts occur in discourse, we have found that, except in the case of language-conscious Chicano speakers, morphosyntactic shifts generally do not occur. Phonetic shifts, on the other hand, are numerous as are lexical shifts. Thus a speaker may say "tá" for "está" or "lo'o" for "luego" as he slips into an informal style but immediately afterwards or later in the conversation as the individual becomes conscious of being taped or being interviewed he will "correct" himself and carefully pronounce each sound or syllable. On the other hand, speakers whose codes are characterized by particular morphosyntactic variants retain these throughout the taped conversation even though they may shift phonetically or lexically.

Thus a speaker who uses -*nos* (instead of -*mos*) as the person-number morpheme of verbs which are *esdrújulos* (i.e., words with antepenultimate stress) generally retains this form throughout the verbal interaction. Those speakers saying *comíanos* also consistently say *salíanos, fuéranos, comiéranos* and *íbanos*. It is of course possible for an *íbanos* user to shift to *íbamos* after undergoing language training. Given the limited number of years of Spanish instruction in transitional bilingual programs today, it is questionable whether formal language instruction will now lead to the rejection of *íbanos* among a large segment of the population using it. Unfortunately emphasis is often placed on producing a permanent shift rather than on expanding the students' repertoire. A student, made to feel inadequate for using a particular variant, may adopt the school's norm as the one and only correct form and reject not only the -*nos* morpheme but the cultural context within which it is used as well. In what follows we will specify in more detail the morphosyntactic, phonetic and lexical variants which characterize popular Spanish varieties of the Southwest.

RURAL VARIETIES

In view of continuous and widespread immigration from Mexico, popular varieties in the Southwest could be subdivided into as many types as there are regional urban and rural dialects in Mexico. As we said previously, these Chicano varieties share many of the characteristics of similar varieties in Mexico and the rest of Latin America, with one exception: the degree to which these popular codes have incorporated loanwords from the English language.

Rural varieties of Spanish are to be found in Texas, New Mexico, Arizona, Colorado, California, Oregon, Washington and sometimes the Midwest, where rural workers have migrated, often after stopping briefly, or for a generation or two, in Texas and New Mexico. It is important to recall that today about 80% of Chicanos reside in urban areas but that only California is heavily industrialized; there are thus many urban centers with a semi-rural flavor dependent on an agricultural economy throughout the Southwest. Only Dallas and Houston in Texas share metropolitan characteristics with Los Angeles.

Up till now far too many studies of Chicano Spanish have summarized linguistic features within isolated sentences or examples. It is important that we analyze these popular varieties within a discourse context. In the pages that follow, phonological, morphological and lexical characteristics of rural varieties will be analyzed within the context of particular exchanges, beginning with a conversation recorded by Yolanda Roblez in Austin, Texas, in an interview with a University of Texas student who was a former migrant worker (Episode A).

Interview of G. V. from Dallas, Texas by Yolanda Roblez. Episode A.
YR: — ¿Dónde vives?
GV: — Dallas, Texas.
YR: — De . . . ¿cómo creciste?

GV: — Yo ha tenido ganas de platicarle algo . . . a alguien de esto porque . . .
en las clases que tengo todo el tiempo dicen que, migrant workers . . .

YR: — ¿Quién, los estudiantes? ¿los estudiantes o los . . . ?

GV: — No, toda la gente piensa eso, el maestro, los estudiantes, los libros,
todo el tiempo dicen que los migrant workers y que, 'tán muy este oppressed y
todo eso . . .

YR: — Que viven una vida bien difícil . . .

GV: — Ajá, bueno y, y la vida que yo conocí . . . la que . . . lo que yo sé de esa
vida, no es así . . . este, cuando estábanos chicas, íbanos con, con mi papá,
bueno íbanos, el era troquero y nos llevaba a las piscas de algodón y íbanos
primero pa ' Sinton, es un pueblo que está cerquita de Corpos y . . .

YR: — ¿De dónde, de acuál pueblo se iban?

GV: — De Devine, porque entonces vivíanos en Devine, vivíanos en Devine.
Ibanos a las piscas . . . y cuando . . .

YR: — ¿Toda la familia?

GV: — Toda la familia. Y este . . . vivíanos en unas casitas viejas pero no . . .
estaba . . . como dice en los libros, que parecían gallineros y todo eso, pero
este . . . no estaban muy buenas pero comoquiera estaban limpias y to'os los
mejicanos que las tenían limpias y to'os, to'os los sábados íbanos a . . . al
pueblo y teníanos y nos . . . y íbanos a las vistas y comprá'anos to'o el tiempo
comprá'anos ropa y comprá'anos zapatos y íbanos a comer y el domingo
íbanos a Corpos a la laguna. Bueno, pero . . . del trabajo . . . yo, yo vendía
sodas. Y yo tenía mucho fun haciendo eso porque, porque este . . . podía
hablar con todos los guys que andaban . . .

YR: — Heh, heh, heh, ¿Qué tantos años tenías?

GV: — que 'taban, que andaban en la pisca . . .

YR: — ¿Qué tantos años tenías?

GV: — Cuando comencé, bueno primero . . . ¿cuándo comencé? Yo creo que
no tenía diez, yo creo, once, once, yo creo tenía once cuando comencé a
vender sodas. Pero hacía, hacía mejor dinero que los que andaban piscando y
de . . . me podía, me podía sentar en la sombrita, cuando no estaba
trabajando, me podía sentar en la sombrita y de veras, este . . .

YR: — ¿ Cómo le hacían . . . ?

GV: — eran, la gente era muy alegre, no andaban que, que, que no les gustaba
el trabajo y que nada. Quién sabe no les gustaría pero and . . . eran muy
alegres.

YR: — Quizás porque no conocían otra vida, porque así, así se impusieron
desde chiquitos, y ellos, y la gente grande también, así le hacía. ¿Cómo le
hacían pa' pa' tener las sodas frías, las tenían en algo . . . caja o qué?

GV: — Era una hielera de esas grandes, como las que tienen en la tienda.
Nomás que no era eléctrica. Le teníanos que echar hielo y . . . teníanos que ir
a comprar el hielo y echarle . . . libras de hielo y . . . y . . . con eso, con eso
teníanos pa to'o el día.

YR: — ¿Y se llenaba la, la refrigeradora de, de sodas?

GV: — De sodas y después le tenían, cuando se acababan esas, tenía que echarle más y . . .

YR: — ¿Compraban bastante, entonces?

GV: — Sí, mi, mi apá las iba a comprar a una . . . a una fábrica de sodas que había en el pueblito, él y él y las iba a comprar y necitábanos, este . . . entonces las usábanos.

YR: — Y ¿cómo le hacían pa, como le hacías tú para, pa, de feria? ¿Qué hacías? ¿Tenías allí la feria contigo en cajón o cómo?

GV: — Bueno, casi, unos me daban, eh, las vendía a daime las sodas y, y casi to'os, los que traiban, me daban un daime, casi todo el tiempo tenían un daime que me daban pero muncha gente este . . . nomás era más fácil que . . . yo tenía una, un . . . un cuaderno y . . . las, las apuntaba, las apuntaba por nombre cada quien que vinía, las apuntaba, y después el sábado cuando . . . o el viernes en la tarde, cuando este . . . mi papá les pagaba, lo que 'bían ganáo esa semana, entonces allí 'staba yo tamién esperándolos pa que me, pa que me pagaran las sodas y así no tenía nada de dificultad en que me pagaran las sodas, de andar coletando pa que me pagaran.

YR: — Allí 'taba tu papá lo'o luego.

GV: — Allí 'taba mi papá y él les pagaba y lo'o ellos me tenían que pagar a mí. Y este . . . en veces este . . . en sábado, no, en viernes, nos, nos íbanos pa la casa a mediodía o despué . . . en o temprano, cuando ya la gente ganaba lo que querían ganar y si ya habían trabajado bastante esta semana se iban temprano y era lo que, una de las cosas que a mí me gustaba . . . de irnos pa la casa temprano para comenzarnos a, a arreglar pa salir. Y tamién me gustaban los días que llovía porque esos días tamién este . . . no teníanos que ir a trabajar y me la pasaba, me la pasaba'llí por las casas platicando con toda la gente pero más, más los muchachos, especialmente los muchachos.

ANALYSIS OF EPISODE A

Possibly the most outstanding variant in the rural varieties of West Texas and New Mexico is the use of the first-person plural morpheme -*nos* for -*mos* found also in the rural varieties of Mexico and among rural migrants from Texas and New Mexico in the other Southwestern states. As is evident in the episode recorded by Yolanda Roblez, the -*nos* morpheme is constant in all first-person plural verb forms in the imperfect tense:

teníanos	estábanos	necesitábanos
usábanos	vivíanos	comprábanos

Other recordings and personal observations indicate that this phenomenon occurs in other tenses as well, as follows:

Imperfect tense:	vivíanos	estábanos
Conditional tense:	comeríanos	estaríanos
Imperfect subjunctive:	estuviéranos	hubiéranos

All of these forms share one feature: they are all *esdrújulas,* that is, the stress falls on the antepenult syllable. All of these forms are normally stressed in the antepenult syllable in Standard Spanish. There is one more form which through rule simplification regularizes the verb stems and produces verb forms with proparoxytonic stress. Consider the following examples taken from Standard Spanish:

Present subjunctive:	pueda	podamos
	puedas	
	pueda	puedan

Verbs in Spanish with an underlying O vowel diphthongize when stressed:

$$O \rightarrow \text{we} / \underline{\hspace{3cm}}.$$
$$+ \text{stress}$$

For this reason the *standard* first-person plural form which takes the stress in the penult syllable does not diphthongize. In *popular* varieties of Spanish in both Latin American and peninsular Spanish, the first-person plural forms are regularized to conform to the rest of the paradigm as follows:

pueda	escriba	venga
puedas	escribas	vengas
pueda	escriba	venga
puédamos	escríbamos	véngamos
puedan	escriban	vengan

In the Southwest these newly regularized verb forms fall into the pattern of forms with the stress in the antepenult syllable. Consequently we have the following first-person plural forms:

Present subjunctive:	vénganos
	vuélvanos
	piénsenos

The reason for this morphological change is probably found in the stress rule, for none of the other popular verbal tenses have shifts of *-mos* to *-nos.* This particular proparoxytonic stress is peculiar to verbals with enclitic pronouns as in:

viéndonos	Vénganos tu reino (from "The Lord's Prayer")
hablándole	Tráiganos una

It is probably the case, then, that this shift is purely phonetic and involves a rule at the lower levels which changes a *-mos* to *-nos* when it appears in a verb form with the stress on the antepenult syllable.

The Roblez interview also contains a number of other changes typical of popular Spanish varieties and of intimate, familiar and informal styles throughout the Spanish-speaking world, such as the following:

a) loss of voiced fricatives in intervocalic position after stressed vowel:

ganado	→	ganáo
comprábamos	→	comprá'anos
luego	→	lo'o
todo	→	to'o

b) loss of initial syllable or vowel = apheresis:

estaba	→	'taba
había	→	'bía

c) simplification of consonant clusters:

también	→	tamién
colectando	→	coletando

d) loss of final syllable or sound = apocope; syncope = loss of middle sounds:

para	→	pa	necesitábamos	→	necitábanos

e) change of verb stem:

verb:	venir	standard:	venía	vino
		popular:	vinía	vino

f) change of conjugation pattern:

traer conjugated like -ar	verb:	traiba
	standard:	traía

g) old case of epenthesis:

mucho	→	muncho

h) epenthesis: insertion of palatal glide between two vowels:
me cayí   for   me caí

i) prothesis: addition of preposition *a* to interrogative pronoun:
¿de acuál pueblo se iban?   for   ¿de qué pueblo se iban?
                            or   ¿de cuál pueblo se iban?

Another example of paradigm regularization appears in the informant's rule simplification of the verb *haber*. Where the standard conjugation has an *e-a* distinction, the popular variety has regularized the stem as follows:

Standard:	he	hemos	Popular:	ha	hamos
	has			has	
	ha	han		ha	han

A popular variant that appears in many of these varieties is the contraction of *alguna otra* to produce *algotra* (algún otro = algotro). Another frequent rural form is *en veces* rather than *a veces*. Some of the rural markers are lexical and semantic. Thus, for example, "ir al pueblo" is a frequent phrase in small towns or rural areas where Saturday's shopping means going into town; the phrase has been retained in urban life to mean "to go downtown" or "to go shopping." Another frequent term in Texas is the use of the term *huerco* or *huerquito* or *huerquillo* to refer to a child when one is annoyed. Episode A contains a few loanwords which we will discuss separately in another section.

This episode illustrates the maintenance of Spanish as a code for communication among young (university undergraduate) Chicanos in Texas. The text at the same time reveals the interviewee's status as the *troquero*'s (truckdriver-contractor) daughter, whose housing was better than that of the workers and who profited from sales of soft drinks to the migrant workers. The interviewee cannot understand how Chicano Studies classes (Mexican American Studies at the University of Texas–Austin) can speak of the oppression of migrant workers; for her it was an idyllic time; the housing was poor but clean; they worked hard during the week but had a good time on the weekends; there was a sense of community with several families residing in the same migrant quarters where the children could gather around a tree for storytelling and the death of a baby was a communal tragedy. Yet her higher status allowed her to go to school when the other children didn't go and to pay for her lunch at school when the other children received free lunches. For her it really was a pleasant experience, but she is aware that there is something wrong with that interpretation. Yet she is able to laugh off her discomfort by recalling falling off her father's truck as he moved the vehicle around the ranch. It is the fall that made her forget the bad part, she says.

Thus her rural experiences as a migrant worker indicate lifelong contact with the Mexican-origin community in a context of relative isolation, although she was one of the few partly integrated into larger society through the school system, as a consequence of her relatively better economic situation.

The conversation is narrated primarily in an informal style, but there are cases when her friendship with the interviewer leads her into an intimate style, with increased use of an intimate pronunciation or vocabulary as in the following examples:

Informal: íbanos con mi *papá*
Intimate: mi *apá* las iba a comprar
Intimate: me cayí de la troca de mi *daddy*

Clearly these texts are proof that rural Spanish is alive and well in some parts of Texas.

The next episode recorded by UCSD student Wendy Borst presents a New Mexican woman, the descendant of immigrants, who resides now in California. The first part of the text is presented to give the woman's background. She grew up in a Spanish-speaking home and began her process of acculturation in the school system, as related in the anecdote recalling the Anglicization of family names. This New Mexican woman no longer functions within a Spanish-speaking context and feels uncomfortable with her Spanish. The interview was conducted in English except for the translation of several phrases which are partly reproduced here as samples of rural Spanish. This type of elicitation can only be valuable if one is able to recognize the sentences as authentic; otherwise the researcher would not know whether the translations reflected a widespread use. Since these sentences reflect a rural variety spread throughout West Texas and New Mexico and are part of our own community's repertoire, we have included a segment of this interview here (Episode B).

Recording of a New Mexican Chicana by Wendy Borst. Episode B

WB: — Your brothers' and sister's names, tell me what they were when they were born.

NMC: — My oldest brother's name was Casimiro but they called him Cas ... another brother was named Onofre, but they called him Joe; uh another brother's name was, uh what was Dale's name? Delaidio, Delaidio.

WB: — Delaidio?

NMC: — And they called him Dale; uh, the sister's name was uh Dulcinea and they called her Daisy, uhm,

WB: — And your name?

NMC: — My name is María Inés; all my school records are Mary Agnes.

WB: — And probably all your brothers' and sister's school records were changed.

NMC: — Uh huh.

. . . .

WB: — ... but, why don't, tell me why you don't speak Spanish.

NMC: — Because I'm not comfortable with the language.

WB: — Just because you haven't spoken it in so long?

NMC: — No, uh, for instance if I listen to uh the news I could pick up a lot of what's being said, but then there's a lot of, a lot of the words that are foreign to me.

WB: — ... When you were little and first went to school, how was your English?

NMC: — ... I believe that my English was quite poor.

WB: — Really?

NMC: — I really do, because we, you know, we spoke Spanish at home.
     (Interviewer requests translations of vocabulary and sentences.)

. . . .

WB: — Did you go to church already?

NMC: — ¿Juites a la iglesia?

WB: — Where did you put the light bulb?

NMC: — ¿Onde pusites la luz?

WB: — My teacher taught us in English.

NMC: — Mi maestra los enseñó en inglés.

WB: — What did you buy?

NMC: — ¿Qué mercates?

WB: — What did you do in school today?

NMC: — ¿Qué hicites en la escuela?

WB: — We had a good time.

NMC: — Tuvimos un buen tiempo.

WB: — He brought the books.

NMC: — Trujo los libros.
WB: — I saw the boy.
NMC: — Yo vide el muchacho.

Since these sentences were asked out of context, we cannot comment on the style or function of particular usage. The first sentence, however, besides reflecting aspiration of the labiodental fricative *f,* a common phenomenon throughout Latin America, also reveals a common rural variant for the II person-number morpheme in the preterit tense. Consider the person-number morphemes in the Spanish of Latin America and Mexico:

	Singular	Plural
I	-	-mos
II	-s	
III	-	-n

As we can see, Standard Spanish has an-*s* person-number morpheme. It occurs in all verb tenses except the preterit. Thus we have:

Present tense:	com - e -s
Imperfect tense:	com - í - a - s

but:

Preterit tense:	com - i - ste

Extension of the person-number morphological rule explains the following preterit forms common in the Southwest:

Rural:	com - i · tes
Urban:	com - i · stes

Here the -*s* morpheme rule has been extended to apply in the case of all tenses without exception. The loss of internal-*s*- could be a case of aspiration followed by loss. More likely it is a rejection of the consonant cluster in initial morpheme position, with metathesis (-ste → tes).

We thus have the following forms in the Borst interview:

Rural:	juites	pusites	mercates	hicites
Standard:	fuiste	pusiste	mercaste	hiciste

The text also includes two archaic forms prevalent in the rural Spanish of West Texas and isolated rural areas of Latin America: *vide* and *truje.* It would be important to recall that *truje* was once part of the *español culto* spoken by members of the king's court as indicated by Juan de Valdés in *Diálogo de la lengua* (1536).[2] In addition to a loan translation (tener un buen tiempo) and some laxing of initial voiced stops to the point of total loss (donde = onde), we also have a case of nasal lateralization, frequent in rural Spanish:

Rural:	Mi maestra *los* enseñó en inglés.
Standard:	Mi maestra *nos* enseñó en inglés.

As we have mentioned previously, first- and second-generation Chicanos are more likely to be bilingual, with Spanish functioning as the language of the home, while third-generation Chicanos often have adopted English as their usual language. The degree of social and language contact, however, is stronger than the generational factor as is evident in the next episodes recorded by Robyn Richter in Stockdale, near San Antonio, Texas. Here we find a 63-year-old third-generation Chicano who grew up in South Texas and had limited contact with the English-speaking community. He had only six years of segregated schooling, five months out of the year. Despite little instruction in English, he was able to develop his proficiency in English as contact increased in work situations:

RR: — ¿Dónde aprendió su inglés? Porque habla muy bien.
JF: — Pues mayor, la mayoría lírico. Lírico es, por ejemplo, aquí en el trabajo, porque yo la id . . . no estudié mucho la gramática en inglés, nomás yo, llegué nomás al seis, en esos tiempos las, las escuelas 'taban muy lejos, no daban más que cinco meses de escuela, 'taba muy lejos la escuela.

This Spanish-dominant Chicano however has grandchildren who no longer use the language. Only the grandchildren who are in daily contact with the grandparents, while their mother works, speak some Spanish, but as he observes their Spanish is jumbled:

JL: — los niños los cuida mi esposa; esos sí le entienden . . . ésos sí hablan, revuelto, pero les entiende ella [ea]. Porque hablan al revés, la idioma, como decir, "ya vine" dicen "ya vino *me*," que ya volvió a la casa, pero comoquiera se le entiende; necita uno mucho trabajo pa hacerlos que entiendan derecho, parejo, la idioma español; la inglés sí la hablan bien pero como comienzan aquí a la edad de cuatro años en el Head Start, well, kindergarten, de mo'o que ya pa cuando entran a la escuela ya saben hablar bien inglés y lo hablan en la casa pero hablan al revés el español, lo hablan al revés. Se entiende uno, pero no pueden ellos desarrollar una conversación.

Urbanization, education and occupational shifts affecting both men and women have placed the fourth and fifth generations in positions where English is the usual medium of communication. In this case, the impact of Spanish-speaking grandparents will no doubt enable some of his grandchildren to have a limited proficiency in Spanish but their usual and dominant language will be and is already English.

This older Chicano also speaks a variety of rural Spanish, as is evident in the previous and the following text:

JL: — Y una gente que aprende la idioma inglés asina, nunca va a hablar bien porque le faltan muchas palabras . . . . Los que hablamos aprendemos lírico. Hay mucha gente que nos habla asina para que entiéndamos, bueno, y asina va aprendiendo uno la idioma inglés. Lo mismo que el que va estudiar español y el que le está hablando, le está hablando mocho pa que le entienda y lo'o así va a hablar él porque así lo aprendió.

. . . .

Nosotros dicemos "pa" y la palabra es "para" p-a-r-a "para" y nosotros la mochamos a "pa" [. . .] . . . . Por eso el que estudia, bueno, habla correcto y el que pesca de aquí y de allá pos no, porque, no están las palabras completas. Lo mismo que una cosa le nombran de dos, tres maneras. Por ejemplo, unos dicen miel de colmena. Unos le nombran de un modo y otros de otra manera. Y el propio nombre es miel de colmena. Otros dicen miel de abeja y hay diferencia entre la abeja y la colmena; son diferentes los animales. La colmena es la que nombramos que fabrica la miel aquí y como en el valle donde está la abeja y hace los panales así lo mismo que l'avispa, los yellow jackets, son más chiquitas y prietas y hacen miel igual a esa pero no tienen cajón.

Some variants found in rural Spanish are, of course, typical of informal varieties or styles of Spanish, like for example the reduction of *para* to *pa,* the reduction of the diphthong *ue* to *o* in *pos* and various cases of apheresis, syncope and laxing of voiced fricatives to produce glides or loss of glide, as in *ella*: [eya] → [ea]. His Spanish, however, includes some rural markers like the use of the archaic *asina.* His Spanish also has the stress-shift rule in the present subjunctive tense that produces proparoxytonic forms, but here the *-mos* morpheme has been retained: *entiéndamos.* Another case of regularization is evident in the gender assigned to nouns ending in *-a*; these are automatically marked as feminine: *la idioma.* The last text presented also includes a common rural variant of present tense *-ir* verbs: "nosotros dicemos." To understand this phenomenon we have to look at what happens to *-er* verbs in the present and preterit tenses:

verb:	comer	Present tense	Preterit tense
		como	comí
		comes	comiste
		come	comió
		comemos	comimos
		comen	comieron

In the case of *-er* verbs we see that the thematic vowel *-e* shifts to *-i* in the preterit tense. The *-ir* conjugations however maintain the *-i* vowel in the present tense:

verb:	vivir	Present tense	Preterit tense
		vivo	viví
		vives	viviste
		vive	vivió
		vivimos	vivimos
		viven	vivieron

As we can see, the conjugations of both -*er* and -*ir* verbs are identical in the present tense except for the first-person plural form. In the popular rural varieties, however, the -*ir* verbs follow the -*er* patterns without exceptions to produce the following forms. Note that verbs with mid vowels in the stem (-*e*- and -*o*-) dissimilate to the mid vowels that follow in the next syllable:

	Present tense:	*Standard*	*Popular*
		vivimos	vivemos
		decimos	dicemos
		sufrimos	sufremos
		sentimos	sintemos
		salimos	salemos
		morimos	muremos
		dormimos	durmemos

These shifts thus regularize the -*e* vowel for all present tense -*er* or -*ir* verbs:

Popular present tense	*Preterit*
salgo	salí
sales	saliste, salistes, salites
sale	salió
salemos	salimos
salen	salieron

The last episode from Stockdale also gives evidence of shifts occurring at the semantic level. Thus for our senior Chicano, *colmena* denotes a type of "bee," the type that is artificially set up in a man-made beehive, rather than the hive itself as in other Spanish varieties. We then have the following denotations:

colmena
    d. "hive"
    d. "bee" (circ.) Mexican varieties in Texas
(d = denotation)   (circ. = circumstance)

In some parts of Texas (West Texas, for example), the only word for "bee" is *abeja.* For the Stockdale Chicano, *abeja* refers to a smaller, darker bee that makes its own honeycomb, its *panal,* a term common throughout the state. Where denotational shifts occur, meanings assigned to lexemes previously are subsequently denoted by other signs. We can represent these semantic differences in terms of sign-vehicles (s.v.) assigned to different denotations or connotations:

    d. "hive" —————— s.v. *colmena*
    d. "honeycomb" —— s.v. *panal*
circ. Tex. d. "bee" ———— s.v. *abeja* (context: *panal*)
                           s.v. *colmena* (context: *box-cajón*)

Regional variants exist for numerous lexical items. Selecting the appropriate term becomes a problem in the preparation of bilingual materials for educational programs, for common items like "kite" can have several sign-vehicles:

d. "kite"————— s.v. *güila,* circ. Texas, Mexico

s.v. *papalote,* circ. New Mexico, Mexico, California

s.v. *cometa,* California, Latin America, Mexico

s.v. *kite,* Southwest

All of the terms may exist in one region but with different denotations. A term like *papalote* for example, is very common in Texas, but generally with the denotation "windmill" and "pinwheel." Some vocabulary in the Southwest is typically rural in origin, but immigration, industrialization and urbanization have also changed the denotation as in the following examples:

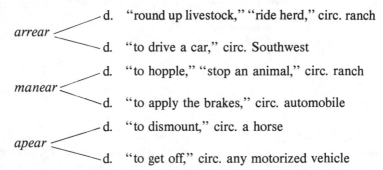

arrear

d. "round up livestock," "ride herd," circ. ranch

d. "to drive a car," circ. Southwest

manear

d. "to hopple," "stop an animal," circ. ranch

d. "to apply the brakes," circ. automobile

apear

d. "to dismount," circ. a horse

d. "to get off," circ. any motorized vehicle

Thus the rural origin of many of the Mexican immigrants who have come to this country, especially during the first half of this century, is marked clearly in the Spanish of a large number of Chicanos, whether it be in the vocabulary, the archaic terms which have disappeared in urban, metropolitan Spanish, the regularized verbal forms, the cases of epenthesis and metathesis (pared → pader), and the aspiration of labiodental fricatives. Rural varieties are undoubtedly the base of the Spanish spoken in the Southwest.

URBAN VARIETIES

As we have stated before, most persons of Mexican origin in the United States are presently residing in urban areas. Yet we cannot automatically speak of "urban" Spanish varieties, for urbanization is a fairly recent Southwest phenomenon which has concentrated Chicanos, in many cases, in urban barrios and ghettos and thereby allowed them to preserve their rural varieties. Let us recall that available statistics on undocumented workers indicate that these are primarily but not entirely farmworkers from rural areas and that during the first half of this century Mexican labor was recruited especially for agricultural work, drawing largely from a pool of displaced and landless peasants. Immigration, both documented and undocumented, and the development of runaway shops or *maquiladoras* by U.S. enterprises on the Mexican side of the border have led to increased border urbanization and massive migration to the northern frontier zone itself. Thus, although Mexican immigrants come from all parts of Mexico, a number of them have spent months or years in Juárez, Matamoros, Piedras Negras, Ciudad Acuña, Nogales, Nuevo Laredo, Agua Prieta, Reynosa, Mexicali, Tecate or Tijuana, attracted by border industrialization or simply waiting for the opportunity to cross over into the United States. Among documented immigrants there are of course skilled and professional workers from urban areas and, as we have mentioned before, Spanish-language radio station announcers who use formal varieties of standard Spanish and have generally received their training in Mexico. These urban Mexican immigrants are one source of our urban Southwest Spanish varieties.

Undocumented workers who go back and forth from Mexico to the United States are thus forced to spend a great deal of time in urban centers like Tijuana. Consequently, despite their involvement in rural work here in this country, their Spanish may be urbanized. The following excerpts are from a taped interview by M. Salas of an undocumented worker who has spent many years working in the flower gardens of the Northern part of San Diego County, for periods of up to six months a year:

Excerpt A.
MS: —¿Te pagan en cheque o te pagan en puro dinero?
UW: — No, en cheque. Hay otra cosa, que aquí el ranchero nunca da . . .
MS: — ¿Moneda suelta?
UW: — No, no, no da cheque de este . . . que se quede uno con el talón. Nunca. Yo estuve trabajando aquí la primera vez en este rancho, pero eran otros dueños, ¿no? Y aquí sí me pagaron, yo tengo mis talones, ¿no? cuando yo estuve trabajando aquí en este rancho. Pero él nunca daba cheque, con cheques personales, ¿no?
MS: — De parte de él nada más.
UW: — Sí, no hay, porque no hay ningún comprobante con que . . .
MS: — Son tramposos estos tipos.
UW: — Digo, sí pues sí, porque digo, ¿con qué le comprueba uno que estaba trabajando ahí?
MS: — Con nada, entonces él, Ud. no puede comprobar nada con él, con nadie.
UW: — Con nadie.
MS: — Y si viene la Migra, él sale limpio, claro.
UW: — Digo, con nadie puedo yo comprobar que estoy trabajando ahí, ¿no? porque no hay ningún comprobante de nada.

Excerpt B.
UW: — Digo, como habemos muchos, ¿no? Muchos trabajadores queremos quedar bien con el ranchero y muchos trabajadores, ¿no? O sea que yo

inclusive por mi parte, ¿no? yo nomás trabajo, digo, pues nada más por lo que me está pagando, ¿no?, digo, no puedo trabajar más, entonces hay algotros que trabajan más recio, eh, o que ganan más, eh, porque en un rancho, donde hay cinco trabajadores, no todos ganan igual.

MS: — La división entre . . . se pelean entre . . .

UW: — Sí, allí donde estaba trabajando yo, un señor que se llama L., ése, gana más, gana igual que otro que se llama B. y otro que se llama R., esos tres ganan igual.

MS: — Ganan dos la hora.

UW: — Sí, yo soy el que sigo, ¿no? a mí me pagaba. 1.65 y luego había otro que le pagaba creo 1.50.

MS: — ¿La hora?

UW: — La hora. Y luego otro, le daba cien dólares quincenales, trabajando domingos y todos los días, diez horas.

MS: — Y el otro, que le pagaba treinta a la semana, ¿quién era ése?

UW: — Ese es otro que precisamente lo acaba de desocupar, el señor ése, no sé qué dificultad tendría con él, ¿no? Y yo me, yo me salí primero, y luego hora que fui, precisamente ayer fui para allí, yo, pasé por allí y no, ya no estaba. Le pregunté a otro señor y ya no estaba.

Excerpt C.

MS: — ¿Y qué hacen los trabajadores cuando no tienen trabajo entonces?

UW: — Porque como te digo, como hay bastante gente aquí, ilegal, ¿no?, entonces no les cuesta a ellos trabajo volver a ocupar al trabajador.

MS: — ¿Pero qué hacen los trabajadores cuando no tienen trabajo?

UW: — Oh, algotros se van, se van para el sur, algotros se van para algotra parte.

MS: — ¿Para el norte?

UW: — Digo, encuentran trabajo en algotro lado o la migración los saca, algunos o digo, no falta, ¿no?, el problema; de todos modos, los trabajadores, esos que desocupan ya no vuelven. Ya no vuelven a trabajar allí hasta vuelta de año, ¿no?, hasta que este mismo tiempo . . . otra vez.

As is evident from these excerpts, this flower garden worker speaks an urban variety of Mexican Spanish. His use of *algotros* (from *algunos otros*) is a popular variant common to both urban and rural varieties, as is the form *habemos* (for *hay*). What is noticeable is his conservation of voiced fricatives in intervocalic position and the lack of apheresis (except for *hora* rather than *ahora*) or apocope. These undocumented workers who have migrated from rural to urban border areas, residing for long periods of time in areas like Tijuana, are a rich source of popular urban varieties, whether they penetrate the farm labor market or the industrial sector in this country.

Urban varieties can also be found among Chicanos whose parents immigrated from urban zones in Mexico. As examples, we will present excerpts from an interview with an eight-year-old girl, second generation, of Mexican origin who at the time of the interview was a second grader in a National City elementary school. Her father works in construction and her mother in the school cafeteria. An eleven-year-old older brother with whom she converses in both English and Spanish is also a student in that school. The language of the home is Spanish. The family has a number of relatives in Tijuana, including an uncle who is a medical doctor there.

Excerpts.

a) Int: — Y ¿cómo te vienes a la escuela?
    IV: — Mi mamá me trae en el carro.
    Int: — Ah, ¿todos los días?
    IV: — Sí.
    Int: — ¿Y en la tarde?
    IV: — No, en la mañana.
    Int: — ¿Y cómo te vas?
    IV: — Me voy con mi abuelita. Mi mamá me lleva pa trás pa la casa.

. . . .

b) Int: — Y tu abuelito, ¿qué hace?
    IV: — Trabaja en el yonque, arreglando carros o algo así.

. . . .

c) Int: — ¿Qué es esto?
    IV: — Un troque.
    Int: — ¿Para qué se usa?
    IV: — Para trabajar o para sacar la tierra; levantan la tierra.

. . . .

d) Int: — ¿Y acá?
    IV: — Se está desayunando, tomando un vaso de leche.
    Int: — Oye, y tú esta mañana; ¿te desayunaste?
    IV: — Sí.
    Int: — A ver, ¿qué comiste?
    IV: — Comí un pan y huevos y leche.
    Int: — ¿Te levantas temprano?
    IV: — Sí.
    Int: — ¿A qué hora te levantaste?
    IV: — Como . . . ahora, a las seis de la mañana, como mi mamá; se levantó a esa misma hora porque tiene que hacerle lonche a mi papá pa que se pueda ir a trabajar.
    Int: — ¿Y tú te levantas también a esa hora?
    IV: — Hmmmhmmm, a ayudarle a mi mamá, a ver pa qué me necesita, a ver, para lavarle los trastes.
    Int: — ¿Tú lavas los trastes ya?
    Int: — Hmmhmm, le ayudo a lavar los trastes.

. . . .

e) Int: — ¿Y ésta? ¿Qué está pasando aquí?
    IV: — Se está quemando una casa.
    Int: — ¿Qué pasaría?

IV: — A lo mejor tiraron un cerillo.
Int: — A lo mejor. ¿Qué más pudo haber pasado?
IV: — Tiraron un cigarro.
Int: — Hmmm ¿o?
IV: — Dejaron la estufa o el calentón prendido y se quemó toda la casa.

. . . .

f) "Gilligan's Island"
IV: — Se trata de siete, de siete personas que se jueron, a, a ver cómo se puede decir eso.
Int: — ¿Se fueron a qué? ¿A una isla?
IV: — Sí, fueron a una isla y luego se les quebró el barco porque había, 'taba lloviendo mucho y luego ellos chocaron en una isla y ya no se podían baj . . . salir porque ya tenía un hoyo muy grande el barco.
Int: — Hmmhmm
IV: — Y luego hicieron casitas para ellos, para, para dormir y no sé, de ésa, muchas cosas como, como hace la gente en una casa y . . .
Int: — ¿Y se quedaron allí a vivir?
IV: — Hmmhmmm.
Int: — ¿Y qué comen?
IV: — Pues comen . . .
Int: — ¿Cómo, cómo viven allí? ¿Qué, pescan o qué?
IV: — Pescan, comen pescado y, y bueno, lo tienen que cocer, ¿verdad? porque si lo van a comer crudo.
Int: — ¿A tí te gustaría vivir en una isla?
IV: — Hmmhmmm.
Int: — A ver, ¿por qué?
IV: — Porque puedes respirar el, el aire.
Int: — Y aquí, ¿aquí no?
IV: — Sí, aquí también. Y puedes ir a la playa, así como hay una playa allí también.

. . . .

g) Int: — ¿Y este hombre?
IV: — 'Tá leyendo un libro en la cama, en el sillón.
Int: — En el sillón. ¿Qué estará leyendo?
IV: — Un libro.
Int: — ¿De qué?
IV: — A ver. De las brujas.
Int: — ¿De las brujas? ¿Tú, tú sabes algo de brujas? A ver cuéntame.
IV: — Que no existen.
Int: — Que no existen, heh, heh. ¿Por qué crees que está leyendo un libro de brujas?
IV: — Que . . . a lo mejor se lo está leyendo a su muchachito pa que . . . A ver si cree que sí hay . . . brujas.

Int: — ¿Tú crees que hay espantos?
IV: — No.
Int: — ¿Por qué?
IV: — Porque espantos no existen.
Int: — ¿Cómo sabes?
IV: — Porque me dice mi hermano que espantos ya no existen ni nunca existaban, exis., exis., ¿existaban?
Int: — Existieron.
IV: — Existieron en el mundo.
Int: — ¿Nunca existieron?
IV: — No, porque yo ví una película de vampiros y yo tenía miedo que me mordiera un vampiro.
Int: — Vampiro, heh, heh.
IV: — Y luego mi hermano me dijo, "no creas en esas cosas porque no hay, no hay, nunca han existido los espantos."
Int: — Ay, muy bien. Así que tienes un hermano muy inteligente.
IV: — Hmmhmmm.
Int: — ¿Cuántos años dices que tiene?
IV: — Once.

. . . .

h) Int: — ¿Qué harías si tuvieras mucho dinero?
   IV: — Lo gastaba como ir a Disneylandia, al zoológico, o si no, ir a unas vacaciones a Hawaii o si no, gastarlo pa comprar un barco.

In these excerpts the eight-year-old girl shifts between some formal and informal variants, as for example between *pa* and *para* or *está* and *'tá*. On the other hand this second grader used *mamá* throughout the thirty-minute interview rather than *amá*; she used *abuelito* and *abuelita* rather than *güelito* or *huelito*; she used *desayunar* rather than *almorzar,* a rural variant for "to have breakfast"; she used *huevos* rather than *blanquillos,* a euphemism among rural residents; she used *cerillo* rather than *mecha*; she used *película* rather than *vista* or *mono*; and she used *pues* instead of *pos*. Yet she also reflects contact with Chicano Spanish, particularly in her use of a number of loanwords, common now along the Mexican border as well: *yonque* (from *junk*), *lonche* (not only as *lunch,* but as equivalent to *sandwich* or *torta*), *troque* rather than *camión,* and a loan translation like *llevar pa trás* ("to take back") rather than *llevar de nuevo* or simply *llevar*. Only on one occasion does she aspirate a word initial *f-*: *se jueron.* When asked what she would do if she had a lot of money, she answered with the imperfect indicative tense rather than a conditional or subjunctive tense:

Int: — ¿Qué harías si tuvieras mucho dinero?
IV: — Lo gastaba como ir a Disneylandia. . . .

This variant could possibly be interpreted as the variant of an eight-year-old who has not yet fully developed an adult variety, except that we find it in the repertoire of adults in the Southwest as well. Consider the following exchange between two Chicana graduating seniors at UCSD. They are discussing a smog device that needs to be checked on a car that one of them is considering buying:

A: — But it might be faulty.
B: — Pues vale más que le preguntes, de to'os modos cuando venga. So you have to have that checked. And how are you gonn . . . you should have asked. Si te 'bieras acordado, le 'bías preguntado al hombre ayer.
A: — Se me olvidó.

This construction: *Si te hubieras acordado, le habías preguntado,* with loss of initial syllables (apheresis), is common throughout the Southwest in both urban and rural varieties. The following variants are common:

> Si te hubieras acordado, le hubieras preguntado.
> Se te fueras acordado, le fueras preguntado.
> Si te hubieras acordado, le habías preguntado.
> Si te habías acordado, le habías preguntado.

Various combinations of these occur in both rural and urban popular varieties. Like the university senior, the second grader always responds with an imperfect indicative:

Int: — Oye, ¿a tí te gusta la nieve?
IV: — Sí.
Int: — ¿Qué te . . . qué sabor?
IV: — De . . . de chocolate.
Int: — De chocolate. ¿Qué harías tú si no hubiera nieve?
IV: — Tomaba agua nomás.

As in the previous case, the structure is: *Si no hubiera nieve, tomaba agua nomás* as opposed to the standard: *Si no hubiera nieve, tomaría agua nomás.* Thus the context implies a conditional function for an imperfect indicative verb form. This function can also be served through the use of adverbial phrases, as in excerpt (e):

Int: — ¿Qué pasaría?
IV: — A lo mejor tiraron un cerillo.

Here again *a lo mejor tiraron* functions like *tirarían.* The child is thus able to demonstrate knowledge of language use and language functions despite the fact that she does not use particular forms. The use of nonsystemic equivalents is of course common in all languages. In short, we see that her urban informal variety does not have a high number of morphological and phonological variants found in rural codes. Her code is distinguished by the use of loanwords within a popular urban variety. Since both rural and urban varieties of Southwest Spanish are characterized by the incorporation of loanwords, our next section will deal with this phenomenon.

LOANWORDS

In analyzing codes we must take into account the different levels of signification and the various fields of content that are reflected in the units which make up the content of the signs. An analysis of loanwords from the English language into Spanish would thus involve an examination of the various cultural units (whether historical, social, economic or literary) which make up the semantic properties of these loans. Other studies on loanwords in the Southwest have focused on form and dealt with types of loans: loans, loan blends, loan shifts, loan translations, compound loans or hybrid loans.

Here, however, we are especially interested in examining the content behind these forms and the function of loanwords in the Spanish of Chicanos. We will study those loans which have displaced or coexist with other Spanish forms to see if these forms share some or all semantic properties and wherein they differ. We will try to determine whether the various possible readings are limited to contextual and circumstantial features and whether the connotations differ in such cases, since the cultural properties that make up the semantic units of the loans reflect the contexts within which the population lives and works, the degree and type of acculturation and the type of language contact. For this reason, before analyzing the phenomenon in terms of denotative and connotative markers we will look briefly at the context within which these loans occur.

A study of context requires not only examining the cultural content reflected in these loans but a brief look at this phenomenon in loans from other sources found in the Spanish language.

LOANWORDS: HISTORICAL CONTEXT

Loanwords are common in the history of all languages. Spanish, for example, has numerous terms taken from Greek, Arabic, French, Italian and early Germanic dialects. It is interesting to observe the types of loans borrowed through contact with these various groups. Germanic loans in Spanish are primarily related to warfare as in words like *guerra, heraldo, robar* and *dardo*, reflecting the relationship of early Roman and peninsular colonies with attacking Germanic tribes.[3]

Arabic words on the other hand, fall into several domains. There are agricultural terms (as in *acequia, alberca, noria, acelga*), domestic terms (as in *almohada, azotea*), commercial terms (*almacén, quilates, quintales*), occupational terms (*alfarero, albañil*) and governmental terms (*alguacil, alcalde*). These reflect over 700 years of coexistence on the Iberian peninsula. It is interesting to note that the language of the peoples inhabiting the peninsula before the Roman invasion (except in the case of the Basques) has all but disappeared. Traces of these early languages are sometimes found in the roots of some place names or river names. The impact of Roman colonization throughout seven centuries reached the full extent of the peninsula in the process of urbanization and *latifundismo* and in the extension of its communications network and economic system, obliterating most linguistic traces of the past.[4] Thus political, military and economic conquest determined language choice by increasing and forcing language contact. The type of contact is also very important as it determines those areas or domains where language shifting or borrowing is likely to occur.

These factors are also significant in our study of the language contact situation in the Southwest. We can trace the status of Spanish as a minority language in contact with a majority language back to 1848 when the United States took the Southwest territory from Mexico. As in the case of the Iberians, the presence of this Spanish-speaking population is obvious in place names (El Paso, San Diego, Los Angeles, Santa Barbara, Sacramento, San Juan, Salinas, San Jose, San Antonio, etc.). The type of language and social contact between the two groups is also evident in loans taken from Spanish by the English-speaking colonizers who learned their early cowboy and mining trades from Spaniards, Mexicans and Indians. In ranching, English incorporated *buckaroo*, *lariat, rodeo, corral, burro, stampede, chaparral, calaboose, mesa, canyon, ranch, barbecue.* From the mining experience it absorbed *placer* and *bonanza.* By the end of the nineteenth century the former Mexican territory was totally in control of the English-speaking immigrants who determined the language of schools, courts, government and commerce. Other factors, however, like continued immigration from Mexico, residential segregation, occupational segregation and racism helped to maintain the Spanish language.

We can get an idea of the historical changes in the last century and their effect on the Mexican-origin population by looking not only at studies describing this period of urbanization, mechanization of agriculture, industrialization and growth of agribusiness in the Southwest but also by looking at linguistic studies of the period. An article on New Mexican Spanish written by Aurelio Espinosa and published in 1909, lists approximately 135 loanwords out of a total of 300 found in Spanish language research of New Mexico.[5] These loans reflect not only linguistic impact but social impact as well. The acculturation of the Mexican population as it adapted to its new environment is indicated by terms which reflect areas basic to survival. There are loans indicating measurement: *bonche, cuara, nicle, peni, dola, bil.* Some refer specifically to occupations: *jobe, deschachar, cuitiar, parna* and some refer to consumer goods: *bogue, esprín, guincheste, overoles, sinque, suera, balún, ploga.* A few refer to American foods: *aiscrín, bísquete, jeli, greve, lonche, queque, sángüiche.* Acculturation is evident, although in a humorous vein, in the incorporation of English expressions like: *al bechu, enejau, evrebore, fain, fon, fone, ful, fuliar, gurbai, jeló, jarirú, olraite.* As Espinosa states, "in the brief period of 50 years, the English language had already influenced New Mexico Spanish in many respects, especially in vocabulary."[6]

Let us recall that during this early period, the Southwest was still primarily dependent on ranching, agriculture and mining. As Mexican immigration to the United States increased after the turn of the century and during the Mexican revolution of 1910, these people were also incorporated into the agricultural economy, picking cotton in Texas and fruit and vegetables in California. The period around World War II brought increased industrialization and urbanization to the Southwest, particularly to California. Eventually the Mexican immigrant was also absorbed into the low-wage sectors of the service and blue-collar labor market. Conditions which have concentrated and segregated Chicanos have enabled the developing loanwords to take root and spread, maintained by succeeding bilingual generations. The loans have taken a similar form throughout the Southwest although a few variations occur. In California, for example, where there has been more of an international labor force involved in farm work including Filipinos, Arabs, Portuguese, Chinese, Japanese and Mexicans, the word designating place of work is *fil* for field. In Texas where the field hands were primarily Mexicans (although in East Texas there were also Black farmworkers), the word is the Spanish term *labor*. Differences in form can thus be traced to different labor situations, that is, to different referents.

Loanwords then reflect historical conditions. The geographical and occupational mobility of Chicanos, for example, is reflected in the language. Spanish has incorporated a number of terms reflecting the transition into the service and blue-collar categories with terms like *weldeador, emplastador* (plasterer), *dompero, factoría, canería, londres, meid, cuitear, descharchar, troquero.* The continued presence of Chicanos in the fields can be seen in words like *fil, migrante,* and *brocle.* Loans also reflect areas of residence on the other side of the proverbial tracks: *traques, dipo, dompe, treila.* The barrios, though segregated and poor, copied the gringo house-style with *yardas, miras de la luz, lotes, sinks, sure, plogues* and *carpetas* while *las huayfas dosteaban, waxeaban* and *mapeaban.* Chicanos were also integrated into the consumer society as indicated by *mapiador, mapiar, juila, teni, guayín.* Acceptance into the totally English-speaking public school system brought numerous terms associated with school activities and subject matter: *rula, espelear, taipear, mistear, ponchar, ringuear, espiche, faite, sainear, jaiscul.* Chicanos joined the automobile generation as indicated by *troca, cranque, cloche, estare, estarear, suiche, huachas, millaje, treila, saine, puche, yaque, parquear, raite, bos* and *bloques.* Acculturation meant shoes were *chaineados* rather than *lustrados,* people were *fuleados* rather than *engañados*; housewives paid *biles* rather than *cuentas* and instead of saying *se sale el agua* they say *la llave liquea.* Chicanos started eating *greve, lonches, sánguiches, harina de flor, aiscrín, binsones* and drinking *birria de la grocería o la marqueta* while they were *wachando la tele* or reading *el magasín.*

These loans reflect acculturation at the same time that they reflect resistance to shifting entirely to the English language. For all of these terms, once incorporated into Spanish, are as much a part of the local varieties of Spanish as Italian loanwords like *pibe, chau, bacán, laborar* are a part of Argentine

Spanish or Nahuatl words, like *elote, cacahuate, petate, hule* and *aguacate,* are part of Mexican Spanish. The difference is of course not the phenomenon itself as it exists worldwide in all languages. The difference is the type of borrowing and the extent of borrowing given the social and economic status of Chicanos in a country where English is the dominant language.

These loanwords must therefore be studied in terms of the historical content they reflect. In fact a few choice loans like *migrante, fil, weldeador* and *welferero* could serve to trace the history of the Mexican-origin population in this country. School-related loans reflect the lack of Spanish-language instruction in the public schools for many, many years. Loans reflecting agricultural work also point to a lack of educational opportunities for today's parents and grandparents who spent their school seasons in the fields. Consumer goods which were new around the turn of the century made their way to Chicano marketplaces as well, as evidenced by the loans. Immigration meant penetrating a different society with different values. Survival meant adapting to a certain extent and these loans indicate that the population did.

LOANWORDS: FUNCTIONS AND SEMANTIC PROPERTIES

In cases where loanwords coexist with popular and standard forms, the semantic properties generally differ in terms of denotative or connotative markers and contextual and circumstantial features. Consider the following pairs:

camión / troca, troque
cuadra / bloque
interruptor / suiche
enchufe / plogue, ploga
cuenta / bil
patio / yarda / solar

In most of these cases the loanword has become the general local term among second and subsequent Chicano generations. Possibly among the early immigrants, and even as late as the early forties in Southwest barrios, gadgets like light switches were not familiar objects constituting part of their cultural repertoire. In some rural areas, in both Mexico and the United States, there was either no electricity or lights were turned on by pulling on a small chain or string hanging from the ceiling. It was then logical that as these new commodities were introduced by an English-dominant society, they be denoted by English terms adapted to Spanish phonology and morphology. Charge accounts also introduced a new phenomenon: monthly bills, permeating all aspects of daily life in the United States. The term *cuenta* which is the standard Spanish equivalent for "bill," was already part of the repertoire of Mexican immigrants but with different denotations as is evident in the use of this term today. Consider the following:

1. Saca la cuenta.
2. Vamos a sacar las cuentas.
3. Tengo cuentas pendientes con él.
4. Vamos arreglando cuentas.

In sentence 1, *cuenta* denotes "sum" or "answer to some computation." This utterance may occur at home in doing math homework or in any kind of computation. Sentence 2 has a similar but more specific meaning; here *cuenta* refers to a computation of expenses or itemized figures. In figuring out monthly expenses one can say the following in the barrio:

Vamos a sacar las cuentas pa' pagar los biles.

Thus "sacar las cuentas" means adding up expenses and figuring out the budget for the month. Sentences 3 and 4, on the other hand, refer to "personal accounts to be settled" and generally connote an affront or disagreeable affair which requires revenge or retribution. Thus for second, third and subsequent generations, *cuenta* does not denote the actual invoice or statement of charges, a function reserved for the word *bil.* The term incidentally is not used to denote a piece of paper money as in "dollar bill"; this denotation is reserved for *billete.* We can then describe the different readings of *cuenta* and *bil* in the Southwest as follows:

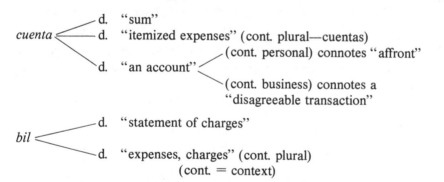

It is thus primarily the contextual features that determine the use of *bil* and *cuenta* although it is evident that from denoting a statement of charges the term *bil* has undergone an extension of semantic readings to refer not only to the statement itself but to the content of the statement, the charges themselves. At this point it appears that both terms refer to general expenses, but in fact the term *cuenta* has been completely displaced here and retained only in the sense of the actual figures or computations involved in an expense. Thus it is always "sacar las cuentas" but "pagar los biles" or even "tener muchos biles"—to have many debts. The plural *biles,* on the other hand is not synonymous with *gastos* which denotes personal expenses as opposed to household expenses, expressed by *biles.*

In the case of terms like *patio* and *yarda,* the semantic features are also different. *Yard,* according to Webster, is a "small, usually walled and paved area open to the sky and adjacent to a building," but in the context of Southwest homes, a yard is generally the open space in front of a house, covered with grass or flowers. In the barrio, *trabajar en las yardas* means to work as a gardener, generally for the Anglo middle class homeowners who have large houses and lots of greenery. *Patio,* although it also refers to the open space adjacent to a building, in the context of home, refers to the backyard. In Mexican or Latin American towns or cities where houses come up to the sidewalk, the backyard is often paved or covered with cobblestones and decorated with flowers. In Chicano Spanish the empty backyard is designated with the term *solar,* which also means "lot." All three terms thus differ in denotations.

yard ———— d. 1. open space adjacent to buildings.
         d. 2. open space with greenery and flowers around a home
                 (context: Southwest house-styles)
yarda

solar ———— d. 1. lot
         d. 2. empty backyard

patio ———— d. 1. open space adjacent to buildings
         d. 3. open space paved or cobblestoned behind a home

Other loans could be studied in terms of their connotations. Some particular loans and loan translations connote youth and unconventionality, especially when they are translations or borrowings from English slang. Consider the following:

1. Le voy a tener que enseñar inglés a mi chamaco nomás *pa que la haga* en la escuela.
2. Por ejemplo, *de cincho* que vinieron cocineros.
3. Anduvimos por el barrio *watchando la movida.*
4. . . . como yo conozco como son los *porasos* de la ganga.

These expressions from a young Chicano male are borrowed from: "to have it made," "it's a cinch," "watch this," and "big party."

In other cases, the loans connote "being one of the people," a sort of folksiness as opposed to the pretentiousness that can be connoted by use of a standard term. Compare the following examples:

1. Misteó mucha escuela.
2. Faltó mucho a la escuela.

3. Te misteo mucho.
4. Te extraño mucho.

5. Tengo que taipearlo primero y luego te lo llevo.
6. Tengo que pasarlo a máquina primero y luego te lo llevo.

7. Le dieron esa chansa de patrolman.

8. Le dieron una oportunidad de trabajar de policía.

In each of these cases, the utterance with the loan connotes familiarity while the standard expressions connote distance or coldness and in some cases, pedantry. All of these denotations and connotations are examined strictly within a Chicano context in intragroup exchanges. Once there is interaction with Spanish speakers outside the Chicano circle (which may include non-Chicanos), these denotations and connotations do not hold.

The loans that we have discussed are all examples of English lexical items adapted to the Spanish phonological, morphosyntactic and semantic system. Oftentimes the meaning of the English term is maintained while it is adapted phonologically and morphologically (spell = *espelear*; push = *puchar*); in other cases a Spanish term extends its meaning by borrowing a denotation from an English cognate ("false cognate") (realize = *realizar*; library = *librería*) or by translating an English phrase and retaining its English idiomatic meaning (call back = *llamar pa'tras*; to have a good time = *tener un buen tiempo*). In all of these cases the English lexical item is adapted to all the components of the Spanish grammar. Borrowing is a worldwide phenomenon affecting all societies in contact with another language, particularly when the source language belongs to a politically or economically dominant group. The reaction of other Spanish-speaking minorities in the United States to the extensive borrowing in the Southwest is generally directed not against the dominant society which has limited the possibilities of continued enrichment of the Spanish language through contact with Spanish-language activities in the arts, music, theatre, literature and academic instruction, but against the Chicano population whose survival has depended on its ability to adapt to a new environment and a new language. Far from simply succumbing to the English language, the Spanish-speaking Chicano population has dealt with the limiting situation by wielding the English language and transforming it for its own purposes and its own survival. The presence of loans in Chicano Spanish is a natural consequence of language and social contact; but it is not simply a sign of acculturation nor is it a tragic sign of language decadence. It is contradictorily both a sign of acculturation and a sign of resistance, for it is the subjugation of the English language to Spanish grammar as much as it is the penetration of American culture into Chicano Spanish.

Much has been said about the extent of English interference in the Spanish of Chicanos. We will discuss this topic further in our next chapter on code-switching.

The whole question of loans is quite complex but we hope to have suggested a new direction for the study of these terms in the Spanish of Chicanos. Loans can be further classified as general or restricted in terms of the various codes within which they appear. In the next section we will look at borrowings which are part of *caló*, the slang code or argot of Chicano youth.

CALÓ

Caló as an urban code is a synthesis of the different varieties spoken by Chicanos in the Southwest, for it incorporates standard Spanish, popular Spanish varieties, loanwords from English and even code-switching. It is primarily characterized by its penchant for innovativeness in its expansion of the lexicon to produce an argot, the slang of young Chicanos, primarily male. Thus in *caló,* the language acquires its highest level of semiotic elasticity as grammatical rules suffer rule extensions in all components of the grammar: sounds, structures and vocabulary. Many words associated with this code have become part of the general repertoire of the Mexican-origin population and ceased to be exclusively *caló* terms. In some cases, words associated with this variety are in fact lexical items taken from the standard language of other Hispanic areas. Fusing standard and popular urban and rural varieties, *caló* sprinkles in a handful of terms borrowed from the argot of Mexico and other Hispanic areas, overcodes (assigns additional meanings) the lexicon and undercodes it (simplifies the meaning) as well.[7] In this section we will be especially interested in looking at the functions and levels of meaning found in this code. First we will look briefly at some important historical events affecting its status.

In the Southwest *caló* achieved a certain degree of notoriety during the decade of the forties, a period marked by geographical and occupational mobility in this area. While the eastern part of the United States had initiated its process of urbanization and industrialization during the nineteenth century, the western part of the country had remained primarily rural and dependent on agriculture, mining and the railroads till the second world war, when the war effort led to increased production of consumer goods, war matériel and agricultural products. Along with the large numbers of people migrating west came thousands of persons of Mexican-origin, especially from Texas, Arizona and Mexico. These new California residents of Mexican origin were concentrated in areas of low-income housing where other Chicanos already resided. As is well known, particular styles of dress and language codes can develop among isolated communities. These metropolitan ghettos and barrios allowed the codes of young men from the strongly Spanish-speaking urban and rural areas of Texas, especially El Paso, and the general Southwest to flourish, particularly in the Los Angeles area. The dress of these young Mexican men imitated the style made famous in Harlem, the zoot suit. In documents compiled by Carey McWilliams during this period we find the following information:[8]

> Zoot suits were made by manufacturers all over the country and sold like hot cakes. . . . They went for them in the foreign districts; in fact the name seems to derive from a mispronunciation of the word "suit."
>
> The zoot suit gained its original fame in New York's Harlem district, but became infamous on the basis of antics of its wearers on the west coast. Los Angeles police arrest about a dozen of the city's long coated, baggy panted Mexican residents each week for minor violations of the law.

This type of reporting was produced by an inflammatory press which incited the public against a growing Mexican-origin population and later supported the beating of young Chicano males by Navy servicemen during the now famous zoot-suit riots. Other media versions of the situation also appeared, as in this sample of other articles compiled by McWilliams:[9]

> The zoot suit is no label of juvenile delinquency. Many a young Mexican in a zoot suit works hard and takes his money home to mamacita for frijoles refritos and many a young zoot-suited Negro never shoots craps and goes to the Baptist Church every Sunday.

These young men with their wide-brimmed hats, long coats, ankle-tight trousers and duck-tail haircuts were called pachucos because the style was assumed to have been brought from El Paso (Pasuco → Pachuco), by young male migrants. However, it is known that the style was not limited to Mexicans and Blacks although it became an identity symbol for ghetto and barrio dwellers. Since minority groups in this country have always lived side by side in slums and other areas of low-cost housing, Chicano males were also able to incorporate numerous lexical items from Black English. According to information collected by McWilliams, the Black population of Los Angeles also increased tremendously, doubling in a period of about ten years to the point where the National Urban League was concerned with the "jive language" of young Blacks. Young Chicanos also had access to the argot of urban Mexico as Mexican immigration increased in the form of documented, undocumented, and temporary agricultural (Bracero) immigrants.

Caló is thus an urban phenomenon but it is important to recall that even though this period marks the urbanization of the Mexican-origin population, this population had always consisted of families who migrated from the fields to towns and cities during the off-seasons when no harvesting or farm work was available. Urbanization, as previously mentioned, brought increased contact with the English-speaking communities, both Black and White. The *caló* spoken today in the Southwest continues to reflect features of the *caló* of the forties but it has also made new lexical additions. It continues to be the slang of young Chicano males but oftentimes what passes for *caló* in the language of young Chicanos has only a trace of those rare exotic argot terms[10] and numerous cases of overcoding and undercoding, as we shall see. Oftentimes all that remains is the peculiar intonation and a sprinkling of ornamental *órale-ése-vatos* added for effect.

Let us compare four varieties of *caló*: one reflecting the language of the Pachucos from El Paso during the forties, recorded by Olga Villanueva with the help of her father, Benito Villanueva; one recorded by Norma Elena Corvera in San Diego with the help of a friend; one recorded by Lynne Sullivan with the help of a friend in Tijuana and one recorded by Rey Gomeztagle of friends from Los Angeles. These texts will be followed by a list of interesting lexical items taken from the excerpts:

A) El Paso Caló:
— Guacha, ¿por qué no me alivianas con un aventón y me dejas en el chante? Y
   mientras que vas por el Chente, yo tiro claváo, me rastío la greña y me

entacucho. Te trais al Chente a mi cantón y le digo a la jefa que nos aliviane con un calmante porque a mí ya me trai la jaspia y quiero refinar. Le dices al Chente que 'stoy invitáo a un borlo y pa que se desagüite el vato le digo a mi güisa que le consiga una jainita para irnos a borlotear todos. ¿Cómo la ves?

— Pos 'stá de aquella la idea pero, pos tú sabes que el Chente va andar muy quebradón porque acaba... va acabar de desafanar y no trai garra de aquella. ¿Cómo la ves?

— O, dile que no se agüite, le dices que no hay fijón por la feria y si necesita garra, yo le empresto pantas, lisa, taiya, carlangos, calcos y hasta calcetas si quiere. Sirve que cuando 'stemos refinando quiero que oiga una rolas que aparé ora, ¿ves? ¡'Tán a todo güelo, tú sabes las songas que hay orita 'tán a todo güelo!

— Orale pues, 'tonces allí te guacho en tu cantón. Pero también le dices a la jefita que me aliviane con un refinazo, ¿eh? Y que no se le olvide los biroles, porque tú sabes como me cain de aquéllas los biroles, ¿eh? Tá de aquélla.

— Simón que yes, ése. 'Tonces aquí te... allí te calmo después que me dejes, ¿eh? ¡Tá de aquélla!

B) Two Young Chicano Males at Work in San Diego:

P: — Y qué ondas con las jainas, ¿dónde cantonean?

M: — Aquí en Carlsbad. Ahi estudia la ruca en un college, no sé cómo se llama.

P: — Y ¿te iba a hablar ahora?

M: — Ayer, loco. Ayer me habló, ése.

P: — ¿Sí?

M: — Pero le dijieron que no vivía aquí, ése, ¡fíjate!

P: — Y ella, ¿no te dio el teléfono de ella?

M: — No, porque se agüitan los jefes si le habla uno, ¿ves?

P: — ¿Y qué onda, pero qué andaba haciendo esa onda allá?

M: — Andaban dos moras, y como estaba mi primo, pos, órale, no' fuimos a cotorriarla, ¿ves? Le di mi número de teléfono para que me llamara. Chulas, loco, las dos moras.

C) El Pachuco Tijuanense:

— Y para no hacértela tan agüitona, pues decidí treparme a la burra que iba para el taun a agarrar otro tipo de patín. Y fíjate que al estarle dando la marmaja al cafre, que mi pupila se endulza al palpar una beibi (wow, ¡qué beibi!) que iba bien trenzadota con su bato. Y pos, la neta, decidí agandallársela al ruco que ya pertenecía a la momiza más que a la chaviza—y por mi jefita que no aguantaba para ella, que era un mangazo. Mas de pronto que me pongo a carburar y me dije, "No aguanta el cambalancho porque la ruca se ve muy popis y furris... y de esas pulgas—no brincan en mi petate." Así es que calmerón y chale a mi plan. Bueno, bato, con esto creo que ya estuvo suave, ¿no? Así es que—ai nos vidrios.

D) Vatos Locos from Los Angeles:

A: — Se cree muy chingón, ése.

B: — ¿Qué trae, ése, aliviánate, ése, llévatela suave, calmontes, ése.

A: — Ese, ¿cómo están las rucas allá por la Mariana?

B: — Las rucas, ése, chingáo, ése, 'tán de aquéllas.

A: — ¿'Tán buenotas las rucas entonces?

B: — 'Tán de aquéllas, man.

A: — ¿Bien firmes?

B: — Firmes, carnal. Nobody fucks around. If anybody tries to get it on with any of our jainas, tú sabes, se lo descontamos, ése, porque . .

A: — ¿Muy bravotes?

B: — Sabe, carnal, we just, we don't think that we're bravotes, carnal, we just don't like to fuck around. Somebody fucks around, pues ponle, carnal.

A: — Chingazos, ése.

B: — Chingazos, carnal. A la brava.

Vocabulary used in these four texts:

A

agandallársela — ganársela
agüitar — entristecer, deprimir
agüitona — pesada
alivianar — ayudar, ofrecer
aquélla (estar de aquélla) — magnífico
aventón — levantón, acción de llevar en el auto

B

bato (vato) — hombre
biroles — frijoles
borlo — baile, fiesta
borlotear — celebrar, festejar
burra — camión

C

cafre — chofer
calcetas — calcetines
calcos — zapatos
calmar — ver, esperar (calmontes = i.e., cálmate)
calmante — bocado, comida ligera
calmerón — calmarse
cambalacho — cambio
cantón — casa
cantonear — vivir
carburar — pensar
carlango — saco, abrigo, chaqueta
chale - no
chante — casa
cotorrear — hablar

D

desafanar — salir de la cárcel
desagüitarse — alegrarse

E

emprestar — prestar
entacucho — vestirse bien
ése — tú

F

fijón (no hay . . .) — nadie se fija, no importa

G

garra — ropa
greña — pelo
guacha — mirar
güelo — vuelo, a todo vuelo — fantástico
güisa — chica, muchacha

J

jainita — chica, muchacha
jaspia — hambre
jefita — mujer, mamá, esposa

L

lisa — camisa

M

mangazo — de mango, mujer linda
marmaja — dinero

moras — muchachas, chicas
momiza — de momia, muy viejo (más momiza
   que chaviza — más momia que chaval)

N
neta — netamente, sinceramente

P
pantas — pantalones
patín — andada, movida, diversión
popis y furris — rica y presumida

Q
quebradón — sin dinero

R
ratió — rastrillo, rastrillar — peinar
refinar — comer
refinazo — comida

rolas — discos
ruca — mujer
ruco — hombre

S
Simón — sí
songas — canciones

T
taiya, taya — corbata
tirar claváo — bañarse
taun — centro
tramos — pantalones
trola — cerillo

V
vato (bato) — hombre, muchacho
vidrios (Ahi nos vidrios) — nos vemos

The vocabulary we have itemized cannot all be called *caló*. Some of the items listed are standard, some popular and some, loans from the English language. A few, however, are strictly *caló* items. The *caló* vocabulary includes a combination of several elements which are added to the popular varieties so that the effect is that of an authentic code. Before we look at the specific elements, let us first examine the functions of *caló* in the previous excerpts.

Excerpt B is the best example of the incorporation of *caló* lexical items in the language of young Chicano males in everyday conversation. Both use a popular variety interspersed with familiar expressions and a few *caló* items when referring to the young girls (*moras, rucas, jainas, chavala*) one met on Saturday, what they drank (*pistiamos*), how they felt (bien *agüitado*) and where they lived (*cantonean*). Everything else is common in the popular varieties of adults and children in informal contexts. In conversation A, which involves two young Chicano males discussing a friend's release from jail, we again find the popular variants (*claváo, rastío, trais, pa, 'stá, cain, 'tá, 'tonces, güelo, empresto*) as well as the presence of *caló* markers. Here the particular *caló* elements include terms which fall in these general semantic areas: grooming, clothing, food, women and sex, recreation and crime. The Chicanos' camaraderie is signalled through the use of these *caló* lexical items, which in fact serve as reinforcement of their solidarity.

Episode D is a good example of the use of *caló* in what is commonly called *cábula* or *vacilada* among Chicanos. The exchange is meaningless at a denotative level since the whole purpose of the interaction is an empty boast about the women of their territory and their own ability to defend them, with blows if necessary. In this kind of jive, the medium, that is, the subcode itself—*caló*—becomes the message. In excerpt B, once again, the *caló* terminology connotes virility and allows speaker M to boast about his latest conquest.

Excerpt C, although recorded as a monologue by a young man from Tijuana, is more of a literary discourse where every other word is a figure of speech and the phraseology is both from popular speech and *caló*. Here the entire narration is marked by *caló* items although again the topics themselves do not trigger the shifts to *caló*. It is the intent to entertain and boast about these manly pursuits in discourse with other males that determines its usage. Thus the message in *caló*, beyond the denotations, can be expressed in terms of speech acts: challenges, boasts, insults, reinforcement and requests for solidarity. Young men who use this code with their friends generally do not use it with their families, women or older adults. Some of the more common *caló* terms, as we mentioned before, have been incorporated into the general repertoire of the Chicano population and are used in any intra-group informal context.

One technique used in *caló* is the introduction of unfamiliar terminology taken from standard Spanish varieties. It is their unfamiliarity which allows them to qualify as *caló* terms. In this category are words like *apañar* (to take); *calcetas* (stockings) and *chaval, chavalo, chavala* (boy, girl), common in other Hispanic areas. Some standard lexical items are overcoded or undercoded, as occurs in all rhetorical language. Eco has defined overcoding as either the assignment of additional meanings to expressions, or the assignment of different shades of meaning to a unit of the code to form more analytic subcodes. Undercoding occurs when an imprecise coding leads the speaker to make general assumptions and interpretations for lack of precise coding rules.[11] Assuming that *apañar* always means "to steal" would be a case of undercoding since the term has other meanings in other contexts. Undercoding also takes place when someone who does not know the *caló* code (nor the other codes in the Southwest), but who is aware of the existence of the argot, assumes that all terms used by young Chicano males in informal domains are *caló* terms, as occurred in the work of Lurline Coltharp, who characterized common loanwords from the English language as *caló*.[12]

Overcoding is a much more common phenomenon in the *caló* variety. Cases where additional meanings are assigned are common in all codes in the use of metaphors, metonyms and synecdoches. An example of an extension of meaning is a word like *cantón*, which denotes "a region or area" of a country. In particular circumstances, as for example in application forms or interviews, it denotes the county or region of origin and connotes "home." This particular process is part of the history of *caló* rather than a current reality since the term used for *county* in the Southwest is *condado*. In South America, however, the word *cantón* is common. An example of overcoding that is current and continuous is that of *vidrios*, which in the context of "Ahi nos _____ " means "vemos" rather than "glass." This rule extension is context-restricted and involves *caló* conventions which determine synonyms if initial sounds are homophonous. Popular expressions also undergo overcoding as in the case of *jalar* (from *halar*) when its denotation is extended from "to pull" to the meaning "to work" through the addition of a circumstantial selection feature (circumstance: employment). A word like *carburar,* for example, which denotes the action of a carburetor, also is overcoded when it is assigned a particular shade of meaning in the context of a human subject. In this case, it means "to think." There are many other examples of overcoding; some involve forming new words and categories from other forms: thus *liviano* ("light") becomes *alivianar* ("to help, offer; to steal"); *perico* ("parrot") produces *periquear* ("to talk"); *talón* ("heel") gives *talonear* ("to walk, go"); *garra* which denotes "rag" in popular Mexican Spanish is extended to mean "clothes," and *rastrillar* ("to rake") in excerpt A means "to comb."

Caló also replaces a number of worn-out phrases with words that have homophonous beginnings. It is in this area where new coinings take place every day. The rule in *caló* is that if the meaning is clear, the context is known and the word starts with a similar sound or syllable, then a synonym can be coined, as in these examples:

Standard or popular phrases	*Caló phrases*
1. Ahi nos vemos.	Ahi nos vidrios.
2. Ya estuvo.	Ya estufas.
3. Sí.	Simón. Sirol.
4. ¿Qué pasó?	¿Qué pasión?
5. Ya sabes.	Ya sábanas.

Caló, like the popular varieties of the Southwest, also incorporates a number of loans from English. These are distinguished from the common loans by their limited use, primarily by young males in verbal interaction with other Chicano young people, and their identification with *caló.* These loans include words like *chante* (from *shanty*), *songa* (*song*), *taya* (*tie*), *biroles* (a combination of *beans* and *frijoles*), *birria* and *bironga* (*beer*).

And finally, *caló* includes a number of terms whose origin can be traced to the language of gypsies and to other Latin American argots. These include words like: *lisa, jaina, jaspia, entacucho, güisa, chale, calcos, tramos* and *trola.*[13]

Caló then is a highly creative code which utilizes a number of techniques to produce an effect of authenticity. Many of the phrases utilized in the *caló* excerpts are in fact found in the popular varieties as well. The uniqueness of the *caló* variety lies in the quantity, in the number of colorful expressions, combined with *caló* lexical items, used in the discourse of Chicano males rather than in the type of expressions created. *Caló* is not a secret language. As an intra-group subcode, it is an element in group solidarity, whether it forms part of the verbal interaction of gangs or of youth in general. Culturally, it has also been an expression form within Chicano poetry, short stories and novels. Years ago it was common in the Mexican movies of comedians, like Tín-Tán, or on Mexican radio comic hours. Today, it continues to be part of the daily discourse of Chicano males but in the artistic and literary fields, Chicanos have raised it to another level and made it a literary code as well.

SUMMARY

Let us now summarize the principal types of varieties found in the Southwest. There are basically two codes: a standard code and a popular code. The popular code is further subdivided into urban and rural codes because in many cases there are marked differences between the two although many urbanized Chicanos originally from rural areas fall into both categories. Within each category there are sub-codes, as for example, *caló,* which is an urban sub-code. We are postulating that differences between these three varieties occur at the morphosyntactic level primarily, although code differences may also involve lexical differences, as in the case of archaic terms, English loanwords or typically rural variants. Sub-codes are primarily stylistic variations involving pronunciation and vocabulary. In Table 4.1 we contrast a few of these forms. Often there will be no distinction between an urban and a rural popular form, but the same may be true for urban popular and standard forms.

Table 4.1   Contrast Between Standard and Popular Urban and Rural Codes

Standard	Urban popular	Rural popular
1. Fuiste.	1. Fuistes.	1. Juites / Fuites.
¿Qué hiciste?	¿Qué hicistes?	¿Qué hicites?
2. Salimos a las tres.	2. Salimos / Salemos.	2. Salemos a las tres.
Decimos.	Decimos / Dicemos.	Dicemos.
3. No traía nada.	3. No traía nada.	3. No traiba nada.
4. No traje nada.	4. No traje nada.	4. No truje nada.
No vi nada.	No vi nada.	No vide nada.
Somos la nueva ...	Somos la nueva ...	Semos la nueva genera-ción.
5. Ibamos todos.	5. Ibamos todos.	5. Íbanos todos.
6. Cuando volvamos ...	6. Cuando vuélvamos ...	6. Cuando vuélvanos ...
7. muchos padres	7. muchos papás	7. muchos papases
muchos papás		munchos papases
8. ¿El libro? Se lo di a ellos.	8. ¿El libro? Se los di a ellos.	8. ¿El libro? Se los di a ellos.
9. Nos lo dio ...	9. No los dio ...	9. No los dio ...
10. Nos trajo a nosotros.	10. Los trajo a nosotros.	10. Los trujo a nosotros.
	Nos trajo a nosotros.	

Our hypothesis is that shifts within individual repertoires occur primarily at the stylistic level rather than at a code level for most of the population since the shifts that we have noted are of a phonetic and lexical nature, at least in most of the cases observed. The one exception is the case of the self-conscious university Spanish literature and language student, who tries to shift entirely to the standard but is sometimes betrayed by his other code rules. The true exception is the individual who consciously and willingly shifts from one code to another.

Before proceeding to examine stylistic shifts occurring within Chicano Spanish discourse, we need to acknowledge our lack of concern with phonological variants in the Chicano Spanish varieties. There are of course phonetic variants in the Southwest, phonetic rather than phonological as they all have the same underlying form. Traditional dialectological studies have focused on the presence of particular variants rather than on when they occur in terms of context, function and speakers. Resnick's synthesis of works on phonological variants, as we have mentioned before, is a good example of the classification of isolated variants. Although we find that phonetic shifts occur as shifts in style in most cases, we will note the presence of some phonetic variants found throughout the Southwest for those concerned with second language acquisition and the existence of particular sounds in Chicano Spanish. This brief summary (Table 4.2) will follow somewhat the variants list used in Resnick's study.[14]

Table 4.2   Phonetic Variants Found in the Spanish of the Southwest.

Form	Possible urban variant	Possible rural variant
/s/	alveolar [s]	alveolar [s] aspiration of some sibilants [h]
trill /r̄/	trill [r̄]	trill /r̄/ [ɹ̃] combination trill and fricative
/x/	[x] and [h]	[x] and [h]
palatal fricative /y/	palatal glide [j]	-palatal glide [j] -loss of glide /ø/
labial fricative [ƀ]	[ƀ] or [v]	[ƀ] or [v]
alveo-palatal affricate /č/	[č] (ch) or [š] (sh)	[č] (ch) or [š] (sh)
[đ] in -ado	[đ] retained /đ/ lost: ø	[đ] lost
labiodental /f/	[f]	[f] or [h] before ___ w

This chart does not note the extensive laxing of voiced consonants in all positions nor the appearance of epenthetic glides between certain *hiato* combinations, which we have discussed elsewhere. The neutralization of simple and trill /r̄/ we have only heard sporadically among English-dominant Chicanos who were limited in their Spanish. None of these phonetic variants are unique to Chicano Spanish since they all occur in other areas of the Spanish-speaking world as well.

STYLISTIC SHIFTS

Stylistic shifts from one sub-code to another occur primarily at the phonetic and lexical levels. Table 4.3 gives some idea of the type of shifts that occur in Chicano Spanish. In the next chapter we will examine several texts to pinpoint

Table 4.3   Some Examples of Styles in Chicano Spanish

Formal	Informal	Intimate	Familiar
1. Usted es	1. Usté es		
2. Todo el día	2. To'o el día	2. To'o el día	
3. No he tomado	3. No he tomáo		
4. Y luego	4. Y luego luego	4. Y lo' luego; Y lo' lo'	
5. Mi padre	5. Mi papá	5. Mi 'apá	5. Mi jefito ~ mi apá
6. Está bien	6. Está bien	6. 'Tá weno	
7. ¿Qué hora es?	7. ¿Qué hora es?	7. [Kjorés?] [Kjorasón?]	
8. Está cerca . . .	8. Está cerca . . .	8. 'Tá cerquita . . .	
9. ¿Dónde estaba?	9. ¿Dónde estabas?	9. 'On 'tabas?	9. 'Ontablas?
10. Se fue al trabajo	10. Se fue al trabajo.	10. Se fue a chambear	10. Le talonió pal jale
	11. Metí la pata	11. La regué	
12. ¿Qué pasó?	12. ¿Qué pasó?	12. ¿Quiubo?	12. ¿Qué pasión? ¿Qué ondas?
13. ¡Está fenomenal!	13. ¡Está fenomenal!	13. 'Tá a todo dar!	13. 'Tá de aquellas!
14. la policía		14. la ley la chota los "impleáos"	14. la jura la placa
15. Empújelo	15. Empújalo	15. Púchalo	

some factors affecting shift. The four styles that we have noted are the following: formal, informal, intimate and familiar. Distinctions between formal and informal are primarily differences in the care with which one pronounces, although there are sometimes lexical differences. The familiar style incorporates all types of slang that facilitate peer interaction and group adhesion. The intimate style is the family style characterized by loss of fricative endings, voiced fricatives as well as initial syllables in some cases.

Stylistic shifts occur with shifts in topic, speech act, addressee and context. These shifts are distinctive in nature as meaning changes when style is changed. Thus it is not the same to say "Hazme esquina" (*caló* for "Back me up") and "Apóyame" ("I need your support," lit. "Support me"), for the first connotes cultural and generational ties between the interacting participants that the second phrase cannot convey. Stylistic shifts are thus partly related to the composition of the group interacting. Consider the following examples:

Inter-group:	Está bromeando.
Intra-group:	Está vacilando.
Intra-sub-group:	Está cabuliando.

All of these sentences express that someone is kidding around but only the two intra-group expressions convey the idea of "jive." The third example from *caló* also conveys participation in an "in-house" activity. For an equivalent phrase we would have to go to the popular expressions of other areas, like the Argentine: "Está macaneando."

The next chapter will present several cases of shifts in style accompanied by shifts in language and language varieties. A study of shifts in style and code is a study of the relation between *what is said* and *what is done,* where the meaning (or content) determines the expression form or style one uses.

Notes

1. Melvyn C. Resnick, *Phonological Variants and Dialectic Identification in Latin American Spanish* (The Hague: Mouton, 1975).

2. Juan de Valdés, *Diálogo de la lengua* (Madrid: Espasa-Calpe, 1964).

3. Ramón Menéndez-Pidal, *Manual de Gramática Histórica Española* (Madrid: Espasa-Calpe, S.A., 1962), pp. 15–24.

4. J. Vicens Vives, *Aproximación a la Historia de España* (Barcelona: Editorial Vicens, 1968), pp. 39–46.

5. Aurelio Espinosa, "Studies in New Mexican Spanish, Part I, Phonology," *Bulletin University of New Mexico,* Vol. I, No. 2, December 1909, pp. 141–150.

6. *Ibid.*

7. Umberto Eco, *A Theory of Semiotics* (Bloomington: Indiana University Press, 1976).

8. Carey McWilliams, "Zoot Suiters. A Compilation of Correspondence, Clippings, Reports and Documents." Microfilm. UCLA Research Library.

9. *Ibid.*

10. Adolfo Ortega, *Caló Tapestry* (Berkeley, CA: Editorial Justa Publications, 1977), pp. 1–5.

11. Eco, *op. cit.*

12. Lurline Coltharp, *The Tongue of the Tirilones: A Linguistic Study of a Criminal Argot* (University, Alabama: University of Alabama Press, 1965).

13. Ortega, *op. cit.*

14. Resnick, *op. cit.*

CHAPTER 5

Code-Switching Discourse

Code-switching is a particular type of verbal interaction characteristic of bilingual populations in the midst of social change. One type of code-switching evolves in places of *elite* bilingualism where snobbishness leads to isolated shifts to the prestige language. The code-switching that we are interested in here occurs in areas where we find *mass* bilingualism, as in the Southwest, where code-switching is the common communicative code among bilingual Chicanos who with varying degrees of proficiency function in both English and Spanish in informal domains during interaction with other bilingual Chicanos. The reasons for this lingual duality are obvious: language contact of a subordinate lingual-national minority with a politically, economically and linguistically dominant majority. This scenario leads first to the overlapping of functions for the languages and eventually to transition from the subordinate to the dominant language even in those areas previously reserved for the minority language. It is during this dynamic period of bilingualism marked by a great deal of mobility, geographical and social, where role differentiation and appropriation prepare the ground for assimilation and language loss that mass code-switching sets in; its duration is determined by those same social, economic and political factors which create class antagonism and maintain social distance between the two lingual societies as well as force the subordinate community to assimilate to the language of the dominant population.

It is one thing, however, to understand how code-switching originates and another to analyze the functions that language shifts have in the verbal interaction of Chicanos. Since code-switching functions as a "code," although it necessarily implies the use of two codes within the same discourse, this phenomenon must be analyzed as part of the total social, cultural and linguistic systems of Chicanos. This study will thus combine a semiotic approach which analyzes codes as components of a total communicative system with that of discourse analysis in order to analyze a given verbal exchange from the perspective of the understandings and reactions of the participants within particular contexts. As we have discussed in Chapter 3 we will be using the discourse model presented by Labov and Fanshel[1] as well as Halliday's[2] study of functions and cohesion in our analysis of Chicano code-switching. Recalling our branching tree from Chapter 3, we will look at verbal interaction as a form of social interaction where discourse content and functions and linguistic choices and shifts are seen to be manifestations of social, political and ideological processes determined by labor relations in society.

Let us first define the term: code-switching involves shifting from one grammatical system to another. It is distinguished from borrowing in that the latter involves taking a term from another language and adapting it to one's own grammatical system, phonologically, morphologically, syntactically or semantically. Where the two systems are maintained as distinct entities but juxtaposed within the same discourse, we have a case of code-shifting. The examples below distinguish between borrowing and code-shifting:

1. Púchalo pa' trás.
2. Me dio un *ride* pa'l pueblo.

In the first sentence "push" has become an -*ar* Spanish verb, the back vowel has become high, tense and rounded and the alveo-palatal voiceless fricative /š/ has been transformed into an alveo-palatal affricate /č/. The verb *puchar* is now a Chicano Spanish verb, conjugated like any other verb. In the second example, "ride" is a case of code switching, for the retroflex [r], the diphthong [ay] and the alveolar [d] are all English sounds. As Bowen and Stockwell have explained, Spanish diphthongs have higher glides than English ones. Although the English term is preceded by an article assigning it masculine gender, plurality of the term would follow English rather than Spanish morphological rules:

$$un \; ride \qquad [rayd]$$
$$unos \; rides \qquad [raydz]$$

Maintenance of English phonological and morphological rules in shifts constitutes code-switching rather than borrowing.

An analysis of code-switching necessarily requires postulating linguistic as well as semantic rules accounting for cases of code-switching. In a previous study ("Nuestra Circunstancia Lingüística") we began with an inventory of linguistic contexts within which code-switching occurred in taped discourse. In this study, however, we base our analysis of code-switching on the functions of these shifts within discourse. In effect we will focus on the interactional content rather than on linguistic forms, as the latter is determined by the former.

CONTEXT, STYLES AND CULTURE

An analysis of discourse must necessarily take into account the relation between context, culture and language since there is a direct connection between the socio-economic and political standing of a population and the functions and status of its language. The inter-relationship of all these factors operates in the selection of codes for given speech acts in particular situations. In the Southwest the presence of contradictory social and economic factors (which account for the segregation of the Mexican-origin community and the concentration of its work force in low-wage categories as well as the occupational and social mobility of the population) and the use of English in all formal, technical domains have helped preserve Spanish for use in informal, intimate situations, especially in the home and neighborhood. Improvement in educational attainment, urbanization and incorporation into blue-collar and service sectors of the Mexican-origin population led, on the other hand, to increased contact with the English language to the point where it is now assuming the informal functions of the Spanish language. Existing social and economic contradictions which impede full assimilation yet promote desires for social mobility have created conditions propitious for code-switching and for language loss. Today, with renewed interest in the Spanish language and the implementation of bilingual education, it is possible to find academic and formal sessions attended by Chicanos where code-switching is the dominant rule of expression. Generally these sessions are set up to function in Spanish but switching is inevitable for several reasons: the language proficiency of the speakers, the speech acts involved and the style of expression. Code-switching also occurs in conferences and meetings where English is the medium of interaction and the audience is Chicano. Here shifts to particular speech acts—jokes, nostalgic narrations, inducements—call for brief code-switching discourse.

In examining different cases of code-switching, we have found that the discourse model for analyzing verbal interaction offers meaningful insights into this socio-linguistic phenomenon. Past attempts at establishing constraints for code-switching on the basis of topics and themes have failed. Among bilingual Chicanos all topics of discourse, whether they relate to Chicano experiences or not, are discussed in either language. The reason for the shift lies in the *effect* that the speaker wishes to produce with the switch to another code as well as in the *function* of the language choice within the speech act involved. Knowing that verbal interaction, as Labov and Fanshel have pointed out, always communicates information about the speakers, we can then examine code-switching as a study of the speaker's linguistic and cultural system.

The term *culture* is often defined in terms of ethnicity but in our presentation it refers to a person's total experiential and ideological context. Thus within one ethnic group, like the Mexican-origin population, we can find different experiences and different life-styles, i.e., different cultures. The life of a working-class Chicano in a segregated barrio differs in significant ways from that of a middle-class, university-educated Chicano living in the suburbs and from that of a farmworker or undocumented worker living on a farm. Though all of these Chicanos may code-shift, the constraints determining the shifting sequences may vary in relation to particular social, economic and cultural factors. These larger factors which affect all groups in this society must be considered in investigating constraints on code-switching.

Two of the factors that affect the degree of code-switching and the extent of loss of functions for a language are nativity and generation. For a segment of the younger generations of Chicanos today, English has begun to assume all of the functions of Spanish; as we have seen, Spanish language maintenance is strongest among the older generations. Thus a significant number of younger people seem to be shifting from Spanish to English as their primary language. The intermediate step is often code-switching. Glyn Lewis has pointed out that where two languages have overlapping functions, the dominant and literate language will gradually eliminate the subordinate language.[3] When we recall that in the Southwest there is primarily an oral proficiency in Spanish, it becomes important to assess the degree to which the English language has assumed the functions of Spanish. A study of code-switching in relation to age and nativity will allow us to examine the extent of shifting within the various age levels, be they first, second or third generation, and the frequency with which the Spanish language is retained in informal discourse by Chicanos.

In a conversation recorded by Jaime Salazar in Los Angeles, we find that code-shifting is determined in many cases by the addressee, although it is not the sole variable. Shifts in style and speech act also trigger code shifts as evidenced by the following conversation between Jaime and a family of three. The parents, born in Mexico, came to the United States in 1920 and 1934; their son was born and raised in Los Angeles:

Episode A
Mother: — Luego tenemos un tío en Salamanca, el que . . .
Son: — Ese es millonario.
Jaime: — Ah, chi . . .
Son: — Tiene unos, tiene unos terrenos. I mean, just acres and acres. As far as the eye can see.
Mother: — Bueno, a un hijo de regalo le dio su casa, con carro, con tractores, con, ¿cómo se llama? ése pa desgranar, la mazorca . . .

Episode B
Mother: — Esos tíos son por parte de . . .
Son: — ¿De mi abuelita?
Mother: — Siempre vienen siendo parientes.
Son: — Pos, que son, L _____ o R _____ ?
Mother: — L _____ pero como . . .
Son: — ¿Qué no, qué no es mi grandma M _____ L _____ ?
Mother: — Sí.
Son: — Se casaron entre la familia.
Mother: — Bueno, sí, el tío, el muchacho de él es mi primo.

Episode C
Father: — Le sale una plaga al trigo, que se come el granito . . . Y otro día iban a fumigar porque hay un avión que fumiga y . . . los trigos. . . .

Jaime: — ¿Esto lo hace el gobierno o . . . ?
Mother and Son: — No, él, él.
Jaime: — ¿Es de ellos el aeroplano?
Father: — No, no, ellos rentan. Sí.
Jaime: — You gotta have those. In Mexico they do that . . .
Mother: — Y luego tienen una cosa pa hacer agujeros . . .
Son: — About a half a million dollars, Jaime, American money, worth of farming equipment from the United States.

In these interactions, the son shifts to English each time he specifically addresses his peer, Jaime, although he addresses his parents in Spanish. There are some occasions in which he initially addresses Jaime in Spanish and then shifts to English. His shifts occur whenever he wishes to boast about the vastness of his uncle's land and in episode B, about his uncle's wealth. Thus boasts, as much as age, trigger the shift, for an evaluative style seems to call for a shift among bilingual second-generation Chicanos, as we shall see later.

In the case above, the two code-shifters are in their early twenties and shift only when they address each other. Peer code-shifting among young Chicanos, however, is not the only case found in the Mexican-origin community. We will now consider a series of interactional episodes recorded by Yolanda Guerrero during dinner at a Chicano home in National City, California. In this particular border area household, there are two generations present: first-generation parents born in Mexico, who have resided in National City for over twenty years, and second-generation children, all born in the United States. A third generation, a visiting grandmother, also appears in the recorded episodes. Although she lives in Tijuana, her role in the interaction is much like that of any older foreign-born resident in this country who has lived primarily in a segregated Mexican-origin community, who speaks only Spanish but understands and responds to English discourse. The daughters are all bilingual and their ages are as follows: D-1, 23 years old; D-2, 19 years old; and D-3, 14 years old:

Episode A-1
D-2:   — Vente a comer, abuela.
D-1:   — Andale, abuelilla, vente a comer. (to Mother) Oh, háblale a tu mamá.
Mother: — Andale, Merilú.
D-3:   — Hee, hee.
D-2:   — Merilú.
D-3:   — ¡Merilú! Andale, *Marylou*.
D-2:   — Se me afigura la Merilú A . . .
All: — Ha, Ha, Ha.
Mother: — El otro día la vi muy acompañada.
Father: — ¿La chaparrita?
Mother: — ¿Tú quieres caldo? ¿Quién quiere caldo?

Episode A-2

D-3: — Mom . . . I'm worried. I can't find my ballet shoes.

D-2: — Stupid, you always lose everything, huh?

D-3: — No, but the last time, Saturday, he says I didn't take 'em.

Father: — ¿Por qué . . . ?

Mother: — ¿Por qué no lo encontraste? Me habló a la tienda.

D-3: — No, Saturday, Saturday . . .

Mother: — ¿No lo llevaste?

D-3: — No, Saturday, I didn't take 'em because it was jazz, just jazz. I took my regular shoes. The last time I took 'em was Thursday. And then I had to tell my Dad to pick 'em up.

Mother: — El lunes, nn'ayer, me llamó por teléfono.

Father: — Eso porque es muy cuidadosa.

. . . .

D-1: — Ha, ha, ha.

Episode A-3

Grandma: — No tiene ningún sabor.

Mother: — No tiene ningún sabor.

D-1: — No, ¿sabes por qué? porque cuando uno las hace boil, se le sale el sabor.

Grandma: — Y de todas maneras, no sé a mí . . .

Mother: — Pero estuvieron a vapor, no boil.

D-1: — No, pero de todos modos se le sale.

Episode A-4

Father: — ¡Que te esperes!

D-3: — No, I just want to answer the phone.

Father: — Te voy a prohibir estrictamente que le des tu número de teléfono a muchachos y a muchachas.

Episode A-5

Mother: — No te estés columpiando, vas a . . .

Father: — Están chuecas las sillas, las patas de las sillas.

D-3: — Oh, well, M _____ 's weighing on it.

Episode A-6

D-3: — Coffee, coffee, coffee.

D-2: — Cada día se lleva su coffee pot upstairs.

D-1: — ¿Y qué tiene que me lleve mi coffee pot upstairs?

D-3: — You think you're studying. Acting like she's studying.

Mother: — And she's asleep.

D-3: — I know.

Mother: — Ha, Ha, Ha. With a book like this; she's . . . with a book on the side.

The six episodes under A indicate that Spanish is the usual language of the parents and the grandmother. The bilingual daughters, on the other hand, shift from Spanish to English or vice versa throughout the dinner conversation. We can then make the following generalizations:

a) if the grandmother is the addressee, all use Spanish.

b) if the father and mother are addressing each other, they use Spanish.

c) if the parents are addressing the children they use Spanish.*

(*This particular rule does not apply however in episode 6 where the mother is teasing D-1 in the presence of her English-speaking boyfriend.)

d) the shifting of the daughters varies according to speech act, style and connotation of signs used, as well as to addressee, as we shall see in additional episodes.

SHIFTING OF DAUGHTERS IN EPISODES A-1 to A-6:

From these recorded episodes, it is evident that the youngest daughter prefers to use English, although in addressing the grandmother she uses Spanish. We have learned that D-3 was monolingual in Spanish when she began her schooling and in fact spent several years with her babysitting grandmother in Tijuana before she entered elementary school. In these episodes, D-3 used English in responses to Spanish reprimands (A-4 and A-5) and to requests in Spanish (see questions in A-2). She does however tease her grandmother in Spanish (A-1). For the youngest daughter, English appears to be not only the usual language but also the code of an indulged adolescent who easily disarms her elders in English. As we shall see in other episodes, she is bilingual and can shift easily to Spanish when she desires.

In the A episodes D-2 uses Spanish consistently except in A-2 where she shifts "to insult" her younger sister. Here it is the addressee as well as the speech act which calls for the use of English. The term *stupid* in the language of American teenagers does not carry the force of *estúpida* in Spanish. In fact, in the context of a tag question, the term denotes an act of teasing rather than an insult. The older daughter, D-1, uses only Spanish in these episodes. Her only shift occurs in the phrase "uno las hace boil" in reference to the cooking of the eggplant. Even her mother responds with the same phrase: "estuvieron a vapor, no boil," although the word *hervir* is as common in that household as *boil*. The parents, both Spanish dominant, received their public school instruction in Mexico. Thus this particular case of shifting must be studied in terms of connotation since the shift responds to an attempt at assuaging the criticism of how the eggplant turned out. Thus the English term *boil* softens the culinary impact and the critical impact. If "boiled eggplant" sounds distasteful, so does *berenjena hervida. Hacer boil la eggplant* however makes the combination tolerable and more importantly introduces a sense of humor in the discussion where the mother's cooking is being evaluated.

The phrase *hacer* + *English infinitive* is common in Chicano code-switching, particularly in the Arizona area but not exclusively. Thus in addition to phrases like *hacer boil* in the recorded episode we commonly have phrases like *hacer go* and *hacer write*. Expressions in Spanish of *hacer* + *infinitive,* however, do not necessarily belong to the same category as those in the shifted phrases. In *hacer hervir* we have a specific Spanish phrase where no intervening noun phrase need appear, although it is possible as in *hacerlo hervir.* In the English translation, a noun phrase is necessary as in *make it boil,* although expressions like *make do* also exist. Expressions like *make write* or *make go* as in **I'm going to make go* for "I'm going to go" do not occur. Obviously expressions like *make it go* do occur. In the recorded episode, the English *boil* is thus a substitute for *hervir* within the grammatical context *hacer hervir.* In what way does this case differ from the other *hacer* + *English infinitive* expressions? At the surface level Spanish *hacer* + *infinitive* expressions are very much alike:

1. Lo hice salir.   (I made him leave./I made it come out.)
2. Lo hice sacar.   (I made them/someone take him/it out. i.e., I had him/it taken out.)
3. Lo hice hervir.   (I made it boil/I boiled it.)
4. Me hizo hit.   (He hit me.)
5. Lo hice write.   (I wrote it.)

In the first two sentences the subject of the main clause and the subject of the subordinated clause are not equivalent. In the third case, although the meaning with equivalent noun phrases is common at the surface level, it can be derived from structures where the noun phrases are not equivalent (b), even when the sense is inchoative as in (a):

Lo hice hervir
- a) I made it boil/I boiled it./I made it come to a boil.
  (i.e., I made $_S$[It + inchoative + boil]$_S$)
- b) I had it boiled (i.e., I had someone boil it.)

In the case of sentences 4 and 5 the subordinate clauses have equivalent noun phrase subjects. Were these to be expressed totally in Spanish, the meaning would correspond to structures like those of sentences 1 and 2:

   a. Me hizo pegar.   (He had someone hit me.)
   b. Lo hice escribir.   (I made him write./I had it written by someone.)

Thus the *hacer* + *English infinitive* are not mere translations of Spanish sentences, although *hacer* in Spanish can have a similar function as in the case of *hacer hervir* which could easily be expressed as *poner a hervir* (to bring to a boil, to make it boil), where *hacer* indicates starting or actively initiating an activity. In the code-shifted sentences the *hacer* not only functions as an auxiliary element which indicates tense for the non-conjugated English verb but denotes inchoateness as well. Thus *Me hizo hit* would be equivalent to *Se puso a pegarme* (He began to hit me). In the last example, *Lo hice write,* the expression indicates completion of an action. Thus *hacer* in these code-shifted expressions not only indicates tense but aspect—perfect aspect—as well for unmarked English infinitives.

The code-shifting of the three daughters in a home context where the parents communicate primarily in Spanish reflects a common practice in the majority of Chicano homes. For despite the fact that the daughters are native speakers of Spanish, with the competence to tease and insult in the Spanish language, today English has become their usual language, and Spanish, a second language. In spite of the fact that the family resides near the Mexican border, that both parents are foreign-born and Spanish-dominant, and that there is a great deal of contact with Mexicans because of close relatives residing in Tijuana, language shifts are quite evident, with the two languages having overlapping functions for some roles in the home. Increased language contact and social mobility have obviously been stronger determining factors than proximity to the Mexican border or the foreign origin of the parents in deciding language choice in the home. The particular types of code-switching which occur require a closer look at the factors triggering these shifts.

FAMILY CONSTRAINTS IN CODE-SWITCHING

In the next three episodes we will be primarily interested in examining the extent of code-switching within the home domain in an informal situation and the types of shifts involved in relation to family roles and speech acts:

Episode B
Father: — Dame una tortilla mientras que estoy co . . .
D-2:   — Ah, ¿Qué es esto? ¿Tortillas?
D-3:   — Tortillas de harina.
Grandma: — No te dije que había hecho tortillas calientitas, que vinieras a comerlas.
D-3:   — . . . Pass me . . . the . . . filet . . . mignon. Pass me the beaners. Uh.
D-1:   — Yo quiero ensalada.
D-3:   — . . . Ah, it's hot.
D-2:   — Here you are.
Grandma: — Pásame una a mí.
D-3:   — Uh. Toma, 'tá caliente de abajo.
Grandma: — No, no quiero tortilla.
D-2:   — Here, Y _____ , want some beans?
D-1:   — No, thank you.
D-1:   — ¿No vas a comer carne, abuelilla?
D-2:   — Pass la ensalada.
Grandma: — Es que voy a comer sin ganas.
D-2:   — I've never even tasted that before.
D-3:   — How do you eat it? Whose idea was it you buy it?
D-2:   — Has to be Y _____ 's idea. Ha, Ha, Ha.
D-1:   — No, ha, ha, ha.
Mother: — M _____ , pon esto.

D-1:   — My grandmother brought it.
D-2:   — Oh, that takes care of it.
Mother: — Allí hay gravy en la ollita.

Episode C
D-3:   — Eh, Mom, ¿cómo se come la eggplant?
Grandma: — Lo que quiera.
Mother: — ¿Cómo?, con la boca.
D-1:   — Son frijoles de, de bote, ¿verdá?
        — [Dishes]
Mother: — Porque los otros son con chorizo.
D-1:   — Saben de bote.
Mother: — No sé qué hago.

. . . .

Grandma: — Ponle tantita de esta, mantequilla.
D-3:   — No quiero.
Grandma: — Mira.
Mother: — Le gustó.
Grandma: — Mira, es que no la has probado.
Grandma: — Yo, no más te la puse pa que la probaras, niña, pero así no te va a gustar, ándale.
D-1:   — I think it'll probably taste a lot better frita.
Grandma: — Esta no comió nada; está rebuena, ésta.
Mother: — Mira, así con mantequilla.
Grandma: — Mira, mantequilla o lo que sea.
D-3:   — Does it taste good with butter on top?
Mother: — . . . [Aside to Father]
D-3:   — Doesn't taste like nothing to me!
Mother: — A ver deja probarlo.
D-3:   — You know what it tastes like?
Grandma: — Sabe a lo que le pongan arriba.
D-1:   — ¿A qué?
Mother: — ¿No quieres café? (background)
Father: — Un poquito aquí.
D-3:   — That, that stuff my Mom makes. What's it called?
D-2:   — No, no he comido.
D-3:   — It's soft like this, like . . .
Grandma: — Pos, si le pones esa sal arriba, sabe a esa sal arriba, si le pones crema, pos sabe a crema . . .
D-2:   — Tú nomás frijoles y carne. Ni ensalada te apuesto que te has servido.
Mother: — No, nada.
D-3:   — That's it. Like zucchini.

Episode D
Father: — Tú, cómo comes tú, bárbara; todos acabamos y . . .

Mother: — ¿Estás contando la comida? Que coma yo más despacito es otra cosa. Pero . . . tú y la Y _____ comen como máquinas.

D-3:   — I'm gonna go look for my ballet shoes.

Grandma: — Allí, don Luis llega y brum [hand-slap], vámonos.

D-3:   — They don't walk away, they tip-toe away.

Mother: — Ora esta semana fuimos a comer la Y _____ y yo. A los cinco minutos ya tenía limpio el plato y yo tenía a penas empezado.

Grandma: — Se acostumbra uno.

Mother: — Y yo no. A mí me gusta masticar y saborear.

D-1:   — Ay sí, they call her the expert taster, Miss Taste Bud. Ha, Ha [sarcastic].

Grandma: — Le duran así más los dientes, ¿verdá? El aparato digestivo.

If we look at the number of interventions in episodes B, C and D, we will find that there are twice as many exchanges in Spanish as in English in this National City household. There are 45 exchanges in Spanish and 22 in English but most of the Spanish verbal interaction is produced by the parents and the grandmother, since they account for 32 of these exchanges. The three daughters apparently use Spanish at home about one-third of the time. Most of their exchanges in Spanish are addressed to their parents and grandmother except when reinforcing their comments; with each other they interact in English.

In episodes B, C and D, the youngest daughter's usual language is still English except when she addresses her grandmother directly (B and C) or when labeling ("tortillas de harina"). In episode C, however, she addresses her mother in Spanish, although as we saw before in A-2, she also addresses her in English. In that episode we saw that she mitigated her negligence in losing her ballet shoes by shifting to English. In analyzing her Spanish request in episode C ("Eh, mom, ¿cómo se come la eggplant?"), we must consider the entire conversational context. This request had previously been stated in English in episode B ("How do you eat it? Whose idea was it you buy it?") without receiving a response, for a simple reason: she had made two requests of no one in particular and only the second one was answered. In episode C, then, reinforcement of her request calls for a repetition of the question, now addressed specifically to her mother, in Spanish. It is thus reinforcement of the speech act that triggers this shift from her usual language, English.

The middle daughter, D-2, on the other hand, shifts much more often between the two languages. She addresses the family as a whole in Spanish, as evidenced by her request for information on the food in episode B. Although no one in particular is being directly addressed, she could be expecting a response from her mother who cooked the dinner: "¿Qué es esto? ¿Tortillas?" When she makes a comment questioning the choice of vegetable with an assertion: "I've never even tried that before," she shifts to English. Thus questioning of judgments calls for an amelioration or a mitigated statement in English. In episode C, however, annoyed by her younger sister's insistence on determining the taste of the eggplant, she intervenes in Spanish. Here an English intervention would sound like support of her carrying-on, as it would place her at a peer level. Her negative reply in Spanish is meant to put a stop to her sister's insistence. When her sister persists in asserting that there *is* another vegetable that tastes like eggplant, she attacks her by suggesting that she would not know what anything else tasted like since she only eats meat and beans. Thus in sibling rivalry when the older sister tries to belittle D-3, she (D-2) shifts to the non-peer language: Spanish. By so doing, she assumes the role of a "wiser" sister and is reinforced by her mother who agrees with her appraisal.

The oldest daughter, D-1, also shifts often between English and Spanish. In these episodes we find that whenever she addresses her parents and grand-mother, she uses Spanish, except when she uses an evaluative style during that interaction. Thus in response to her mother's teasing in Spanish about eating so fast that D-1 resembles a machine, the oldest daughter retaliates with sarcasm about her mother's gourmet airs in eating slowly. Again the English expression mitigates the cutting edge of her remark and reduces it to the level of teasing. In her interaction with her sisters she generally answers in the language of the request. In episode C, she shifts from English to Spanish at the end of the utterance: "I think it'll probably taste a lot better *frita.*" "Fried eggplant" is not as appetizing as "eggplant *frita*" just as previously boil was preferable to the humdrum *hervir.* The semantic combinations that can be produced through the shifting of codes is boundless.

Thus in this family, shifting is determined by two major constraints: the addressee and the connotation of the sign or utterance involved. These shifts often function metalingually and metaphorically. As is evident, they allow the discourse of bilinguals to have a broad range of readings and allow the speakers to inject a broad range of connotations into their speech. A study of code-shifting is thus a study of the semantic or cultural features that make up the various semantic fields in the codes of Chicanos.

METALINGUAL AND LINGUISTIC FACTORS

Another factor that must be considered in analyzing code-switching is the individual's grammatical proficiency and sociolinguistic competence in both languages, that is, his ability to use the languages appropriately in given situations, whatever the varieties. Native speakers of a language do not automatically have command of all the varieties or styles that exist in that language. As we have noted, the acquisition of some varieties requires special instruction or contact with speakers of those varieties. In the Southwest, Chicanos have been deprived of formal instruction in Spanish for many, many years until recent implementation of transitional programs in the early years of elementary school. It is then not surprising that some Chicanos lack the more technical and formal styles of standard Spanish. It is also true that some Chicanos have a comparatively higher proficiency in English; thus formal, more technical situations call for a shift to English. In the presence of speakers of standard varieties of Spanish, some Chicanos will shift immediately to English lest they be criticized for particular conjugations or word choices. This type of code-shifting reflects the social standing of the Spanish varieties spoken in the Southwest and the disdain with which these are viewed by educated Mexicans, Latin Americans and other Hispanics. Aware that all of these cases of code-switching are common, we are nonetheless primarily interested in the code-switching that occurs among Chicanos who accept and in fact enjoy shifting from one language to another, who are able to express themselves in both languages about a given topic, and who automatically code-shift whenever they interact with compatible bilinguals.

Although formal situations call for care in speaking, speakers in informal situations may also be conscious about their language. Thus a speaker who feels uncomfortable about a given pronunciation may shift to the other language, even in informal situations, as in the following examples:

1. He's working there as sheepsh . . . , de trasquilero, pues.
2. Lloró porque lo pelis . . . pellis . . . he pinched him.

Oftentimes frequency of use in particular contexts and domains automatically triggers a shift to the other language. In these cases, if the medium of interaction is Spanish, for example, and a shift to English occurs, a speaker may "correct" himself and repeat the utterance in Spanish, as in the examples below:

1. But when you have the chance . . . cuando tienes la chansa . . .
2. Que . . . it's our fault. Es la culpa de nosotros.

If however code-switching is the accepted mode of interaction, no such "self-correction" occurs, as in the case below.

En términos de publications, la cosa no se ha hecho bien, bien, tal vez, porque hemos hecho muchos errores y estamos confusos y we got to straighten ourselves out because we are the ones who are doing it. But when you think in terms of TV, radio, films, entonces la cosa cambia— there is an audience that is easier to move.[4]

A Chicano whose proficiency is greater in English than in Spanish often feels himself pressured by his peers to code-shift, especially if that is the mode of interaction or if Spanish is the primary language of discourse. In these cases the speaker may simulate Spanish discourse through the introduction of Spanish connectors and adverbials, as in the example below:

I've been interested in this as a sociologist pero también as a person who has lived in an area of dynamic transition en los últimos años y I explain it this way. This is discounting that there is a lot of negative feeling por los gringos toward things that are traditional.[5]

This exchange occurred during a Chicano workshop on language and related issues. Since the meeting was conducted primarily in Spanish, the speaker of the interaction above later apologized for shifting to English in the following way.

What is happening is that the vast system is swallowing us up. Excuse me for not having expressed myself in Spanish, *but this is an important thing.* [our emphasis][6]

The speaker felt that his comments were important enough that they had to be expressed in his dominant language. The message, whether intended or not, is that the Spanish language is for non-serious discourse while English is the language for serious and important discourse.

Code-shifting can also function metalinguistically to initiate or end discourse and as a transition device to allow continuity of the narration. In the following exchange, for example, the discourse is initiated and ended in English. The Spanish discourse functions as an expansion of the English utterances which form the skeleton of the speech event. In fact the Spanish part offers no new information and is a filler which allows the speaker a chance to control the floor for a few extra seconds and to reinforce her point. Thus the speech act of reinforcement triggers the switch. This reinforcement also allows the speaker to introduce local color into the conversation, as we can see in the discourse marked off by braces:

> When a Chicana in El Paso brought a bookmobile [y que biblioteca del pueblo, que quién sabe qué.] all of a sudden circulation of books in El Paso went up by a thousand percent in two weeks. [Entraron a los barrios. Y no nada más las chavalas; las viejitas y los viejitos estaban leyendo. Lo que está pasando es que la gente está leyendo porque se entra a los barrios y una bola de chavalitos primero y de repente de todo tipo de gente.] People want it.[7]

The English discourse is thus a synthesis of the intended message while the Spanish is an expansion which focuses on a description of local details. As a transitional device, code-shifting often allows for repetition of each point raised. This technique of shifting for elaboration in a narrative exchange is evident below:

Uncle: — El estuvo allí, en el San Quintín, ún tiempo de, de d'ese cabrón de guard. Allí se voló cuatro cabrones.
Mariana: — Killed them?
Uncle: — They made a riot, you know, and he came in there and . . . mean, he was born, they're born, them kind of a people are born, cómo diré . . .
Aunt: — Que no tienen miedo . . .
Uncle: — No tienen miedo a la vida, you know. They're not scared of, they're not scared of, of their life. They risk their life on anything. No tienen miedo . . . this came out in the paper. El mismo me platicó.
Aunt: — Las muchachas ya están casadas.
Uncle: — El salió en . . . estuvo bastante en el papel. He went in there, you know, he settled things down.
Mariana: — What?
Uncle: — Allí en San Quintín. Tenían al warden agarráo y todo, ¿ves? Y éste se metió. Risk his life. Y luego estuvo mucho tiempo todavía allí . . .

In this episode the first exchange sets the stage in Spanish: a man who worked as a guard in San Quentin killed four prisoners. The subsequent English and Spanish discourse offers an elaboration: there was a prison riot, the warden was held hostage, the Chicano guard risked his life by going into the danger area and settling things down. His evaluation of this man's bravery appears in English first, with a repetition of the innateness of the attribute. As he grasps for a better expression, he uses a Spanish crutch-phrase— cómo diré"—and his wife supplies a phrase in Spanish. Although he repeats the phrase, he immediately translates it and continues to repeat it, for his evaluative style is in English. As a transitional device and to conclude the evaluation, he returns to the Spanish phrase. The role of the press is expressed in both languages, in English first; the guard's personal relation of the story to him is announced in Spanish. Additional praise about the guard's accomplishments appear in English but once he returns to the narration, he shifts back to Spanish. In this final exchange he again praises the guard in English. Thus the shifting, in addition to marking shifts in speech acts or discourse styles, also functions metalinguistically and allows for a continuation of the narration linking attributes and narrative details.

Semantic constraints thus appear to be fundamental in triggering code-switching. "Semantic" of course covers a broad range of meanings and levels of signification. Linguistic structures and categories are useful, however, in the analysis of discourse, as structuralist critics analyzing literature have discovered. In the exchange which follows, the discourse may be divided into functional categories or units, à la Greimas, much like a sentence is divided into grammatical categories: actants, actions and adverbials:

> That's not the way we write; most Chicano writers in all fields, whether we talk about history, sociology, you name it, most están escribiendo en inglés porque reconocen que el producto de lo que escriben va a ser más fácil distribuirlo en ese nivel porque digamos hay una marqueta más grande. Yo lo veo como un problema porque a cierto grado dice uno you want to be effective at the highest level that you can, so, do you include as a criterio say, a publication component that all materials be published bilingually? And, eso es fácil, pero una vez que están entretejidos, ¿cómo?[8]

This verbal interaction begins with a challenge of a previously stated position about the language of Chicano writers. (The other participants at the Las Cruces meeting were characterizing the Chicano as bilingual and for them bilingualism meant code-switching. One of the participants had specifically asserted: "No puedo escribir just in one language.") This challenge is followed by specific information on the publication and distribution of Chicano works. The subject of his argument—the Chicano writer—and all the qualifications pertaining to the actant, appear in English. In fact we could say that the elements functioning as a noun phrase are in English. The introduction of the verb phrase, or the action, marks a shift to Spanish. The adverbial clause indicating the reason for the action also appears in Spanish. In the next sentence the adverbial is rephrased in terms of principles of excellence and effectiveness, in English. In proposing these high "standards," he uses the English language, for his comment reflects the values of American business: "you want to be effective at the highest level." This shift in fact marks an introduction to a cultural code (à la Barthes),[9] that of the managerial class, which in this country, is primarily English-speaking. Interestingly enough, the discourse answers the following questions bilingually: Who = English, What = Spanish, Why = English. Metalinguistically, the English language also serves to bring his interaction, initiated in English, to a close.

COHESION AND COHERENCE IN CODE-SWITCHING

Metalinguistic functions can also be studied as cohesive functions. Halliday has defined cohesion as a relational concept where "it is not the presence of a particular class of item that is cohesive, but the relation between one item and another."[10] Coulthard notes the Widdowson distinction between cohesion and coherence as parallel to that made between sentence and utterance:

> Sentences combine to form texts and the relations between sentences are aspects of grammatical cohesion; utterances combine to form discourse and the relations between them are aspects of discourse coherence.[11]

This distinction between cohesion and coherence will be explored further as we examine code-switching discourse.

Halliday identifies various types of cohesion which provide links between sentences and propositions: reference, conjugation, substitution, ellipsis and lexical.[12] For Halliday cohesion is not a structural relation but rather a semantic relation effected in the text through repetitions, omission, occurrences of certain words and constructions which signal the need to relate one passage to something else in order to interpret it.[13] These relations can be subdivided in terms of the type of reference within a text or beyond the text: anaphoric (pointing back to some previous item), cataphoric (pointing forward to the following element) or exophoric (pointing outside the text).

As we shall see in the following examples, cohesion is one of the functions of code-switching, for language shifts serve to lend cohesiveness to the verbal interaction and coherence to the social interaction taking place.

In interaction between Chicanos, often the reference is strictly exophoric in that it points to a reality outside the text, that is, to the social and ethnic conditions of the speakers. In these cases the shifts are primarily at the junctural level and merely serve to link sentences as well as link the speaker to the other participants in t   conversation, as in the previously quoted example:

> I've been interested in this as a sociologist *pero también* as a person who has lived in an area of dynamic transition *en los últimos años, y* I explain it this way. This is discounting that there is a lot of negative feeling *por los gringos* toward things that are traditional.

These junctures, whether they be conjunctions or prepositional phrases, are not merely ethnic markers, but elements relating various propositions.

Code-switching also allows for cohesion through reiteration, which is a form of lexical cohesion involving the repetition of a lexical item, synonym, near-synonym, a superordinate or a general word. In code-switching synonyms are provided through translations of various elements. Often these occur at the level of exchange, with one participant encouraging the other to proceed by translating the last remark of the other participant or it may occur within the utterances of the same speaker. Consider the following interaction between two bilingual Chicanos:

A. — ¡Híjole! ¡qué buena co . . . , ¡qué suave huele!, C., smells really good, huh?
    — It is really good.

B. — ¡A quién me fui encontrar!
    — I know, of all people, ¡ah que d'ésta!

In the first example, the reiteration reaffirms the speaker's approval of the cooking but in the second case, the second speaker provides an English equivalent of the Spanish meaning, expressing surprise and amusement, although it is not a literal translation. What is established then is a continuity of meaning or coherence. Code-switching thus has a double function: it provides both cohesion and coherence.

The function of code-switching as a relational element, however, cannot be studied in isolated examples but rather in entire episodes. What follows is an analysis of two episodes featuring interaction between two former UCSD Chicana students about to graduate. The interaction takes place in the apartment shared by several students; here we will focus on two episodes, one dealing with a home topic—bottled water—and one dealing with a public agency—the employment office. Our primary intent is to examine the function of code-switching in terms of the underlying propositions in order to determine its role in providing coherence between utterances and in the interaction. We will examine both implicit and explicit propositions as well as the sequencing of speech acts and the actions and reactions of the speakers to the underlying propositions:

Episode 1. (Recorded by María Rojas)
1. M: — ¡oh, C _____ , vino el del agua!
2. C: — Uh huh.
3. M: — Y le dije, le dije que sí, te acuerdas que me dijites que le dijera, que tú querías que te dejaran otro, otra botella.
4. C: — Mmhuh.
5. M: — Pues le pregunté que si le 'bías dicho y me dijo que no, que he hadn't heard from you or anything like that. And . . .
6. C: — I called the office though.
7. M: — Oh, but so, no but this guy didn't know anything, so I told him, I told him, you know, le pregunté, que cuántos, cuántas botellas te dejaba antes y me dijo que dos.
8. C: — ¿Que dos? ¿a cada cuándo?
9. M: — Me dijo.
10. C: — Dos al mes.
11. M: — Ajá, dos al mes, y le dije, 'pues ella dijo que quería una botella más.
12. C: — Y dejaste otra más . . . te dije. (chuckle)
13. M: — Es lo que tú dijistes.

14. C: — ¿Cuándo?

15. M: — Te acuerdas que dijites que se nos 'bía 'cabado muy pronto las dos éstas y que we should have another one.

16. C: — Oh yeah? I said that? Uh-uh.

17. M: — Yes, you did, and then you said you were gonna call 'em up and tell 'em.

18. C: — Oh, no me acuerdo, pero, pero pues tres al mes, son mushas, because they're, they're ah . . . two seventy-five each.

19. M: — Really?

20. C: — Ah-há.

21. M: — Oye, pero, pero, este, entonces . . .

22. C: — Because I don't cook with them, I just drink 'em.

23. M: — Pero, pero, entonces dijo que, que . . .

24. C: — Pero ¿qué le hace?

25. M: — 'bía dejado estas dos botellas 'horita, puso una aquí y dejó otras dos y dijo, dijo, depende de lo que quieran next month.

26. C: — Yeah, I mean, it doesn't matter. I can always tell 'em not to leave that many, pero, porque, es mucho, voy estar pagando como diez al mes, de pura agua.

27. M: — ¿Sabes qué?

28. C: — ¿Eh?

29. M: — Pero, pero no dijites que we were gonna divide it among us?

30. C: — Well, I don't know if you guys want to.

31. M: — Well, of course, if they're all, we're using it, we should.

32. C: — Then o.k., then.

33. M: — Oye, pero, ¿sabes qué otra cosa, este, 'staba pensado?

34. C: — ¿Qué?

35. M: — Que allí donde venden l'agua, las venden las esas cosas a seventy-five cents.

36. C: — I know, that's what I want to do, pero, pero es que no sé dónde, es que nosotros a veces en la casa como, cuando, when we ran out of water, it's ten cents per gallon and that's . . . no, ten cents per, uh, half gallon and that's five gallons so you can fill it up with one dollar, you can fill one up with one dollar, and it's a lot cheaper if you, if you take it to ah . . .

37. M: — Yeah, well there's one over there, over at Fed Mart, over on Genesee and Balboa.

38. C: — Oh, uh-huh.

39. M: — And it has a sign up there and it says "seventy-five cents for five gallons."

40. C: — Oh, then it's seventy-five cents for five gallons, this is less than half what I, what we'll be paying if they deliver, but, uh, we have to have a bottle, that's the problem.

41. M: — ¿Pos no te puedes robar una 'ehas botellah?

42. C: — Sí, pero, if we stop the delivery they wouldn't leave us that cooler either.

43. M: — ¡Oh! ¿se llevan todo pa' 'trás?
44. C: — Sí.
45. M: — ¡Oh! (chuckle)

In this particular episode M. and C. are conversing about the delivery of bottled water. M. initially reports her interaction with the delivery man and states a number of propositions which C. disputes. C. however dismisses the misunderstanding by indicating that the problem can be easily solved. M. then proposes an alternative solution, which C. accepts; M. then suggests another solution, which C. rejects, although seemingly she accepts, by pointing out disadvantages of the second proposal. M.'s response to this last problem is also rejected through the presentation of additional disadvantages.

The entire dialogue involves reference to particular moments and propositions related to those moments. References providing continuity throughout the text are of two types: anaphoric and cataphoric. The following scheme pinpoints the reference points:

Point A is the interaction between M. and C. on a previous occasion.

Point B is the interaction between M. and the delivery man (X), who brought the bottled water.

Point C is the present interaction.

Point D represents a future moment suggested by M.

There are implicit and explicit propositions underlying each previous interaction, according to M. These are outlined below:

Point A
1. M. and C. talked about the bottled water.
2. C. expressed a need for an extra bottle of water.
3. C. said she would call X's company.
4. C. said the water was for everyone.
Point B
1. M. talked to X and requested extra bottle of water.
2. X denied A-3. (see above)
3. X left extra bottle of water.
Point D
1. M. proposes all apartment dwellers split cost.
2. M. proposes water be purchased elsewhere.
3. M. proposes theft of water bottle.

The interaction that takes place at Point C is thus a sequence of references to Points A, B and D and the propositions underlying the recalled interactions or the proposed propositions. In this episode, C invariably disagrees with M.'s propositions; consequently there are a number of reiterations, requests for clarification, denials and requests for confirmation. When M. makes several proposals for the future which presuppose certain propositions of the past, C. requests confirmation of one proposal but rejects two indirectly by providing additional information. This episode is initiated in Spanish and the interaction is primarily in Spanish, as we would expect, given the topic and the context. The English language is used for expansions (lines 5, 22), reiteration (lines 7, 15, 17, 22, 26, 31), questioning of propositions (lines 18, 19) and rejection of the propositions (lines 40, 42). These reiterations or denials are often preceded by Spanish junctures, conjunctions and adverbs to provide cohesion between sentences. As we shall see later, there are ideological implications to using the dominant language to deny, challenge or reject a proposition.

In the next episode, it is evident that both M. and C. share a great deal of cultural information, as their reactions are the same and one can complete the sentences of the other. References to previous conversations allow for ellipsis and substitution. The topic here is the employment office; the primary language for discussion of this technical subject is English:

Episode 2. (Recorded by María Rojas)
M: — I haven't called that fellow to ask him if he got my d'este . . .
C: — He might not even be in when you call.
M: — But I did call the other professor and I told him my d'este was gonna be in late.
C: — And what did he say?
M: — He, he wasn't there, I left a message . . . well I left a message and I left him my phone number.
C: — For him to call you?
M: — Y no me ha llamado.
C: — For him to call you if he didn't agree with it.
M: — Pues ¿verdad? ¿por qué no? . . . y a 'mejor ni agarró el mensaje. (pause)
C: — Mmm.
M: — What a drabby looking office th-uh, ¿verdá? it makes your spirit, your spirit even worse when you go in there . . . y lue'o la puerta 'tá toda mugrosa, and I'm sure si la limpiaran once a week it wouldn't be that dirty . . . pero si, just what you said, C _____ , you can tell right away it was something that was put in there because, because, you know, like, the other place was overcrowded.
C: — I mean, that doesn't have anything to do with women.
M: — Oh yeah, I know . . . pero ¡híjola! ¡qué feo se mira!, ni una matita ni nada.
C: — Te da, te da'l, your . . . spirit goes shiuuuu.
M: — I know, I know, the minute you, it's so ¡híjola! It feels terrible! . . . fíjate y lue'o 'stá pos, un montón de pobre gente te apues . . . te apuesto que mucha de'sa gente tiene familias y . . . y . . . pues gente como yo, pues yo sí ne'sito el dinero pero, mm, si, si no puedo 'garrar dinero, pues no me voy a morir de hambre, you know, pero, pero a mucha gente que tiene gente that depend on

them an', an' que me da más coraje cuando, miro en los periódicos o en ah, ah, eh, en televisión que dicen que . . .

C: — Que la gente no quiere trabajar.

M: — Que no quiere trabajar la gente.

C: — Yo no sé de dónde agarran eso.

(pause)

M: — But at least they weren't, I, maybe, ¡híjola! we got to the point that, the, the people are satisfied with anything ¿verdá? digo que, que at least they didn't get, they weren't . . .

C: — Snobbish?

M: — Snobbish, ajá, at least, porque se me'hace que my spirits would've even gone down worse, if I had met someone that was, had, would be bitchy with me.

C: — But, how could they afford to be bitchy in a place like that?

M: — Well they can, let me tell you, 'cause I've been in the employment office in Indio and los cabrones son ¡híjola! . . . una vez hasta ya mero me hacían llorar.

C: — No, I mean in a little torn down office like that.

M: — Ah . . . no, but I don't mean snobby, C _____ , I meant, you know, que, que, que they just give you a hard time.

C: — Oh . . .

M: — Como que, si l'está saliendo la d'esta de su, de su, mira te embarrates allí en . . . como que's, come que, que'l dinero is coming out of their pockets, or something.

In this episode M. refers indirectly through substitutions (d'este) to a request for unemployment compensation left at the employment office. Most of the propositions are stated by M. while C. reiterates M.'s comments or makes requests for expansions. Only at the beginning does C. question M.'s implicit intent of calling the employment office. Thereafter she merely reaffirms what M. states.

There are a number of propositions underlying the interaction; two of them are implicit, stating the rights of the unemployed and the obligations of the employment office to its clients:

Implicit Propositions:

1. Employment office personnel should serve the public in a courteous manner.

2. Employment offices should be pleasant places for the public.

The other propositions are outlined below, with expansions of these, offering additional information or causes listed to the right:

Propositions:	*Expansions:*
	(summarized in translation)
1. Public employees are not respon-	a. They have not returned my call.
sible to the public.	b. They don't relay messages.

Propositions:

2. The employment office is drabby.

3. It's a make-shift arrangement.

4. The employment office depresses the clients.

5. These people need some sort of income.

6. Employment personnel can be bitchy. At least these weren't.

7. Reiteration of evaluation: They act as if money were coming out of their own pocket.

Expansions:

a. The door is dirty.
b. They don't ever clean up.
c. There are no plants.

— The poor people have to put up with it.

a. The media distort the situation.
b. These people want to work.

a. The ones in Indio were real bastards.
b. Some personnel are boss-minded, act as if they owned the place.

All of these propositions express criticism of the employment office and of society's role and comprehension of the situation of the unemployed. The underlying propositions are expressed in English but expansions giving additional information or detail are expressed in Spanish. Only in one case is English used to reiterate an expansion of a Spanish proposition, which in fact was incompletely stated in Spanish. This combination of English and Spanish utterances provides a continuity where underlying propositions in English are further expanded in Spanish. Concrete examples and anecdotes are offered in Spanish while the general propositions about roles and obligations are presented in English. Here again there are ideological implications since interaction in Spanish is limited to a secondary role, even though Spanish plays a significant part in providing cohesion and coherence to the interaction.

In both episodes shifts occur primarily at the clause level although there are a number of cases where shifts from English to Spanish merely provide juncture to ensure "bilingual" cohesion in what is assumed to be an exchange in both languages. Here then are some examples:

Clause level:
1. I'm sure si la limpiaran once a week . . .
2. Pero a mucha gente que tiene gente that depend on them.
3. Me dijo que no, que he hadn't heard from you.
4. Y que we should have another one.
5. Son muchas, because they're, they're . . . ah two seventy-five.
6. I can always tell 'em not to leave that many pero, porque es mucho.
7. Pero no dijistes que we were gonna divide it among us.
8. That's what I want to do pero, pero es que no sé dónde.
9. A veces en la casa como, cuando, when we ran out of water. . . .

Junctures: Spanish juncture → English discourse
1. Sí, pero, if we . . .
2. Me dijo que no que he hadn't . . .
3. So I told him, I told him, you know, le pregunté que . . .
4. Y que we should . . .
5. Pero, pero no dijites que we were . . .
6. My d'este.
7. I meant, you know, que, que, que they just give you . . .
8. Como que's, como que, que'l dinero is coming . . .

Only in the last case of juncture presented above does shift occur after NP (noun phrase) functioning as subject in these two episodes.

Code-switching thus provides a relational function at the linguistic and discourse levels but these shifts in code also have a mediating function between text and social and ideological context. As the expression form of acculturation and linguistic penetration, code-switching communicates levels of meaning outside the purview of monolingual discourse, as we shall see in our discussion of denotations and connotations in code-switching discourse.

CONNOTATIONS AND DENOTATIONS
IN CHICANO CODE-SHIFTING

A semiotic theory of codes explains how rules of competence permit individuals to form and interpret messages or texts.[15] Given the multiplicity of social codes, context and circumstances, the meaning of a sign depends on particular conditions and conventions. Messages are, of course, only hypothetically open to diverse readings. A semiotic model allows us to incorporate historical factors and social conditions of signification as indispensable components of the content of a sign. These cultural units or semantic properties form therefore the denotative and connotative markers of a sign vehicle. Within the Chicano community there are rules operating on the basis of these denotative and connotative markers which determine code selection and code interpretation. It is then necessary to study the conditions of signification of a given code-switched message and the circumstances under which this shifting occurs.

In an analysis of code-shifting we must also consider the linguistic background of the speaker and addressee involved in the verbal interaction. Since the degree of proficiency in the two languages differs among bilingual Chicanos and since the frequency with which the two languages are used also differs, it is possible to find different types of shifting. The shifting among those who have primarily a receptive competency in the Spanish language and who shift infrequently from English to Spanish occurs in areas of vestigial bilingualism where one language has assumed all of the functions for that community or family or individual. This type of vestigial shifting is not the subject of this study. On the contrary, we wish to analyze the code-shifting of bilinguals who continue to function in both languages within given situations but who are progressively using the two languages within the same domain and within a given verbal exchange. The shifting may occur in the sequencing of speech acts within the utterances of one speaker or in exchanges with another participant. Determining when these shifts occur requires a look at the sequencing of speech acts as well as at the linguistic and semiotic factors involved. In this particular case we must look at the nature of bilingualism itself.

Linguists and psycholinguists who have studied the phenomenon of bilingualism often speak of compound and coordinate bilinguals.[16] Compound bilinguals have been described as speakers who consider a word in Language A as having the same meaning or reference as the corresponding word in Language B. In this definition the two sign-vehicles from different codes are in effect said to have the same denotative markers and the same referent. Coordinate bilinguals on the other hand, are said to perceive a word in Language A as a sign distinct in meaning from its Language B equivalent. In this case the two sign-vehicles can be said to vary in denotative markers. A mixed system is said to occur when "one of the words is perceived as meaning the other rather than referring directly to the object or event in question."[17] In this case the referent is another sign.

In semiotics, however, no two signs are ever considered *identical* in form or reference. Signs or utterances may be *similar* as to referent when denotational markers are identical. If two denotative markers totally overlap we say that the two are synonymous. This synonymity may be limited to particular contexts and circumstances, for a sign may have more than one denotation. What is also true is that two signs may share semantic properties in denotation and yet differ in the connotative marker, in given contexts and circumstances.

Consider the following sentences:

A.
1. Me dio un *aventón* a la casa.
2. Me dio un *raite* a la casa.
3. Me dio un *ride* a la casa.

B.
1. ¡Qué *peace and quiet* sin la televisión!
2. ¡Qué *paz y tranquilidad* sin la televisión!

Although the sign-vehicles within A and B appear to share semantic markers, the referents are not really identical because the entire compositional trees vary, for each is connected to different content systems. There are contextual and circumstantial selections associated with each semantic marker. Thus in A all three signs (*aventón, raite* and *ride*) possess the same pertinent marker (to be borne along in a vehicle) yet are read in different ways. In B, the common English expression refers to an English-speaking cultural system and connotes participation in the cultural values of the dominant group (i.e., acculturation), as well as a light-hearted complaint. The Spanish "paz and tranquilidad" would, on the other hand, convey seriousness and disgust with the TV noise. The connotation of the code-switched utterance is quite evident when we consider that the expression in fact comes from a foreign-born, middle-aged Chicana and was directed to her bilingual family at home. In both A and B the code-shifted expressions and their equivalents in Spanish reflect different social status. Differences in this respect might be clearer with another example:

a) Mi papá es un *bartender*.

b) Mi papá es *cantinero*.

The first sentence was said by a student in elementary school when asked where her father worked.

— ¿Dónde trabaja tu papá?

— En el Hilton.

— ¿Qué hace ahí?

— Es un manager y un bartender.

Whereas the word *cantinero* has no prestige in the community, *bartender* signifies social mobility, especially in connection with the Hilton. *Cantinero* would have signified work at the local Chicano bar.

In the previous examples, *aventón* signals a Mexican speaker or a recent arrival from Mexico; *raite* could be the unmarked item as it is probably the most frequent lexical choice in our communities. But even here *raite* signals an informal, intra-group variety. In a situation where "Me llevas" would be the expected request, "Me das un *raite*" could introduce a trace of humor and familiarity which would detract from the idea of imposing on the car owner. "Me das un ride" could also serve the same purpose, not by introducing humor but by introducing a nicety, a touch of polite elegance. Thus careful pronunciation of code-switching elements in a sentence leads to additional levels of signification. In communication theory the amount of information conveyed by a message increases as the amount of uncertainty becomes greater. At one level code-switching can be seen as conveying little information in those instances where the uncertainty as to the message is diminished. The same thing occurs in a shift from one variety or subcode to another. There are cases in the use of *caló* for example, when the shift to a *caló* item substitutes for an anticipated expression. In the expression "Ahí nos vidrios" ("Ahí nos vemos") or "Ya estufas" ("Ya estuvo") the sign-vehicles have been substituted but the denotational markers remain the same. In those circumstances in which the hearer already knows what the speaker is going to say, however, the substituted sign-vehicle is attributed extra meanings or extra markers. On another level, then, the *caló* substitution conveys more than a denotation. In fact the use of the *caló* item increases the number of possible readings of the message. The same thing happens in code-switching where extensive and frequent shifting is equivalent to greater uncertainty about the total message in terms of both denotations and connotations and thus to a greater amount of information. An examination of these connotations requires familiarity with all the other cultural semiotic fields which interconnect with the linguistic code. Code-shifting then may direct the addressee to the speaker's attitudinal, ideological, affective, social or cultural perspective or views. In Spanish, for example, the word "pasear" implies a fun outing but the word "paseada" when attributed to a girl or woman signals a moral judgment. There are times, however, when euphemisms or the substitution of sign-vehicles changes the connotation. Thus to avoid saying "Es una muchacha muy paseada," that is, "She's a wanton woman," a person may say "Le dan sus *rides*." The use of *aventón* here would merely convey the idea of facilitating transportation. *Ride* on the other hand conveys comfort and pleasure. *Raite* would not fit either but the word *raitecito* would, as in *Le dan sus raitecitos*. Thus the code-shifted item and the loanword in diminutive form convey the intended put-down.

The same connotational differences arise at the level of entire utterances. Consider the following sentence:

Ponlo en el refrigerator so it won't spoil.

This sentence said entirely in Spanish ("Ponlo en el refrigerador para que no se eche a perder") is perceived as a more formal command than the code-switched sentence which can be taken as lightly as a suggestion. Thus any sentence said entirely in Spanish in an informal context could carry a tone of formality and may in fact sound pedantic as in *Tenemos que enumerar los puntos principales,* as compared to *Tenemos que list todos los important points.* The same pedantic effect appears in *Tengo que fotocopiar este cuento* vs. *Tengo que xerox este cuento.* We cannot assume that the speaker who code-switches in familiar situations does not have the Spanish vocabulary to produce the utterance entirely in Spanish, for it is generally only in the case of technical vocabulary which has been learned only in one of the languages that this phenomenon arises.

Code-switching may also serve a rhetorical purpose. In the use of metaphors within the same language where two items have semantic markers in common whether at a denotative or connotative level, substitution is possible. Thus two items from different classes may be substitutable if they share a semantic property, or are associated with a particular class or property (as in a *thousand swords* for a *thousand men*). In effect the use of metaphors is a type of code-switching. Code-switching at the level of two languages may also be a rhetorical code-switching at the level of semantic codes. Consider for example the following sentence taken from a transcribed version of a sociolinguistics conference in Las Cruces, New Mexico in 1974.[18]

"I would fight, no me importa que me maten como a un perro."

Let us focus here on the use of the word "perro." In English the word "dog" possesses two connotative markers:

$$dog \begin{cases} \text{connotes "fidelity"} \\ \text{connotes "being inferior"} \end{cases}$$

Thus "being in the doghouse" means being in disfavor in a society where dogs are allowed inside the house and punished by not being allowed in. At the same time one can be "treated like a dog," i.e., "treated poorly, like nothing." Where dogs are generally protected, one does not "die like a dog"; one dies or drowns "like a rat," or is slaughtered like livestock, sacrificed like a lamb or killed like a rabid dog, perhaps. Dogs in the Mexican or Chicano community belong to a different cultural system, that is, to a different code. In Spanish *perro* connotes "impotence, defenselessness." When applied to a person in power or control, it connotes what the English word "pig" does. In this particular utterance, the speaker was trying to convey his intent of standing up for his rights despite the odds. The particular topic under discussion was the rights of Chicanos to have access to publication of their works. In this case the code-switching exchange was a speech act within a speech event which was an academic discussion of several Chicano academicians and writers on the problems of publication. Because the discussion was not really heated, this particular code-shifted intervention served merely as an exclamation mark which lent dramatic flavor to the discourse. The act itself of shifting added strength to the statement of being willing to die for the cause. In fact the entire utterance is an oxymoron of sorts which fuses two contradictory markers: resistance and defenselessness, resistance conveyed through "I would fight" and defenselessness through "no me importa que me maten como a un perro." Thus the code-shifting here is rhetorical and conveys irony. At another level the whole exchange is ludicrous given the particular circumstances under which it was said: a pleasant retreat area in Las Cruces, New Mexico to discuss sociolinguistics under circumstances not of resistance but of acceptance of Ford funding.

SPEECH ACTS

Denotations and connotations in code-switching can be more closely examined in terms of the particular speech acts within the text. Labov and Fanshel describe four groups of speech actions relevant to their analysis of therapeutic interactions: meta-linguistic, representations, requests and challenges. These are further broken down into more specific speech acts within each category. These speech actions correlate with what they call *fields of discourse* which are subdivided into three styles: Interview style, Everyday style and Family style.[19] On the basis of their description of these styles, we could relabel them: therapeutic, narrative and evaluative. These styles and speech actions are closely related to the functions of different elements within the speech event as discussed by Jakobson, Morris, Halliday and Barthes. All of these semiotic analyses which seek to discover the significant units of discourse are to some extent explicit in the model presented by Labov and Fanshel, which distinguishes between mode of expression, mode of argument and mode of interaction.[20] All focus on an analysis of the form of the content, its intent, its effect, and its context.

In our analysis of speech acts in code-switching, we will borrow from all of these models, but particularly from that of Labov and Fanshel, and refer to the following components and subcomponents.[21]

1. Elements of Expression: English text, Spanish text
                               Denotations and Connotations
                               Chicano interlocutors

2. Interactive Styles: Metalingual, narrative, evaluative, incitive

3. Speech Actions: Assertions, evaluations, interpretations,
                               agreement, denial, support, contradiction,
                               reinterpretation, reaffirmation, reinforce-
                               ment, confirmation, requests, refusals, re-
                               sponses, withdrawal, challenges, questions,
                               disagreement, insults, boasts, apologies,
                               excuses, flattery, threats, promises, etc.

The sequencing of speech acts and their effect on code-switching will be
examined in the following conversation taped by Mariana Marín in Chualar, a
small rural town near Salinas, California. Our contention is that particular
speech acts in the verbal interaction of Chicanos are expressed in particular
forms: English-language forms. The form of the content, which reflects social
functions and speech acts, thus takes a particular form of expression in the
following dialogue:

(Conversation recorded by Mariana Marín, Chualar, California)

Aunt: — Tú no te acordabas lo que tu mamá y tu papá te decían ora de la
llorana ¿verdad?

Uncle: — No, . . . No, es de una mujer que mató sus hijos en un paredón al
pie de la ss . . .

Aunt: — No, era una mujer que mató sus hijos y los tiró al, al río, al río y lo'o
entonces ella estaba . . .

Uncle: — Tú estás . . . just guessing.

M: — What is it?

Aunt: — Yo no me acuerdo de ese . . .

Uncle: — Pos seguro que no te acuerdas. Pos no l'ha leído la historia; hay
historia . . . *There is a story* that de la llorona . . . en español está una historia
de la llorona.

Aunt: — No, era una mujer que, que, que tiró sus hijos al, al río.

M: — How come?

Uncle: — Yo no me acuerdo de la historia esa. Uhh, ya hace muchos, muchos
años la oía, cuando estaba chico, la mentaban, hablan mucho de la historia.
En años pa trás, muchos años pa trás; ya la gente no habla mucho de eso. Pos
yo no me acuerdo, pero mucho, platicaban mucho la historia de la llorona.

Aunt: — No, mi amá decía que . . . que esta mujer tenía tres hijos o . . .

Uncle: — No, ¡al diablo!

Aunt: — Tenía tres hijos.

M: — Uh huh.

Aunt: — Y por no cuidarlos, los agarró y los tiró en el río y lo'o depués y luego estaba en una, como, una, modo de que quería sus hijos para atrás.

M: — Oh, yeah.

Aunt: — Y no los podía recoger; y entonces comenzaba a llorar y por eso le decían la llorona porque comenzaba a llorar. . . .

Uncle: — No, no, no.

Aunt: — Por . . .

Uncle: — No, si es una historia muy grande. Es una historia muy larga, esa de la mujer.

M: — Mmmm.

Aunt: — Pero entonces ¿cómo comenzó? Así es como mi amá me decía.

Uncle: — No, yo, yo, yo me acuerdo, yo me acuerdo de chico que . . .

Aunt: — Tsst, ahh.

Uncle: — Se ponía uno allá en las lumbradas afuera y había unos muchachos ya más mayores que sabían leer, que platicaban, tsst, pos allá en aquellos tiempos, tú sabes, porque, ya, en tiempo de frío está haciendo frío, ponía una llanta uno, prendía una llanta vieja que tuviera, ¿no? Le prendía uno fuego allá afuera, pos allá a Broley yo estaba chico, empezaba a platicar uno, había un hombre allá en . . . allí en onde nosotros vivíamos y se ponía a platicar historias, y también de una mujer que . . . de . . . como.

Aunt: — La llorona era porque tiró los hijos.

Uncle: — Se trata de . . .

Aunt: — Porque tiró los hijos, la llorona . . .

Uncle: — Se trata de una historia que en . . . es que la gente en aquellos tiempos más antes, ¿no?, era muy creída en cuestiones de—de como del día trece, ves, thirteen, el martes.

Aunt: — No es el trece . . .

Uncle: — Pero el martes, pero el martes, and people, man, en aquellos tiempos, el martes, no, no, no salía la gente de la casa.

M: — ¿No?

Uncle: — Oh—no,

Aunt: — Es que el martes trece . . .

Uncle: — Y a éste, le mataron toda la familia, a este hombre, porque salió el día trece y lo'o el coshi, tú sabes, un taxi, el coshi que vino, era también el número trece, pos yo no más me acuerdo ya, 'taba muy chico, cuando ese barullo.

M: — Heh, heh.

Uncle: — Pero esa es un historia también . . .

Aunt: — No, pero se trata de la llorona.

Uncle: — Muy buena. *It's actually, it's actually is,* eh, tú sabes, la llorona y todo, hay libros, de ella. En Mexicali, en México, puedes comprar libros de la llorona, toda la historia de ella *because it is the truth.*

M: — What, that she killed 'er kids?

Uncle: — Mm hmm.

M: — ¿Cómo los mató?

Aunt: — Los tiró . . .

Uncle: — Pos yo, del modo que oí yo, que se fue al cerro y los mató de puras pedradas, pero les llaman otra cosa a las piedras, en los paredones, tú sabes, los agarró a las piedras y los, los hizo garras allí, entre las piedras.

Aunt: — No, no, no.

Uncle: — Eso es.

Aunt: — No es eso.

Uncle: — Es una historia, muy, muy, ah, es larga la historia. It's a . . . it's a, it's a true story.

M: — Did she die?

Uncle: — No, era de, del estado de Chihuahua, la mujer.

M: — A real person?

Uncle: — It was a real person and actually, it did happen.

M: — Aahhh.

Uncle: — Yes, it did, it did happen.

M: — Nooo.

Uncle: — Yes, it did.

Aunt: — No, no, no, no, no, . . . era . . .

M: — Then how come people are afraid of her?

Uncle: — What?

M: — How come people are afraid of her?

Uncle: — People at that time were afraid of her because she sound, because this woman when she died, after she . . .

M: — ¿Se murió entonces?

Uncle: — Se murió la mujer, cuando murió salía allí al paredón y se parecía, se aparecía la mujer con unos lloridos, como un coyote gritaba, y lloraba, verdad, por los hijos. Allí onde los mató, allí se aparecía esta mujer.

Aunt: — No, tu historia es . . .

Uncle: — Andale, pues.

Aunt: — Tu historia es diferente. Como mi amá y mi apá nos decían a nosotros que la llorona era, dice, "si eres malo, si eres mala, viene la llorona por tí" y lo'o decíamos nosotros: ¿por qué? Y lo'o 'icía, porque la llorona agarró . . .

Uncle: — Dale poquito más recio a ese pedo.

Aunt: — Tenía, tenía, tenía tres hijos y lo'o entonces ella, ella estaba muy . . . , ella estaba muy . . . que, que, que . . .

Uncle: — Así es como va.

This particular conversation on the Mexican folktale "La Llorona" involves three Chicanos: an aunt and uncle who are second-generation Chicanos, and Mariana, a third-generation Chicana. The aunt and uncle are bilingual but Spanish is the language of the home.

The context of the conversation is an important ingredient in the analysis. All three are sitting before the television set which is barely audible in the background. The aunt and uncle are older, working-class Chicanos, around 60 years of age. The uncle has been retired from work at the sugar refinery for a while because of ill health. As is evident in the conversation, there is some good-natured competition between the couple and a desire to impress the visiting university graduate-student niece.

The conversation is primarily in Spanish. There are, however, several shifts which occur during the interaction that can be analyzed in terms of the speech acts discussed before, which, as will be evident, correlate with interactive styles and the particular denotations and connotations of the text.

The conversation begins with a request by the aunt for information from the uncle's biography about the well-known and multiple-version folktale "La Llorona." The uncle responds that he cannot provide the information requested from his own biography; however, he is able to inform on the topic itself from other sources. His particular narrative version of the folktale is immediately challenged by his wife who knows another version. As she proceeds to give her version, the uncle interrupts to disagree with an evaluation of her representation of the tale. His affective intervention triggers a shift to English:

Uncle: — Tú estás . . . just guessing.

We thus have the following sequence of speech acts:
   a. request for information from biography of uncle
   b. expression of version A of "La Llorona"
   c. rejection of version A
   d. expression of version B
   e. challenge of version B with negative evaluation of speaker
At this point a challenge in an evaluative style has triggered the shift which occurs in the middle of a verb phrase. Some linguists who have studied code-shifting do not consider cases where single words are shifted, preferring to label these as loans but as we have indicated previously, we consider single word shifts as cases of code-switching as well. In the preceding example, the bilingual speaker could have said:

Tu estás *nomás adivinando.*

If we compare the words *adivinando* and *guessing* we will see that the Spanish term makes reference to a riddle or an unsolved problem and denotes a discovery method through conjecture. Although a similar denotation exists in English, one can also "guess at something," with the added meaning of "making up" or "fabricating" something, even a story. What he in fact suggests is that she is making up the story and that her version is incorrect. Thus a combination of speech act (a challenge), style (evaluative) and connotation (an invention) explain this particular case of shifting.

The conversation proceeds with a question in English by Mariana and a reaffirmation of her version by the aunt through a denial of the uncle's version. The uncle then makes an assertion about the veracity of his version by alluding to the written version. To reinforce his version he again shifts to English:

a. Challenge of her version: "Pos no l'ha leído la historia."
b. Assertion of written version: "Hay historia."
c. Reaffirmation of assertion "*There is a story* that de la llorona."

Thus he reaffirms his assertion in English. This use of the English language is directly tied to the status and role of the English language in this society. In fact, of course, the power does not lie in the language but in ᵗʰe speakers of the language, the dominant class in society.

The conversation proceeds with an account of details recalling the narration of the tale itself in a different context. This interaction, which focuses on the act of narrating itself in Spanish, is followed by the aunt's narration of version B of the folktale with intermittent protests from the uncle who supports his challenge by recalling his childhood days. This historical approach with details about the people of long ago further reinforces his challenge of her version. At this point the uncle introduces additional evidence and discusses a specific attribute of people in the olden days who used to be quite superstitious. Here the uncle recalls an old Hispanic superstition about Tuesday the 13th. To enable Mariana to receive the full impact of what Tuesday the 13th means, he shifts to English in the pronunciation of number thirteen as it evokes an equally ominous connotation in English. The aunt's rejection of this hybrid association of "La Llorona" with Tuesday the 13th is disregarded as he proceeds loudly to narrate a story about a man whose whole family was killed on the 13th.

The aunt's disagreement and reference anew to the "llorona" folktale bring a reaffirmation of the truth-value and authenticity of his Tuesday the 13th story, which like the "llorona" folktale is again argued to be true. Once again he reinforces his argument and attests to its authenticity by shifting to English, while stressing the utterance at the same time:

En Mexicali, en México, puedes comprar libros de la llorona, toda la, la historia de ella *because it is the truth.*

The conversation continues with a more detailed narration of the uncle's version of the folktale. His argument is again reinforced by shifting to English:

Es una historia, muy, muy, ah, es larga la historia. It's a . . . it's a . . . it's a true story.

Throughout the conversation Mariana generally responds to particular assertions in Spanish with additional questions in English. In most instances the aunt and uncle respond in Spanish:

Mariana: — Did she die?
Uncle: — No, era de, del estado de Chihuahua, la mujer.

When Mariana, however, questions the veracity of his story, he responds in English also:

Mariana: — A real person?
Uncle: — It was a real person and actually, it did happen.

The interaction continues with challenges of the story, reaffirmation of the story and further challenges, all in English. Mariana's request in English for additional information about the tale's protagonist leads to an attempt by the uncle to narrate the tale in English but he half-starts and cannot proceed because his narrative style is obviously in Spanish. Mariana's subsequent request in Spanish enables him to initiate the narration again in Spanish.

This conversation indicates that for Mariana's uncle, Spanish is the language of narration, assertion and interpretation. Challenges in Spanish are initially rejected in Spanish and subsequently, in an effort to declare them null and void, in English. The authenticity and truth-value of an assertion can only be expressed in English. Valuative acts are also expressed in English. As the dominant language in this society, English is seen as the language of status and power. This hierarchical relation, with English as the superordinate language and Spanish as the subordinate language, is evident in the choice of English for those speech acts through which the speaker seeks to impose a particular interpretation of the information given.

IDEOLOGICAL CODE-SWITCHING

Shifting from Spanish to English or vice versa is not the only type of code-switching that occurs in the discourse of Chicanos. Other types of shifts offer insights into the function of Spanish-English code-shifting, the contexts in which it occurs, and the sociolinguistic variables which determine its constraints. These other types of shifts have rhetorical value and could be called style-shifting or code-switching (Eco).

Rhetorical shifts occur to increase or restrict the levels of signification by changing the form of expression and the connotations of the sign. These shifts can be metonymic (expressing semantic connections), metaphoric (expressing shared or identical markers) or synecdochic (expressing genus-species relations), but in any case the shifts convey relationships of interdependence through the underlying markers or semantic features. The entire rhetorical operation is made possible by the existence of particular cultural conventions and sets of accepted values. Although this technical labeling of discourse is particularly widespread in literary criticism, rhetorical code-switching is common not only in literature but in everyday discourse as well. Advertising has made good use of these rhetorical techniques in its discourse on consumer goods. Eco has analyzed how the sale of diet foods in the American market shifted its focus when cyclamates were announced to be carcinogenic.[21] The advertising pitch had originally focused on the presentation of cyclamates as dietetic (non-fattening) and counted on its connotation as life-preserving (no heart attacks). This advertising had an underlying premise: sugar means more fat which causes heart attacks. After the cyclamate scare, the original oppositions were no longer functional. Thereafter a new series of correspondences and oppositions emerged and dietetic foods were advertised as having sugar and no cyclamates. Because sugar was not associated with cancer and death, it was now seen as a life-preserving substance. The introduction of sugar into dietetic foods did not however change the advertiser's propaganda about the product's value as a slimming food. In effect, as Eco indicates, sugar was presented as having a positive effect on losing weight. Eco calls this change in connotations an "ideological operation" and a case of code-switching.[22] The whole operation was possible because of the values of American society which allowed the underlying presuppositions.

Thus discourse relies on a cultural and ideological background in its presuppositions; the addressee, moreover, must share this information which is obviously necessary for a "correct" interpretation. In the conversation recorded by Mariana Marín we found that her uncle switched to English whenever he shifted from a narrative to an evaluative style. In effect he was actively engaged in ideological code-switching. For him the following oppositions were operating:

Chicano population — subordinate minority group
vs.   vs.
Anglo population — superordinate majority group

Given this underlying cultural and social background, the following connotations were implicit:

Chicanos — Spanish language — powerless
vs.   vs.   vs.
Anglos   English language   powerful

The discourse itself had an interactive opposition between narrative and evaluative styles. For this speaker, the evaluative style carried more force and was in fact used to give emphasis to his interpretations. Thus the evaluative style and the English language both shared a feature: power. Consequently a narrative style implied the Spanish language and an evaluative style implied the English language. In reality, of course, Spanish can convey emphasis and valuative judgments just as well as English. The Spanish-English code-switching allowed him to shift on an ideological plane, from a subordinate to a dominant position. Thus, his acceptance and expression of the dominant values in society through his code-shifting involved shifts in the use of linguistic, rhetorical and ideological codes.

These three types of code-shifting (linguistic, rhetorical and ideological) are evident in other types of stylistic shifts in the discourse of Chicanos. Since shifts in styles or codes involve changes in expression and/or content and since these changes can be expressed in terms of rules, we will also be using the term *variety* to refer to the subgroups within linguistic codes. Thus the English code, for example, includes several subcodes or varieties or dialects.

Shifts in Spanish subcodes or varieties also constitute a type of code-switching which parallels the English-Spanish shifts. These shifts are found not only in the speech of Chicanos but also in their literary discourse. In the September 1978 issue of *Caracol*, a Chicano literary magazine from San Antonio. Texas, on the bilingual editor's page, we find two columns, one in English and one in Spanish, with a series of notes on current cultural events in the Chicano community. The announcements are not only written in two languages but in different styles and varieties that juxtapose an informal English version with a familiar Spanish *caló* version. Consider the following examples taken from *Caracol* which appear under these column headings: (italics ours)

a. Otra vez pido la ayuda de los subscriptores *pa* que se vuelvan a subscribir y nos avienten un chequecito *pa seguirle dando gas.*

a. Again I continue to ask the support from our subscribers so they may re-subscribe and send us a check to keep us alive.

b. Si alguien quiere vender Caracoles por allá *donde cantonean, pos órale.*

b. Anyone who wants to sell Caracol in your area is welcome.

c. Es imposible *tirar rollo* de todas las películas que vi.

c. It's impossible for me to talk about all the movies that I saw.

d. Nos sentamos y nos paramos juntos *pa hacer esquina* a nuestros cinematógrafos chicanos.

d. We sat and stood together to show support to our movie people.

e. A los bookstores les ofrecemos *la misma movida.*

e. Bookstores are also welcome to the same deal.

f. Lo siento *por las babies . . .*

f. I feel sorry for those beauties . . .

The first opposition evident in these columns is that of language codes: English vs. Spanish. Beyond that we find that although the two columns are supposedly a translation of each other, they in fact communicate different messages, for the connotations differ and the addressees differ as well, even though they may all be Chicanos. The English version matter-of-factly informs the reader about a series of events and assesses them in a superficial way ("an artistic expression," "a deep story," "good") at the same time that it solicits subscribers. Although the style is relatively informal, the presentation is meant to be taken seriously.

The Spanish column, on the other hand, combines three varieties of Spanish as exemplified by these portions of text:

a. Formal/standard variety: — "Les mandamos un paquete de 10 o más a un descuento de 40 porciento."
— "Esta organización es dueña de mucho capital en el mercado mundial."

b. Informal/popular variety: — "Nos avientan un chequecito."
— "Donde los cardinales lambieron manos y cachetes."
— "Pa ponerle la cherry al queque:
"Considerando el mugrero que hacen los gringos."
— "Pura chapusa."

c. Familiar/*caló* variety: — "Periquiando en Aztlán"
— "Pa seguirle dando gas"
— "Por allí donde cantonean, pos órale"
— "Pa hacer esquina"
— "Tirar rollo"

Popular varieties are characterized not only by lexical differences but by phonetic, morphological and syntactic rule differences as well. The *caló* variety is actually a popular variety distinguished from variety B only in terms of vocabulary. Each of these varieties has different connotations in the Chicano community, given the contexts in which they are used and the speakers who use them. In a literary magazine which seeks a broad circulation in the Chicano community, primarily of San Antonio, Texas, but in the general Southwest as well, these varieties have the following connotations:

Formal/Standard variety: Education

Informal/Popular variety: Chicano solidarity, informality, unpretentiousness, lack of linguistic hangups

Caló variety: Virility, defiance of literary norm, artistic innovativeness

The connotations of a particular sign system can of course only be determined in terms of the culture of a given social group. Thus the special connotations of the *caló* variety are only evident in the context of Chicano literary newsletters and magazines. Of course once the same style and phrases are used repeatedly, the text becomes trite. The editor's Spanish discourse is thus fuzzy as he wavers between these contradictions:

Formal	vs.	Informal
Educated	vs.	Popular
Normative	vs.	Defiant
Hackneyed	vs.	Innovative

These sets of contradictions are then opposed to another set, that which polarizes the Chicano and Anglo communities, as we saw before. Within the Spanish column, there are also cases of a fourth "code"—the code-switching mode—where the connotation recalls those noted in the discourse of Mariana's uncle, as in this example:

No se vale crédito, ni consignment, nomás cash.

Here the terms, which denote money, sales and business enterprise, are shifted to English; the presupposition is that they belong to another cultural system, a capitalistic one. Thus another opposition is insinuated: artistic vs. commercial. The English column here, as we mentioned before, is addressed to Chicanos as well as other English dominant readers. The no-nonsense approach in that column implies a more serious readership, thereby creating still another opposition. At the same time, the inclusion of an English column itself which does not produce the same cultural, artistic and solidarity message implies one further opposition: in-group readers vs. out-group readers. The editor then not only shifts from Spanish to English, but from one style to another, from one variety to another and from one level of meaning to another. These too constitute a type of "code-shifting" and often all of these or combinations of these different types underlie Chicano shifts from one language to another.

Code-switching is thus a form of verbal interaction where functions are shared by two codes. The delegation of particular functions to one or the other language appears to be determined by extra-linguistic and extra-textual factors, that is, by the socio-economic structure determining social interaction and language status. Let us recall our branching tree from Chapter 3 (Figure 3.13), now modified to reflect a code-switching context (Figure 5.1). Code shifts noted in the linguistic expression are actually shifts in ideological perspective, manifested as shifts in function and shifts in speech acts. These shifts are

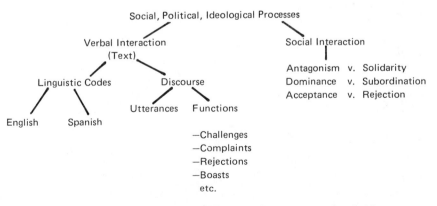

FIGURE 5.1   Social, Political, and Ideological Processes in Code-switching

expressed linguistically but the choice of code merely reflects underlying social and ideological functions channeled through particular speech acts.

Code-shifting in the Chicano community is thus a complex phenomenon, which involves not only shifting from one language to another but shifting from one level of meaning to another. Shifted utterances are never mere translations; they carry additional connotations. In fact, code-switching involves shifts in linguistic, rhetorical and ideological "codes." A study of code-switching entails knowledge of the speaker's cultural background and values as well as close contact with the dynamic bilingualism prevalent in the area, for this information is essential in analyzing the semiotic and ideological constraints determining code-switching.

Notes

1. William Labov and David Fanshel, *Therapeutic Discourse. Psychotherapy as Conversation* (New York: Academic Press, 1977), p. 30.

2. M. A. K. Halliday, and Ruqaiya Hasan, *Cohesion in English* (Hong Kong: Longman, 1976).

3. Glyn Lewis, *Multilingualism in the Soviet Union* (The Hague: Mouton, 1972).

4. National Council for Chicano Sociolinguistics, *Proceedings of the National Exploratory Conference on Chicano Sociolinguistics* (Austin: National Educational Laboratory Publishers, Inc., 1976), p. 161.

5. *Ibid.,* p. 110.

6. *Ibid.,* p. 111.

7. *Ibid.,* p. 171.

8. *Ibid.,* p. 170.

9. Roland Barthes, *S/Z* (New York: Hill and Wang, 1974), pp. 18–19.

10. Halliday, p. 12.

11. Malcolm Coulthard, *An Introduction to Discourse Analysis* (Hong Kong: Longman, 1977), p. 10.

16. John Macnamara, "Bilingualism and Thought," *The Language Education of Minority Children,* ed. Bernard Spolsky (Rowley, Mass.: Newbury House Publishers, 1972), pp. 60–76.

17. Susan Houston, *A Survey of Psycholinguistics* (The Hague: Mouton, 1972), pp. 204–205.

18. *Proceedings of the National Exploratory Conference,* p. 136.

19. Labov and Fanshel, p. 42.

20. *Ibid.,* p. 67.

21. *Ibid.,* p. 61.

22. Umberto Eco, *A Theory of Semiotics* (Bloomington: Indiana University Press, 1976), p. 287.

   Ibid., p. 288.

Conclusion

This work has examined Chicano bilingualism from various perspectives: socio-linguistic, semiotic, historical, cultural and ideological. This approach recognizes that language is a social means of communication and that this communication occurs simultaneously at three levels: linguistic (code), interactional (discourse) and social (ideological and cultural). Within each level language expresses particular meanings. At the linguistic level, these can be summarized as denotative and connotative levels of signification. At the discourse or interactional level, these meanings, expressed in terms of functions and speech acts, reflect relations between participants and the intentions of the speaker through verbal actions. The third level accounts for the fact that discourse and linguistic meanings are produced within a particular social context where given conditions give rise to particular messages. Consider the following example:

> — Es del departamento.
> — ¿Y qué?

In this exchange, the first speaker indicates that something belongs to the department, in this case an academic department in a university. The second speaker responds with a question: "So what?" Thus at the *linguistic* level, the second speaker's answer is a *question*. At the *utterance* level, there is a *request* which functions as a *challenge*. At a *social* level, the interaction reveals *antagonism* or difference of opinion between the two speakers. We would need to know more about the social context in order to understand the underlying reasons for this antagonism. A study of language, then, or of a particular language situation requires an analysis at these three levels. Our study has attempted to encompass these various levels of meaning in order to provide a comprehensive analysis of the various factors determining particular types of bilingualism in the Chicano communities of the Southwest.

The fact that dynamic and transitional bilingualism persists in communities of the Southwest, as we have seen in this study, is a sign of the contradictory material conditions under which Chicanos live. The continued presence of Spanish in verbal interaction that gradually becomes more and more English dominant reflects both language maintenance and language loss, both acculturation and cultural resistance, both maintenance of class boundaries and occupational mobility, both a highly urban population and a large population of rural roots, both recent immigrants from Mexico and third, fourth and fifth Mexican-origin generations in the United States, both largely segregated barrios and highly integrated multi-ethnic urban communities. As material conditions change, so will the language situation of Chicanos. It is man, however, who changes conditions, who transforms the economic structure of society and thereby eliminates class conflict. The role that language choice can play in social transformation is secondary but undoubtedly significant as language is our principal means of communicating ideas to others.

Presently however the Spanish language does not have a subversive function in the community although it does identify a low-income working-class national minority residing in areas of strong Mexican-origin concentration in the Southwest. Its association with a particular class and culture explains rejection of Spanish by those who attribute the vehicular function for upward mobility to English. For this reason, many Chicano parents consciously determine to stop using Spanish in the home. In some cases it is the children who refuse to answer their Spanish-speaking parents in Spanish, shifting totally to the English language. Thus language choice has an ideological function. Where Spanish is seen as identifying a subordinate, low-income population, conscious rejection of Spanish reflects acceptance of the dominant ideology, of the functionalist myths of upward mobility. Rejection of Spanish is thus synonymous with a rejection of class and culture.

Countering this complete linguistic abdication are the resistance efforts of those who consciously seek to retain verbal interaction in Spanish, not only in the home and community but in academic circles as well. Among these are Chicano writers who write and publish in Spanish. Reality, however, has forced most Chicano publication houses to publish bilingual editions as the number of Spanish readers who consume Chicano literature is limited. There are, at the same time, those who see bilingualism as a vehicle for greater employment opportunities. In this case, far from signifying cultural or ideological resistance, bilingualism assumes the functions of English monolingualism, that is, it becomes a two-code vehicle for transmitting the dominant culture and ideology and for achieving a certain degree of upward mobility. Thus contradictions increase, since bilingualism can be co-opted by the system just as well as it can serve to unite a working-class national minority in its struggle against oppressive conditions.

Contradictions in the attitudes of Chicanos towards bilingualism and especially towards the specific Spanish varieties spoken in the Southwest are evident in the texts that follow. In episode A, we have a female undergraduate student from Northern California; in B, a male university senior from San Antonio, Texas; and in C, a male graduate student from California of New Mexican parentage:

Attitudes towards the Spanish Language.
A. Student from California:
— Y ustedes, ¿qué hablaban en la casa?
— Español, mi mamá me hablaba español. Y no me hablaba nada más. Si le hablaba en inglés, no me contestaba. Me dijo, me decía, "ésta es mi casa, en mi casa se habla español y eso es todo." Y de primero cuando era joven, pensaba, qué; ¿está loca o qué? Porque ya estaba, me estaban agringando la sistema y . . .
— ¿En la escuela?
— Yeah. ¿Por qué no habla esta mujer en inglés? ¿Por qué se enoja tanto si hablo en inglés? Y luego yo empecé a entenderlo, porque, porque era la única cosa que teníamos, la idioma, y ya puedo decir que se aventó mi mamá por eso pero por lo otro, fue culpa mía de no aprender más por no poder como se dice, apreciar la idioma hasta que ya entré al colegio.
B. Student from Texas:
— Semos la nueva generación, el movimiento, la nueva inspiración de nuestra gente. Nosotros, de' que nuestros padres vinieron pa cá, a los Estados Unidos después de la revolución, este, se presentaron todos aquí como en el sur de Texas, en todo el Southwest, hasta California y este . . . ellos vinieron, vinieron a . . . , muchos a buscar trabajo, muchos nomás este por buscar otra, otra buena vida y nosotros, nosotros semos el, los hijos de esa gente y ellos son nuestros forefathers, ellos son nuestros padres, ellos son la generación vieja y, y, nosotros, este . . . como en los barrios, en, en las comunidades donde hemos vivido nosotros aquí, hemos este, combináo como, como el estilo americano y el estilo mexicano y hemos hecho un estilo que es nomás de nosotros, que es el chicano, and lo vemos en nuestra lengua, lo vemos en . . . en como hemos cambiáo muchas palabras del estandard Spanish a Chicano y cuando nosotros hablamos en Chicano, nosotros este . . . tenemos más, más este, más feeling que hablar en el standard porque nosotros asina nos criamos con, con esa lengua que inventamos nosotros, y asina nos criamos y asina sufrimos y asina lloramos y asina jugamos y asina dicemos chistes y por eso es que esa lengua es, you know, it's our feelings, asina es como nos hemos criado, hablando así, yo 'toy hablando de esta generación nueva, los chicanos.

. . . .
Dicen que no es español, dicen que está muy americanada que it's too americanized esta, esta lengua de nosotros, en las palabras que muchos dicen que no pronunciamos bien, o que no deletreamos bien. La cosa es

que la deletreamos al estilo de nosotros y al cambio de nosotros. Y por eso que la, la comunicación que tenemos nosotros con our peers son, éste . . . Por eso nos dicen, estos muchachos no hablan correcto español, ¿cómo les vamos a enseñar? Y no hablan correcto inglés. Por eso muchos papases reaccionan y dicen pos, chihuahua, le voy a tener que enseñar inglés a mi chamaco nomás pa que la haga en la escuela pero la cosa es que ni sabemos el inglés bien, ni ellos saben el chicano bien.

El sistema is not geared for us, pal Chicano, y por eso they're always suppressing it, que no, y que no y que no, ves pero. . . . When they're doing that, nos quieren quitar algo que nosotros tenemos. Nos quie-ren. . . . They refuse to say, well, hablen chicano y hablen inglés, hablen los dos, I mean, there's nothing wrong with that. They refuse to say that.

C. Excerpt of a converation with a second-generation, Chicano male graduate student at UCSD:

— Acerca de eso, _____ , también lo que yo he notáo es cuando alguien me llama por teléfono, por ejemplo, y es un Chicano, entonces empezamos hablando español porque nos identi . . . porque por ese medio nos identificamos como parte del mismo, de la misma expe-riencia, del mismo movimiento, but then we find that we've gotta talk about some technical things having to do with education and we don't have the vocabulary to express ourselves in Spanish, so we immediately switch over to (English) and then I've also discovered, or I've seen, I, I observed that as we finish our conversation on the telephone, entonces nos despidimos con el español otra vez, parece como una acción de soli, sola, como solidarity, decimos "adiós," "nos vemos" solamente en, en español y la conversación ha sido casi totalmente en inglés, nomás el principio y el fin ha sido en español.

. . . .

I would consider English my home language, the language to which I return when I'm expressing myself in more difficult terms, or expressing more difficult ideas, so that's my home language.

As we can see, student A has undergone a process of re-acculturation. The language she once rejected has now become a symbol of culture, family and resistance to the point where she recognizes that the Spanish language was their only inalienable possession: "era la única cosa que teníamos, la idioma." Yet this recognition has come many years later, at a stage where she has a limited proficiency in Spanish, which she speaks with an English accent, for she has been thoroughly "agringada." Once this type of student, however, returns to the language, she is able to regain that long forgotten oral production facility. The political and cultural movement of the late sixties and early seventies brought many of these students to college and in some cases to Spanish classes to regain a lost asset.

Student B, speaking a rural variety of Spanish, on the other hand, is proud of his bilingualism, his facility in code-shifting and his adaptation of a number of English words to Spanish morphology and phonology to form what he calls a new language, a Chicano language through which Chicanos can better express themselves. This student has never stopped using the Spanish language and never will as he both loves his Spanish and lives in an area where the language has been maintained. This Texas Chicano sees the Spanish language as an element reflecting history, creativity and acculturation and demands the right to continue speaking his language varieties which he finds appropriate and modern.

On the other hand, student C, who is more proficient in the English language, feels that English is the language for more formal and technical functions. In fact, even though Spanish was his first language, it is no longer his usual language but rather a second language to be used as a cultural code. For this reason he limits his use of Spanish to informal greetings and closing remarks in intra-group exchanges. As a university graduate student, this Chicano could also have increased his proficiency in the Spanish language, had he so desired. It is significant then that he did not. This student thus expresses the views of a good number of Chicanos whose main goal has been to master the English language as it seems to offer opportunities for social mobility. The Spanish language, seen as the code of low-income, poorly educated persons, is thus assigned an inferior status and consciously or unconsciously felt to be insignificant and inadequate for important communication. Shifting to English for particular speech acts, is, as we said before, not only a linguistic matter. It is also an ideological sign, for through these shifts the speakers reflect their adherence to the dominant ideology and their acceptance of the inferior status assigned to the Spanish language and to Chicanos as well.

The future of the Spanish language in the Southwest will undoubtedly be determined not only by all the social and economic factors affecting the Spanish-speaking population in the Southwest but by the speakers themselves who for reasons of resistance or capitulation make their language choices and either lose or maintain the Spanish language.

Author Index

Subject Index